Dear David,

I truly enjoyed the conference in KL, and catching up with your friends again!

You may recall the 'Beer Lao' study I mentioned? The paper associated with that experiment is in this volume.

Best regards,

Jay

Infrastructure and Trade in Asia

Infrastructure and Trade in Asia

Edited by

Douglas H. Brooks

Asian Development Bank Institute, Japan

Jayant Menon

Asian Development Bank, Philippines

A JOINT PUBLICATION OF THE ASIAN DEVELOPMENT BANK
INSTITUTE AND EDWARD ELGAR PUBLISHING

Edward Elgar

Cheltenham, UK • Northampton, MA, USA

Published by
Edward Elgar Publishing Limited
The Lypiatts
15 Lansdown Road
Cheltenham
Glos GL50 2JA
UK

Edward Elgar Publishing, Inc.
William Pratt House
9 Dewey Court
Northampton
Massachusetts 01060
USA

A catalogue record for this book
is available from the British Library

Library of Congress Control Number: 2008930893

ISBN 978 1 84720 941 2

Printed and bound in Great Britain by MPG Books Ltd, Bodmin, Cornwall

Contents

Contributors

P.B. Anand, Reader in Environmental Economics and Public Policy, Bradford Centre for International Development, University of Bradford, UK.

Douglas H. Brooks, Senior Research Fellow, Asian Development Bank Institute, Tokyo, Japan.

Prabir De, Fellow, Research and Information System for Developing Countries, New Delhi, India.

Philippa Dee, Visiting Fellow, Australia Japan Research Centre, Crawford School of Economics and Government, ANU College of Asia and the Pacific, Australian National University, Canberra, Australia.

Christopher Edmonds, Rural Development Economist, Asian Development Bank, Manila, Philippines.

Christopher Findlay, Head of School, School of Economics, University of Adelaide, Australia.

Manabu Fujimura, Professor, Department of Economics, Aoyama Gakuin University, Tokyo.

Haider A. Khan, Professor of Economics at the Graduate School of International Studies, University of Denver, USA.

Jayant Menon, Principal Economist, Asian Development Bank, Manila, Philippines.

Richard Pomfret, Professor of Economics at the University of Adelaide, Australia.

Peter Warr, John Crawford Professor of Agricultural Economics and Director, Poverty Research Centre, Division of Economics, Research School of Pacific and Asian Studies, Australian National University.

John Weiss, Professor of Development Economics, University of Bradford, UK.

Fan Zhai, Economist, Asian Development Bank, Manila, Philippines.

Foreword

Asia's remarkable rapid growth in recent decades, and the resulting poverty reduction throughout the region, has been underpinned by increasing economic integration. Goods, services, financial flows, and ideas now cross borders throughout the region in quantities and values that were inconceivable fifty years ago. The Asian Development Bank (ADB) and its subsidiary for research and capacity-building, ADB Institute (ADBI), contribute to the region's growth and poverty reduction, and to greater understanding of the processes and policy implications of alternative development paths.

The rapid growth in the region's international trade has largely been the result of private sector initiatives, and private sector development is a strategic priority of ADBI. To both facilitate and enhance the benefits of resulting growth and economic integration, countries in Asia and the Pacific have undertaken massive investments in infrastructure. The international fragmentation of production processes and supply chains has spurred both the surge in intra-regional trade and greater regional co-operation. Similarly, increased regional co-operation has led to greater infrastructure investment and economic integration, leading to a virtuous cycle of investment, trade and co-operation.

It is in this regional context of rising trade, infrastructure investment, integration and co-operation that this volume makes its contribution. Chapters explore important concepts relating infrastructure and trade, and measurement issues are carefully discussed. Cross-border infrastructure projects are seen to raise particular challenges in planning and implementation. Since the distributions of costs and benefits are rarely perfectly correlated, a co-operative framework becomes critical for undertaking such activities.

The chapters in this volume were initially papers prepared for the conference on 'Regional Cooperation and Regional Integration in Asia and Latin America: The Role of Regional Infrastructure', held in Seoul, Korea, on 16–17 November 2006. This was the third annual conference jointly sponsored by ADBI and the Inter-American Development Bank under the Latin America/Caribbean and Asia/Pacific Economics and Business Association (LAEBA) initiative. The LAEBA encourages comparative research on the business economics of the two regions and enables researchers to exchange ideas, discuss current research and co-operate with policy-makers and the private sector. The conference was held in collaboration with the Korea Institute for Economic Policy, Korea Trade Investment Promotion Agency, Export-Import Bank of Korea, Korea Council on Latin America and the Caribbean, and the Latin American Studies Association of Korea. The assistance and helpful comments of those organizations is gratefully acknowledged, as is the assistance of ADBI staff.

Masahiro Kawai
Dean, Asian Development Bank Institute

Abbreviations

ADB	Asian Development Bank
ADBI	Asian Development Bank Institute
APEC	Asia-Pacific Economic Cooperation
ASEAN	Association of South East Asian Nations
ASW	ASEAN Single Window
BLS	bank-led system
BOT	build, operate, transfer
CDC	Committee for Development of Cambodia
CER	Closer Economic Relations
CES	constant elasticity of substitution
CGE	computable general equilibrium
CIF	cost, insurance and freight
CPI	Corruption Perception Index
CRS	Creditor Reporting System
ECO	Economic Cooperation Organization
EMS	equity-market based system
ERP	effective rate of protection
EU	European Union
FAO	Food and Agriculture Organization
FBS	family-based corporate governance system
FDI	foreign direct investment
FOB	free on board
FTA	free trade agreement
GDP	gross domestic product
GE	government effectiveness
GMS	Greater Mekong Subregion
HOS model	Heckscher, Ohlin and Samuelson model
HS	Harmonized System of Product Categories
IDB	Inter-American Development Bank
IDFC	Infrastructure Development Finance Corporation Limited
II	infrastructure index
IMF	International Monetary Fund
IMT	intermediate means of transport
INGO	international non-governmental organization

IO	input-output
IRI	international roughness index
IT	information technology
JBIC	Japan Bank for International Cooperation
LAEBA	Latin American/Caribbean and Asia/Pacific Economics and Business Association
LaoGEM	Lao General Equilibrium Model
Lao PDR	Lao People's Democratic Republic
LDE	less developed economy
LECS	Lao Expenditure and Consumption Survey
LGU	local government unit
MCTPC	Ministry of Communications, Transport, Post and Construction
MDG	Millennium Development Goals
MRC	Mekong River Commission
NAFTA	North American Free Trade Agreement
NEC	Northern Economic Corridor
NGO	non-governmental organization
NTB	non-tariff barriers
OECD	Organisation for Economic Co-operation and Development
OLS	ordinary least squares
PACER	Pacific Agreement for Closer Economic Relations
PCA	principal component analysis
PPP	public–private partnership
PRC	People's Republic of China
PTA	Preferential Trade Agreement
RQ	regulatory quality
SAM	social accounting matrix
SOE	state-owned enterprises
TEU	twenty-foot equivalent unit
TF	trade facilitation
TFAP	Trade Facilitation Action Plans
TII	trade intensity indices
UMCT	Urban Maintenance and Construction Tax
UN	United Nations
UNCTAD	United Nations Conference on Trade and Development
UNDP	United Nations Development Programme
UNESCAP	United Nations Economic and Social Committee for Asia-Pacific
UNICEF	United Nations Children's Fund
UXO	unexploded ordnance

VAT	value added tax
VOC	vehicle operating costs
WB	World Bank
WTO	World Trade Organization
WHO	World Health Organization

1. Infrastructure and trade in Asia: an overview

Douglas H. Brooks and Jayant Menon

The remarkable growth of developing Asia in recent decades owes much to the expansion of its international trade, including intra-regional trade. Exports even played a critical role in the region's recovery from the 1997–98 financial crisis. The region's trade expansion has in turn been facilitated and encouraged by the development of supporting infrastructure, including both physical (hard) and institutional (soft) infrastructure. Investment in infrastructure has been complemented, and spurred, by foreign and domestic investment in productive capacity as well as by structural reforms that improve the environment for investment, production and trade.

There are clear signs of a resurgence of interest in infrastructure among developing countries and particularly in developing Asia, where trade has been expanding most rapidly. Inadequate infrastructure can cost an economy significant unrealized gains from trade. Imagine what Singapore would be like without its port facilities, airports or communications links to the outside world. What would the economy of Azerbaijan or Kazakhstan be like without the infrastructure for developing and exporting hydrocarbon resources? On the other hand, imagine what Mongolia would be like with widespread satellite communications, sewage and sanitation facilities, ample well-maintained roads, health-care facilities, and sufficient electrical power to generate greater export earnings and increase domestic living standards.

Infrastructure in many Asian countries is inefficient, if not inadequate. Inability to transport goods and people efficiently or an inadequate power supply to operate machines leads to microeconomic as well as macroeconomic bottlenecks. Infrastructure can also yield positive externalities. For example, developing a new road infrastructure project to relieve congestion produces advantages not only for the users of the project but also for users of other roads where congestion is lessened as a result of the new project. Even non-users can gain through reduction of pollution and improvement of the natural environment, and the country as a whole can benefit through reduction of oil consumption or oil imports.

From 1975 to 1995, developing Asia's port capacity increased from 3 million to 62 million twenty-foot equivalent units (TEU), an average annual growth of over 15 per cent. Airfreight shipments in the region increased roughly 14 per cent annually from less than 2 billion to more than 30 billion ton-kilometres during the same period.

A notable feature of developing Asia's intraregional trade is the growing volume of shipments of parts and components across national borders. Fragmentation of production supply chains and sourcing raw and intermediate inputs from wherever costs are lowest (including related trade costs) has yielded benefits both for producers and consumers, as well as tax revenues for government budgets. To compete for larger shares in these benefits, countries have been striving to lower their costs by increasing the quantity and quality of infrastructure services that support the production, distribution and international trade of a widening array of goods and services.

Analysis of infrastructure's role in facilitating international trade, and consequently regional economic integration, is still rudimentary. This volume aims to help fill that gap in our knowledge by exploring relevant concepts, measurement issues, aspects of the implementation of trade-related infrastructure facilities, and their impacts on poverty, trade, investment and macroeconomic balances.

INFRASTRUCTURE AND REGIONAL CO-OPERATION

Efforts to take advantage of economies of scale in production, procurement or marketing lead firms to look beyond national borders. Promoting efficient financial intermediation, co-ordinating regional public goods, reducing macroeconomic vulnerability to shocks and strengthening security ties offer governments similar incentives to design, develop, and manage regional co-operation and integration. In this context, infrastructure is one of the 'three I's', along with incentives and institutions, that are key determinants of overall growth and the magnitude and productivity of capital inflows as economies open up (Hill, 2004).

As production services become increasingly fragmented and traded internationally, co-operation among the economies participating in those production networks becomes more and more important to maintain or raise a host country industry's competitiveness in supplying those services. Physical infrastructure can convert constraints of the natural environment into economic opportunities by altering comparative advantage (Brooks and Leuterio, 1997).

Infrastructure can not only foster economic growth, but also can strengthen inclusiveness and reduce poverty. Especially, infrastructure investment facilitates regional economic integration through trade and investment expansion, which motivates regional co-operation, including co-operation in infrastructure development, generating a virtuous cycle.

In Chapter 2, John Weiss presents a framework for considering the role of infrastructure in regional co-operation. He utilizes a modified formulation of the effective rate of protection to quantify in a flexible manner the empirical significance of broader trade cost barriers than the familiar tariffs and quotas. Infrastructure investments and interventions, both hard and soft, are then seen to be instruments that reduce trade costs and thereby stimulate closer intra-regional trading linkages. In this manner, the height of barriers posed by different types of trade costs suggests a rough ranking of priorities for infrastructure development to reduce these barriers.

Factors like high freight costs, delays in customs clearance, unofficial payments, slow port landing and handling, and poor governance create barriers to trade. Institutional bottlenecks (administrative, legal, financial, regulatory and other logistics infrastructure), information asymmetries, and discretionary powers that give rise to rent-seeking activities by government officials at various steps of trade transactions also impose costs. These costs can be lowered through facilitation of merchandise and services trade logistics, for both inbound and outbound shipments.

TRADE FACILITATION

Trade facilitation can be defined in many ways. In the context of the World Trade Organization, it primarily refers to simplifying or speeding up administrative documentation procedures at border crossings. In broader usage, it includes measures taken by public and private sectors, non-tariff measures, and physical efforts to facilitate trade by reducing time in transit. Thus, it may encompass both hard and soft infrastructure that facilitates trade.

Philippa Dee et al. (in Chapter 3) include in the scope of trade facilitation all factors affecting the time and money cost of moving goods across international borders. They go on to discuss different methods used to measure the economic effects of reforms aimed at facilitating trade. With this background, implementation options, including institutional arrangements and particularly regional agreements, can be usefully considered.

The success of reforms to facilitate trade depends on their influence on both rent-creating and cost-creating influences. Use of price–cost margins as a performance measure helps to identify rent-creating barriers, while use of cost or productivity as performance measures can identify cost-creating barriers. The identification is important since the treatment effect (as rent-raising or cost-raising) can dominate other factors in the estimated height of barriers with consequent policy implications. The extent to which non-tariff barriers, such as regulation, result in vertical shifts in demand or supply curves and effects on costs and prices can be quantified through antimonde estimation, in which a measure of economic performance is estimated for the counterfactual case with no non-tariff barriers in a market.

Infrastructure quality has a significant effect on trade, and is relatively significant compared with other trade barriers. For example, infrastructure improvements that raise port efficiency from the twenty-fifth to the seventy-fifth percentile can reduce shipping costs by more than 10 per cent (Clark et al., 2004). Infrastructure improvements also generally have the positive effect of applying equally to both foreign and domestic entrants. This is particularly true when infrastructure improvements are complemented by effective competition policy that constrains monopoly power and removes barriers to entry (Brooks, 2005).

SOFT INFRASTRUCTURE

In addition to the administrative aspects of trade facilitation, other forms of soft infrastructure influence international trade. These include (among others) availability of adequate credit and foreign exchange at reasonable rates, a reliable system of legal recourse, effective competition policy and the capacity of existing human capital to process exchanges. Indeed, soft infrastructure may often be more important than hard infrastructure for increasing trade and its profitability.

While difficult to quantify, governance is a critical aspect of soft infrastructure. Definitions vary, but governance can be thought of as the institutions and processes by which collective decisions are made and problems are solved. In Chapter 4, Haider Khan provides a framework for considering how soft infrastructure can contribute to lowering trade costs and strengthening regional co-operation in developing Asia, again modifying the concept of the effective rate of protection. With this formulation, comparing the height of different trade cost barriers allows a rough ranking of priorities in terms of potential soft infrastructure interventions.

Investment in infrastructure is expensive and its realization is relatively slow. Suppliers and operators of infrastructure facilities share a long-term commitment to the host country. Their mutual interest in success leads

them to support a favourable business environment. Ideally, this can translate into a virtuous circle of increased investment, increased growth, and a
further increase in investment. Often the best way to manage the risks
involved is through a public–private partnership. To be successful, the relationship has to be meaningful to both partners. This requires that each
partner has clearly identified objectives and these are understood by the
other. Over time, objectives and markets change, so the relationship needs
to adapt constantly. In this dynamic situation, the transparency of each
partner's business activity is key for maintaining mutual trust.

Advances in technology are changing the potential ownership structure
in some sectors from natural monopolies to competitive enterprises. The
policy environment can either promote or hinder this restructuring. In
many countries, reform of the pricing system is needed to improve investment potential and avoid cost overruns. If pricing and tariff structures are
not properly set, they may affect the commercial viability of an enterprise
or may require supplementary subsidies which may distort resource
allocation. Moreover, subsidies (including foreign aid) may reward or
encourage avoidance of policy reform. Technological advances and policy
reform increase the potential for privatization to improve efficiency, which
also requires a supportive legal, policy and regulatory environment.
Privatization of energy, water, transportation and health-care infrastructure, all have implicit knock-on effects in terms of the relative weights given
to considerations such as the integration of local manufacturers and the
level of efficiency of existing services – both affecting the type and number
of local employees. While there are considerable low-skill tasks associated with the construction phase, maintenance of infrastructure requires
increasingly high-skilled labour.

The underdeveloped financial markets in most developing countries, and
especially the limited availability of debt instruments with a term structure
long enough to match the extended payback period of most infrastructure
projects, is one of the main constraints to infrastructure development in
Asia. Consequently, one priority activity in the region is helping to develop
local capital and financial markets, particularly bond markets, so that the
high Asian domestic saving rates can be converted to long-term productive
investment.

At the international level, co-operation through preferential trade and
investment agreements that strengthen structural reforms and increase the
attractiveness of a destination for foreign investment can leverage domestic policy actions and impact on growth, equity and efficiency, and may
help to reduce corruption. Cross-border co-operation in building and
maintaining soft infrastructure can therefore lead synergistically to a reduction in trade costs and stimulate further investment, trade and growth.

ESTIMATES OF TRADE COSTS

Empirical assessments of trade costs are most frequently derived through estimation of a gravity equation. An excellent survey of estimating trade costs can be found in Anderson and van Wincoop (2004). They estimated that the tax equivalent of representative international trade costs is as high as 74 per cent for industrialized countries, including 21 per cent transportation costs and 44 per cent border-related costs.[1] Costs for developing countries can be much higher.

In Chapter 5, Prabir De estimates a modified gravity equation for eight sectors in ten Asian countries, controlling for distance, to examine the effects of both policy and non-policy barriers to trade. Infrastructure quality and transport costs, along with tariffs, are found to be the main determinants for cross-country variations in trade flows. Infrastructure interventions that reduce the costs of international trade will be crucial for the region to fully realize the gains from recent and prospective trade policy liberalization reforms.

Note that an important component of transportation costs is the time cost involved. This is particularly critical for perishable or other time-sensitive goods. Hummels (2001) found that the time cost of one day in transit for US imports is equivalent to an *ad valorem* tariff rate of 0.8 per cent, implying the equivalent of a 16 per cent tariff on an average ocean shipment of 20 days. Clearly, improvements in infrastructure services that reduce delays in ports, border-crossing procedures or transit times will influence a country's propensity to trade. Developments in containerization and intermodal transport networks contribute to the growth in air shipments and quicker delivery times.

When it comes to infrastructure development in developing countries, there is often scepticism that the benefits do not accrue proportionately to the poor and the very poor. Large-scale infrastructure projects are often viewed as mainly benefiting big business, whether they are domestic or foreign owned. The poor, often also the most deprived of infrastructure services, are generally considered to be secondary beneficiaries, if indeed any benefits at all trickle down to them.

In Chapter 6, Jayant Menon and Peter Warr examine the impacts of road improvement in a poor, land-locked country, Lao People's Democratic Republic (PDR). Lao PDR is also a country with a rugged, mountainous terrain and generally low-quality roads. Because the poorest people often reside far from urban centres, these people are the most disadvantaged by the high transport costs resulting from bad roads. Over the past two decades Lao PDR has made considerable progress in reforming the legal and administrative obstacles to market-based development, which were a legacy of earlier policies. But for people facing very high transport costs arising from inadequate roads, these reforms may be of limited value. For them, markets cannot be accessed except at high cost. Bad roads are clearly an obstacle to attaining the potential benefits from market-based economic reform.

Against this backdrop, Menon and Warr employ a general equilibrium modelling approach to study the effect that rural road improvement has on poverty incidence. They differentiate between three categories of rural villages according to the quality of road access available to them: (1) no vehicular access; (2) dry season only access; and (3) all weather access. They find that, although all forms of road improvement can reduce poverty, the type of road improvement is critical in determining the magnitude of the impact. For instance, when no vehicle access areas are provided with dry-season access roads, the reduction in poverty incidence is about 17 times the reduction that occurs when dry-season access only roads are upgraded to all-weather access roads. The effect on gross domestic product (GDP) is about six times as great. Thus, reducing transport costs for households without road access is highly pro-poor compared with road improvement for households already having dry-season road access.

In determining the most appropriate road-building strategy, however, the relative costs of these two types of road improvement must also be considered. After taking into account the relative costs, they find that these are significantly lower than the corresponding relative benefits, suggesting that there are grounds to reconsider the way in which resources are allocated among these different types of road improvement when poverty reduction is a key objective.

The impact of infrastructure development is a theme that carries over to Chapter 7, but with a few differences. Christopher Edmonds and Manabu Fujimura are interested in the impacts on trade and foreign direct investment (FDI), and so they focus on both domestic and cross-border infrastructure in the Greater Mekong Subregion (GMS). Studies on the impacts of cross-border infrastructure are relatively sparse in the literature, and this study represents the first of its kind for the GMS region.

The way in which road infrastructure, whether domestic or cross-border, affects trade is quite clear, and operates mainly through reductions in transport costs. These reductions in transport costs also underlie the effects on poverty analysed in Chapter 6. But how does infrastructure development affect FDI flows? Reductions in transport costs can have an indirect positive impact on FDI inflows by reducing transaction costs involved in intra-firm vertical integration designed to exploit varied comparative cost advantages across countries. Increases in FDI, in turn, can further increase regional trade and add to the direct effect of reduced transport costs achieved through improvements in the road infrastructure in border areas. When such gains are present, this reduces tendencies towards production agglomeration and, if the advantages of production integration across economies outweigh those from agglomeration, then reductions in transport costs would make FDI complementary to trade. If true, this would define a virtuous cycle of cross-border infrastructure development, trade and investment that fosters increased trade and economic growth.

To do this, they estimate gravity models using panel data from 1981 to 2003 for trade and FDI flows between each pair of the six GMS countries. Their results show that the quality of road infrastructure in the border area between economies has a positive and statistically significant relationship with trade flows between them, and that this relationship is particularly strong when both cross-border and general domestic road infrastructure are included in the estimates. They also find that cross-border roads have distinct effects from domestic road infrastructure, suggesting that investments in cross-border infrastructure have an independent and important role to play in the promotion of regional trade.

Results relating to the impact of road infrastructure on FDI flows are less clear-cut. Cross-border road infrastructure was estimated to have a positive but not statistically significant association with FDI in most models. The poor performance of these models could be due to data shortcomings, however, since the number of countries reporting FDI flows at disaggregated levels is limited. Despite these data limitations, there is some evidence of a positive trade–FDI nexus in which FDI contributes to export growth from the FDI-recipient economies. This is clearly an area that is worthy of further research, especially if a more comprehensive and reliable data-set on FDI can be assembled to facilitate the analysis.

The final two chapters of this book deal with two different aspects of infrastructure: the first relates to the type of infrastructure itself, mainly access to water and sanitation, while the other deals with the financing issue, for all types of infrastructure development.

In Chapter 8, P.B. Anand examines progress with meeting the Millennium Development Goal (MDG) water target in Asia, and considers what role regional co-operation can play in this process. Providing adequate access to potable water should be a high priority for policy from both human development and human security perspectives. Lack of access to water and sanitation has been recognized (through its inclusion in the Human Poverty Index, for instance) as an important characteristic of poverty. Improving access to water and sanitation can also have a significant influence on decreasing the disease burden due to diarrhoeal and other water-related health risks, and on improving overall quality of life.

His findings point to a number of countries missing the MDG water target; however, in most cases, the gap between what is likely to be achieved and the MDG target is less than 5 per cent of the population. The gap is greater than 5 per cent for eight countries, namely, Bangladesh, Vietnam, Turkmenistan, Yemen, Mongolia, Tajikistan, Lao PDR and Cambodia. The results also suggest the following: (1) access to water and sanitation were highly correlated with per capita national income; (2) economic growth has a more than proportionate effect in increasing access to water; and (3) starting point matters: improving access is much harder for countries further away from the target where less than 50 per cent of the population has access to the services.

Anand then moves on to consider how regional co-operation can make a contribution in helping countries achieve the MDG target. The first relates to a regional benchmarking system. A regional-level benchmarking system can help in comparing performance and identifying and sharing best practice.

There is also evidence to suggest that when two or more countries have a significant share of an international water resource, the proportion of the population with access to water increases in countries with stable agreements for such sharing of waters compared with countries without stable agreements.

This highlights the importance of creating a regional infrastructure of 'software' for promoting and sustaining water sector reforms in order to achieve MDG targets. Such networks are clubs that produce regional public goods. Design of incentive mechanisms is crucial for fostering and maintaining such clubs.

Asia needs more infrastructure. A recent joint Asian Development Bank, Japan Bank for International Cooperation and the World Bank (ADB/JBIC/WB, 2005) study estimated that a very large amount – more than \$200 billion per year – is needed to fund estimated needs in infrastructure. New or improved roads, power plants, communications facilities, and water and sanitation systems are urgently needed in most developing countries across the region. The People's Republic of China (PRC) alone is expected to require about 80 per cent of the total investment. Nevertheless, many smaller and poorer developing countries in the region also face severe bottlenecks that call for large amounts of finance.

Where will the money come from to support these investments? Many hope that the private sector will step in to fill the gaps that governments are finding hard to fill. But how realistic is this? What additional steps can cash-strapped governments themselves take to mobilize additional funds? Should governments borrow more to fund domestic infrastructure, or should they raise domestic taxes to meet financing needs? It is important to come to grips with the impacts of different financing options given strong political resistance in some countries to policies such as increased government borrowings and higher taxes.

In Chapter 9, Douglas Brooks and Fan Zhai attempt to answer some of these questions relating to financing infrastructure development. A dynamic general equilibrium model is employed to examine the macroeconomic and inter-generational distributional impacts of increasing public infrastructure investment in the PRC and India. Three alternative financing modes are considered: consumption tax financing, financing through a labour income tax and debt financing. They find that although infrastructure can play an important role in sustaining long-term growth, its effects on the macroeconomy and intergenerational distribution heavily depend on the particular financing mode chosen. In general, the consumption tax financing option is the best in terms of promoting long-term growth and investment, but it involves large short-term transitional costs for existing older generations. Debt financing is more favourable to ensure inter-generational equality, but may have undesirable long-term effects.

There are difficulties in generalizing these results however, which the comparison between the PRC and India reveals. In other words, country-specific factors can be important in determining the magnitude of these effects. In particular, due to its relative scarcity of public infrastructure, India can generally benefit more from increasing the public infrastructure stock. Its current low household saving rate also makes it possible to increase public investment with a smaller crowding out of private investment. However, the high existing stock of government debt in India renders debt financing the least attractive mode of public infrastructure financing.

CONCLUSIONS

In the next few decades, developing Asian economies are likely to make up most of the fastest growing markets in the world. An important part of this growth will come through trade expansion, regional integration through the fragmentation of production networks across national borders, and the broadening and deepening of capital flows to support the trade and production expansion.

The demand for information and related services (such as telecommunications) can be expected to grow faster than the demand for transportation of goods and people. Similarly, as the density of economic activity increases with population and economic growth, and modern flexible manufacturing practices spread, moving production closer to consumers, there may be an increasing demand for short-haul relative to long-haul transportation, at least in the domestic context.

Efforts to expand and enhance infrastructure services will reduce costs of doing business, of achieving economies of scale and of international trade, helping to maximize growth and the benefits of regional trade and investment integration. At the same time, infrastructure improvements, complemented by trade expansion, will attract and facilitate greater investment in productive capacity, expand market access for the poor and broaden the range of consumer choice.

NOTE

1. The costs are not simply additive. The total is $1.44 \times 1.21 - 1 = 0.74$.

REFERENCES

Asian Development Bank, Japan Bank for International Cooperation and the World Bank (ADB/JBIC/WB) (2005), *Connecting East Asia: A New Framework for Infrastructure*, Washington, DC: ADB/JBIC/WB.

Anderson, J. and E. van Wincoop (2004), 'Trade costs', *Journal of Economic Literature*, **42**: 691–751.

Brooks, D. (2005), 'Competition policy, international trade, and foreign direct investment', in D. Brooks and S. Evenett (eds), *Competition Policy and Development in Asia*, London: Palgrave Macmillan, pp. 27 46.

Brooks, D. and E. Leuterio (1997), 'Natural resources, economic structure and Asian infrastructure', in C. Oman, D. Brooks and C. Foy (eds), *Investing in Asia*, Paris: OECD, pp. 155–74.

Clark, X., D. Dollar and A. Micco (2004), 'Port efficiency, maritime transport costs, and bilateral trade', *Journal of Development Economics*, **75** (2): 417 50.

Hill, H. (2004), 'Six Asian economies: issues and lessons', in D. Brooks and H. Hill (eds), *Managing FDI in a Globalizing Economy: Asian Experiences*, London: Palgrave Macmillan, pp. 29–78.

Hummels, D. (2001), 'Time as a trade barrier', *GTAP Working Papers*, 1152, Center for Global Trade Analysis, Department of Agricultural Economics, Purdue University.

PART I

Concepts and Measurement Issues

2. A framework for considering infrastructure for regional co-operation

John Weiss

INTRODUCTION

Regional co-operation has received considerable attention as a means of stimulating 'inclusive-growth' in developing countries in Asia. Conceptually such discussions can be seen as a part of the analysis of the 'New Regionalism'. The focus here is on co-operation through preferential trade and investment agreements that aim to strengthen structural economic reform, aid economic transformation, attract foreign investment and generally raise the international competitiveness of participating countries (IDB, 2002).

It is possible to identify four broad mechanisms and levels for regional co-operation. These distinguish among:

1. co-operation in various aspects of infrastructure in both 'hard' (for example, ports, roads, telecommunications) and 'soft' (for example, social networks, legal frameworks) variants;
2. formal agreements on trade and investment (free trade agreements, investment agreements);
3. monetary co-operation (currency swaps, exchange rate pegs, currency unions); and
4. regional public goods (health and environmental protection).

Here we focus on the first of these mechanisms since the latter three have been examined extensively elsewhere (for example, see Bhattacharya, 2006; Kawai, 2005). The issue we discuss in this chapter is how and why infrastructure can assist in this process. While it may seem intuitively obvious that co-operation and economic activity more generally require infrastructure we seek to clarify more sharply why this might be so and thus provide a framework for subsequent empirical analysis of where policy interventions might be most effective.

INFRASTRUCTURE AND GROWTH

A simple way of thinking about the role of infrastructure in growth more generally is to draw on the distinction made many years ago by Hirschman (1957) between 'social overhead capital' and 'directly productive activity'. The former provides inputs, markets and a working environment for the latter and can be used as a shorthand term for infrastructure in its broadest sense, covering not just 'hard' activities such as roads, ports and power plants, but also the 'soft' institutional side relating to governance mechanisms, social networks and the 'rules of the game' more generally. The notion of social overhead capital supporting market-based productive activity is clearly a simplification, since much infrastructure provides services that are also market based. However, if infrastructure is interpreted broadly to include institutions, the distinction between social overhead capital and productive activity provides a link with the current focus on institutions as a key prerequisite for economic growth.

There continues to be considerable debate on the exact role of institutions in economic growth (see, for example, Rodrik, 2004), with much of the problem a technical one of attributing causation; even if it is agreed almost tautologically that 'good' institutions go with high growth, how far institutional quality is a response to rather than a cause of growth still remains to be resolved in many cases.

There is also a substantial literature linking physical infrastructure with growth. It is possible to use indices of 'hard' infrastructure as explanatory variables in growth regressions, although again problems of reverse causality (what causes what) remain. Jalilian and Weiss (2006) looked at this issue by constructing weighted indices of infrastructure quantity and quality, and then using these separately in growth regressions. The use of best-practice econometrics allows the isolation of the impact of infrastructure, which in this analysis is found to have an independent causal influence on growth, although the actual elasticity of growth to the infrastructure measures is relatively low (see also, Calderon and Serven, 2004).

The common sense of this is that infrastructure impacts on growth through a number of mechanisms: among others by widening access to markets (for example, through better road, rail and port links), by increasing or improving access to inputs (for example, by increased power supplies) and by raising the incentive to invest (for example, by improved communications). These national growth mechanisms will also be relevant when we consider regional co-operation in the form of heightened trade and investment between nations.

'TRADE COST' AND REGIONAL CO-OPERATION

Trade costs are often defined as the range of costs involved in moving a product from a point of production to a market. As such they can refer to both national and cross-border transactions. For example in their authoritative survey Anderson and van Wincoop (2004: 691) define trade costs as 'all costs in getting a good to final user other than the marginal cost of producing the good itself'. Declines in such costs obviously make goods more cost competitive and raise the return on investment. For an analysis of regional co-operation the focus must be on the costs faced by internationally tradable goods. Cross-border aspects of such costs (or 'international trade costs'), can be thought of as the costs of moving a good from the production point in one country to the market in another, and these costs raise barriers to trade and restrict the return on investments in exportables (although they raise it for domestically produced import substitutes). Their incentive effect is similar to other policy-induced barriers to trade (like tariffs and quotas) as they increase protection in the domestic market and create barriers to exports.

International trade costs can be subdivided in various ways, and different components and aspects of infrastructure can be linked with the different types of trade costs. Table 2.1 sets out some of the links to bring out the wide range of infrastructure features that will impact on these costs.

Table 2.1   Illustrations of trade cost and infrastructure interventions

Type of trade cost	Infrastructure intervention
Transport cost	Ports, road, rail, air links
Freight insurance	Insurance regulation
Customs delays	Harmonization of customs procedures
Unofficial payments	Governance reform
Time in transit	Road, rail, air links
Information search	Investment climate
Management of supply chain	Telecommunications, investment climate, regulatory environment
Excess inventories	Ports, road, rail, air links, harmonization of customs procedures
Currency changes (cost of hedging)	Financial sector regulation

The significance of this for regional co-operation is that international trade costs form a potentially important barrier to trade and that improvements in infrastructure, for example through the various mechanisms noted in Table 2.1, can lower these barriers. The theoretical framework that is relevant for an analysis of their impact is an extension of the well known effective rate of protection (ERP) indicator (Balassa, 1971; Corden, 1972). The conventional ERP formulation quantifies how far value added in a line of production is impacted by policy-induced barriers to trade in the form of tariff or quota protection on outputs and inputs. This approach has been extended to incorporate transport costs on outputs and inputs (Amjadi and Yeats, 1995). In principle, however, there is no reason why non-transport international trade costs cannot also be added as they also provide a form of protection that allows domestic producers to capture a higher level of value added, while still remaining price competitive with foreign suppliers.

Formally we can extend the ERP concept so that

$$ERPi = (ti - \Sigma aji \cdot tj)/(1 - \Sigma aji) + (ri - \Sigma aji \cdot rj)/(1 - \Sigma aji) \quad (2.1)$$
$$+ (ni - \Sigma aji \cdot nj)/(1 - \Sigma aji)$$

where i is the final product, j is an internationally traded production input and aji is the (unobservable) coefficient for units of j per unit of i with no policy barriers to trade and no international trade cost; ti and tj are the rate of tariff or tariff equivalent of policy-induced trade barriers on i and j respectively, ri and rj are the transport costs per unit of i and j respectively and ni and nj are the non-transport trade costs per unit of i and j.[1] Coefficient aji is not directly observable and in practice is proxied by actual inputs per unit of output.

The first term gives the potential proportionate increase in value added due to policy-induced protection, the second term gives the proportionate increase due to transport costs and the third the proportionate increase due to other international trade costs. In other words the sum of these gives the increase in potential income to domestic factors in comparison with a situation where there are zero tariffs, no quotas and no trade costs. Trade cost thus potentially increase 'natural' protection and since they can vary significantly between products they can impact on (or distort) relative prices with efficiency implications.

HOW DO WE MEASURE TRADE COSTS?

Before one can incorporate trade costs in a calculation of effective protection one needs an estimate of their magnitude (that is the coefficients ri and

ni in (2.1) above). Quantification of trade costs can be done by case study observation, through surveys of product prices at different stages of the supply chain. This is arguably the most desirable way of quantification and can be seen as a version of 'value-chain analysis' (see Kaplinsky, 2000). However in the literature a number of alternative simpler approaches have also been tried mostly focusing on the transport component.

One approach is to take the difference between cost, insurance and freight (CIF) and free on board (FOB) prices of a commodity as a measure of transport and insurance costs (see, for example, Limao and Venables, 2001). Hence for trade between countries j and k we have

$$ri = (ci - fi)/fi \qquad (2.2)$$

where ri is transport and insurance costs per unit of i, ci is the CIF import price in k and fi is the FOB export price in j.

If an aggregate trade cost measure r is required (2.2) will have to be weighted by the share of i in the total value of trade between j and k (wi), so we have

$$r = \Sigma_i ((ci - fi)/fi) * wi. \qquad (2.3)$$

The difficulty with this approach is the lack of consistency in price data at the CIF and FOB levels, which may be aggregated across different products. This can lead to wide variations in ri between products that appear unlikely to reflect the actual situation. Also there is the issue of bias in estimating aggregate measures when using this approach since the weights (wi) will reflect actual trade patterns that have been influenced by trade costs. Ideally the weights should reflect the potential trade shares in the absence of trade costs (similar to the free trade input coefficients required in theory in (2.1)).

A second approach uses international freight rate data as a direct measure of transport cost; Limao and Venables (2001) for example use quotations from shipping companies and De (2006b) uses freight rates collected by one particular shipping company. Here individual commodity data will rarely be used and r (excluding insurance) will be estimated as a weighted average across commodities so

$$r = \Sigma_i si \cdot qi \qquad (2.4)$$

where si is the shipping cost for commodity i per physical unit shipped from country j to k and qi is the share of i in the volume of trade between j and k.

Although use of shipping rates has the advantage of obtaining direct data on transport costs like the use of the CIF–FOB margin it omits other

elements of trade cost. Hence as a third approach an index of infrastructure quality is often combined with one or other of the transport costs estimates in an econometric model. Infrastructure quality is therefore used as
a proxy for the non-transport components of trade costs. For example,
Limao and Venables (2001) base their infrastructure index on an aggregation of road density, paved road network, rail network and telephone lines
per person. The econometric model used is normally a variation of the
gravity equation so that

$$Y = f(d, \mathbf{Z}, T, I, \varepsilon) \qquad (2.5)$$

where Y reflects trade between two partners, d is distance between them, $\mathbf{Z}$
is vector of country characteristics, such as income per capita, T is a
measure of transport cost between the countries, I covers a separate index
of infrastructure for both countries and ε is an error term.[2]
   The responsiveness of trade to T and I gives an indication of the importance of trade costs. Such analysis will not give a direct per unit estimate for
the impact of non-transport costs, however if the volume effect of I on
trade is combined with an assumed price elasticity this will allow the estimation of an implicit price effect (or tariff equivalent).

HOW SIGNIFICANT ARE TRADE COSTS?

While arguments about the importance of trade costs are widely recognized
there is a lack of empirical evidence, particularly in the Asian context. It is
now widely asserted that trade costs are more important than policy barriers to trade; for example Anderson and van Wincoop (2004: 693) argue that
'inferred border costs appear on average to dwarf the effect of tariff and non-
tariff barriers'. Their 'representative' international trade costs for industrialized countries, a combination of transport and non-transport costs, are as
high as 74 per cent, compared with average tariffs of less than 5 per cent. Of
these international trade costs, roughly one-third are transport related and
the rest cover the various types of trade cost listed in Table 2.1. This rough
figure of 74 per cent, which is no more than illustrative, can be interpreted as
the sum of ri and ni in (2.1) above. If international trade costs for inputs are
below those for outputs the representative effective protection rate created by
trade cost (terms two and three in (2.1)) will be higher still.
   More specific estimates of this type for developing countries are required
to gain a sense of the magnitude of the barriers to regional co-operation
through trade. Work on sub-Saharan Africa some years ago was novel in
deriving effective protection estimates due to transport costs (the second

term in (2.1)) and highlighted the barriers to African exports posed by poor transport infrastructure (Amjadi and Yeats, 1995). For example, while import tariffs facing African goods in the USA were relatively low the tariff equivalent of higher transport costs from Africa was on average eight percentage points above the tariff rate. These are nominal protection figures however, and with low value-added content effective protection afforded US producers from transport costs will be much higher. In an analysis for the early 1990s the authors found an average effective protection due to transport of 25 per cent compared with a nominal one of 15 per cent (Amjadi and Yeats, 1995: table 5).

More approximate estimates of the ratio of freight costs to imports are available for different regions. For the world around the year 2000 these are put at 5 per cent, while for Asia and Africa they are 8 per cent and 11.5 per cent respectively (cited in Mesquita, 2006). These figures are likely to be below effective tariffs (revenue collected divided by import value). Detailed country comparisons for Brazil reveal that for a majority of products freight costs as a percentage of imports exceed effective tariffs, although not for the most industrially sophisticated goods (Mesquita, 2006).

An important part of the argument over the significance of trade costs (not just transport costs) is their variation across products. There has been considerable theoretical discussion on deadweight losses incurred through significant variations in tariffs, and similar arguments apply to trade costs more generally. It is intuitively clear that transport costs per unit of value will vary across products with different weight to value ratios, but other aspects of trade cost also appear to differ substantially between products. We have some approximate evidence on this from trade data that allow a comparison between FOB and CIF values for the same product with the CIF–FOB margin interpreted as a measure of non-policy induced trade cost. De (2006a: tables 4 to 6) for example reports the CIF–FOB margin at the four-digit level for the top ten product categories in trade with very considerable variation between them. For the People's Republic of China's imports from Japan, for example, in 2004 the margin as a percentage of the CIF price ranges from a low of 2 per cent to a high of 123 per cent (De, 2006a: table 4b). Import tariffs on the other hand range from zero to 35 per cent. As we have noted, there are doubts about the accuracy and comparability of this FOB and CIF price data, but nonetheless the range of trade costs implied by this data seems very wide.

Infrastructure stock and its quality also seem to matter considerably for trade flows. In their widely cited study, Limao and Venables (2001) find that deterioration in their infrastructure index from the median score to the 75 percentile raises transport costs by 12 per cent with a subsequent significant impact on trade. Time can also be an important element in trade cost.

Djankov et al. (2006) find that delays in shipment are also a significant negative influence on trade. Each additional day prior to shipment reduces trade by 1 per cent or more. Similarly, for US imports Hummels (2001) finds that one day in transit has a cost equivalent to a tariff of 0.8 per cent, so for an average ocean shipment of 20 days the tariff equivalent is 16 per cent (cited in Brooks et al., 2005).

ARE BARRIERS TO TRADE STILL IMPORTANT FOR ASIA?

Having noted the scale and variability of trade costs, the key question is whether they are currently a significant barrier to regional co-operation and closer trading ties. It is well known that, despite the existence of those trade costs, East Asia has seen a very rapid growth of intra-regional trade ties in recent years, although the same is much less true for South and Central Asia. However, this does not necessarily imply that intra-regional trade cannot expand still further. There are alternative pieces of evidence to support this.

First, we can point to the vast literature in the 1990s that addressed the impact of trade liberalization, in terms of tariff and quota reductions, on trade flows. In general, while there has been dispute as to the impact of trade reform on income growth, in terms of trade flows there is little doubt that trade did expand significantly in response to reductions in policy-induced trade barriers.[3] If trade cost barriers are as high as often claimed, their reduction should also see a significant rise in trade. This is illustrated in the modelling exercise of Brooks et al. (2005), who assume current trade costs raise prices by 120 per cent. They simulate the change in trade if these trade costs are halved. The results show that the impact of this reduction dwarfs the effect of the removal of all remaining policy-induced (tariff and quota) barriers. They conclude that trade efficiency offers much greater growth potential than tariff reform.

Second, we can draw on trade intensity indices (TII) from the very detailed work of Ng and Yeats (2003) on East Asia. The TII is defined simply as

$$TII_{ij} = (x_{ij}/X_{it})/(x_{wj}/X_{wt}) \qquad (2.6)$$

where we have trade between countries i and j and x_{ij} is the exports of i to j and X_{it} is the total exports of i; w is the world, x_{wj} is world exports to j and X_{wt} is total world exports. Thus TII is simply the ratio of j's share in i's exports to j's share in world exports. If it exceeds 1.0 we can say there is an 'intense' trade relation. In this analysis *j* can be a partner country or a regional group of countries. As expected for all bilateral trade flows in East Asia, TII exceeds 1.0 often by a very wide margin. However, if one corrects for distance between trading partners and compares a predicted TII derived from a regression model with the actual TII, in 2001 for about 40 per cent (by number not value) of the possible bilateral trade flows in the East Asian region, the actual index was below the predicted figure (Ng and Yeats, 2003: 23). In other words, given the distances involved, one would have expected the partners to trade even more with each other than they actually did. The analysis is simple as it does not allow for other factors apart from distance, but it does highlight that the apparently high level of trade intensity in the region may not be as strong as it first appears.

Third, this analysis has been extended by the growing number of gravity models that relate trade between partners to distance, a set of country char-acteristics and proxies for trade costs. Invariably the latter prove to be a significant explanatory variable, negatively related to trade levels. For example, De (2006b) examines bilateral trade between 11 partner countries in Asia both aggregated and disaggregated by sector. He tests for the significance of transport costs (measured separately by equations (2.3) and (2.4) above), and for an index of infrastructure stock. Version (2.4) of trans-port costs based on shipping rates works better, and for the pooled total trade data the elasticity of trade to transport costs is -0.12. The infrastructure index for the exporting (but not the importing) country is also significant with a negative sign. Import tariffs are not significant (De, 2006b: table 5).

Fujimura and Edwards (2006) use a similar framework for bilateral trade in the Greater Mekong region, although their analysis has no data on trans-port cost, which they proxy by distance. Their main concern is to establish a relation between road infrastructure, both national and cross-border, and trade. They find a relatively high trade elasticity with respect to cross-border roads of between 0.6 and 1.4, varying with model specification. As in De (2006b), policy-induced trade barriers, as measured by tariffs, do not have a significant influence on trade.

Much more work remains to be done in extending the definition of trade cost to be used in these models, but insofar as higher trade can stimulate income growth there are further potential benefits from infrastructure invest-ment or intervention in these areas to lower trade cost barriers to trade.

THE INCENTIVE TO INVEST

As with any other form of cost, an increase in trade costs of all types will be expected to impact on the incentive to invest. This is reflected in the responses typically found in 'investment climate' surveys which indicate that poor-quality hard infrastructure that provides poor road and air communications, unreliable power supplies and congested ports is a major disincentive to investment. Similarly, weak institutions or poor soft infrastructure are also cited frequently as obstacles to investment (World Bank, 2005).

It is important in welfare terms to distinguish between trade cost elements that act as equivalent to a tax and thus impact on price and those that use up real resources and therefore raise costs with a consequent effect on prices. Unofficial payments in the form of bribes are quasi-taxes. Their effect is redistributive transferring rents (or surplus profits) from producers and consumers to the recipients of these payments. The welfare effect of a fall (or a rise) in such payments is shown by an increase (or a decrease) in the welfare triangles of producer and consumer surplus. On the other hand, trade costs such as freight and insurance charges, delays in transit or search and communications costs require the use of real resources and a fall or a rise in these costs creates changes in welfare rectangles rather than triangles, with the former considerably larger than the latter.[4]

The incidence of the effects of a change in trade costs of either the redistributive or resource-using type will be determined by demand and supply elasticities, so not all trade costs need be borne by the domestic purchaser or importer. In the extreme case in which supply of a good is perfectly inelastic any increase in trade costs will be borne wholly by the supplier. Any attempt to pass on higher trade cost will raise the domestic price above the market-clearing level and the resulting excess supply will bring down the price. At the other extreme, where demand is perfectly inelastic, any increase in trade cost will be borne solely by the purchaser or importer. Most real-world situations will involve less than perfectly inelastic demand and supply schedules, and who bears the largest share of increases in trade costs (or who benefits most by their reduction) will be determined by the size of demand and supply elasticities, and when elasticities are equal the burden is shared equally. However, assuming a less than perfectly elastic supply schedule, the more the elasticity of demand falls the higher will be the proportion of trade cost borne by the purchaser or importer, and hence the greater will be the negative impact on their investment plans.[5]

CONCLUSIONS

This chapter has attempted to provide a framework for considering how infrastructure – both in hard and soft variants – can contribute to the process of regional co-operation in various parts of Asia. It has drawn on the familiar formulation of the effective rate of protection – developed decades ago when tariffs and quotas were serious barriers to trade – and argued that this concept can be modified to quantify the empirical significance of broader trade cost barriers. The effective rate of protection concept is flexible enough to allow the effect of a range of potential trade costs to be addressed. Infrastructure interventions can be interpreted as instruments to lower trade costs and hence are a means of stimulating closer trading links.

We have emphasized specifically the relationship between both hard and soft infrastructure and trade costs. Clearly, much work remains to be done to quantify the impact of trade costs both on domestic value added and through protection on trade flows. The basic policy point is that if we have a clear indication of the height of the barriers posed by different types of trade cost, this will give us a rough ranking of priorities in terms of infrastructure interventions to lower these. While a vast amount of empirical work in the 1960s and 1970s quantified the barriers to trade caused by tariffs and quotas, as yet relatively little has been done to quantify protection from these largely 'non-policy' barriers. More specifically it will be useful to know how high are the barriers to trade created by factors like high freight costs, slow port handling, customs delays, lack of competition in the insurance sector, poor corporate governance, unofficial payments, and so forth. Some of these factors may be intrinsically difficult to quantify but there is a potentially rich field here for further empirical work.

NOTES

1. Here for simplicity we treat non-traded inputs as traded inputs with a zero tariff and assume away the impact of tariffs, quotas and trade costs on their price. Similarly this expression assumes no interaction between tariffs and trade costs, whereas in practice tariffs are typically imposed on CIF values which will include trade costs. With an interaction effect on price the expression becomes

$$ERPi = (ti - \Sigma aji \cdot tj)/(1 - \Sigma aji) + (ri - \Sigma aji \cdot rj)/(1 - \Sigma aji) + (ni - \Sigma aji \cdot nj)/(1 - \Sigma aji)$$
$$+ (ti \cdot (ri + ni) - \Sigma aji \cdot tj \cdot (rj + nj)/(1 - \Sigma aji)).$$

2. When distance and transport costs are closely correlated as may often be the case inclusion of both may lead to error.
3. Weiss (1992), for example, showed the link between tariff reform in Mexico in the 1980s and the growth of exports.
4. Dee (2006) terms the redistributive effect 'rent creating' and illustrates the distinction between welfare triangles and rectangles.
5. Amjadi and Yeats (1995) demonstrate these points graphically in the case of freight costs.

REFERENCES

Amjadi, A. and A.J. Yeats (1995), 'Have transport costs contributed to the relative decline of African exports?', *World Bank Policy Research Working Paper*, 1559, Washington, DC: World Bank.

Anderson, J. and E. van Wincoop (2004), 'Trade costs', *Journal of Economic Literature*, **40** (11), 691–751.

Balassa, B. (1971), *The Structure of Protection in Developing Countries*, Baltimore, MD: Johns Hopkins University Press.

Bhattacharya, B. (2006), 'Emergence of regional trade blocs in Asia: problems and prospects', workshop on 'Understanding the latest wave of regional trade and co-operation agreements', CESifo, Venice International University, 19–20 July.

Brooks, D., D. Roland-Holst and F. Zhai (2005), 'Asia's long-term growth and integration: reaching beyond trade policy barriers', *ERD Policy Brief*, Manila: Asian Development Bank.

Calderon, C. and L. Serven (2004), 'The effects of infrastructure development on growth and income distribution', *World Bank Policy Research Working Paper*, 3400, Washington, DC: World Bank.

Corden, W.M. (1972), *The Theory of Protection*, Oxford: Clarendon Press.

De, P. (2006a), 'Regional trade in Northeast Asia: why do trade costs matter?', workshop on 'Understanding the latest wave of regional trade and co-operation agreements', CESifo, Venice International University, 19–20 July.

De. P. (2006b), 'Empirical estimates of trade costs for Asia', paper presented at the Third LAEBA conference, Seoul, November.

Dee, P. (2006), 'Trade facilitation: what, why, how, where and when', paper presented at the Third LAEBA conference, Seoul, November.

Djankov, S., C. Freund and C. Pham (2006), 'Trading on time', mimeo, World Bank, Washington, DC.

Fujimura, M. and C. Edwards (2006), 'Impact of cross-border road infrastructure on trade and investment in the Greater Mekong Subregion', paper presented at the Third LAEBA conference, Seoul, November.

Hirschman, A. (1957), *The Strategy of Economic Development*, New Haven, CT: Yale University Press.

Hummels, D. (2001), 'Time as a trade barrier', *GTAP Working Papers*, Centre for Global Trade Analysis, Purdue University.

Inter-American Development Bank (IDB) (2002), *Beyond Borders: The New Regionalism in Latin America*, Inter-American Development Bank, Economic and Social Progress in Latin America Report 2002, Washington, DC.

Jalilian, H. and J. Weiss (2006), 'Infrastructure and poverty: cross country evidence', in J. Weiss and H.A. Khan (eds), *Poverty Strategies in Asia: A Growth Plus Approach*, Cheltenham, UK and Northampton, MA, USA: Edward Elgar.

Kaplinsky, R. (2000), 'Spreading the gains from globalization: what can be learned from value chain analysis?', *Journal of Development Studies*, **37** (2), 117–46.

Kawai, M. (2005), 'East Asian economic regionalism: progress and challenges', *Journal of Asian Economics*, **16** (1), 29–55.

Limao, N. and A. Venables (2001), 'Infrastructure, geographical disadvantage, transport costs and trade', *World Bank Economic Review*, **15**, 451–79.

Mesquita, M. (2006), 'Trade costs and the economic fundamentals of the Initiative for Integration of Regional Infrastructure in South America (IIRSA)', paper presented at the Third LAEBA conference, Seoul, November.

Ng, F. and A. Yeats (2003), 'Major trade trends in Asia: what are their implications for regional co-operation and growth?', *World Bank Policy Research Working Paper*, 3084, Washington, DC: World Bank.

Rodrik, D. (2004), 'Getting institutions right', mimeo, Harvard University.

Weiss, J. (1992), 'Trade liberalization in Mexico in the 1980s: concepts, measures and short-run effects', *Weltwirtshaftliches Archiv*, **128** (4), 711–26.

World Bank (2005), *World Development Report 2005*, Washington, DC: World Bank.

3. Trade facilitation: what, why, how, where and when?[1]

Philippa Dee, Christopher Findlay and Richard Pomfret

I. INTRODUCTION

The degree to which trade is facilitated depends on a wide range of aspects of the trading system. In our framework, the scope of trade facilitation includes all factors affecting the full (time and money) cost of the movement of goods across international borders. This performance depends not only on the systems for processing information about goods, but also on systems used for their physical movement.

Trade facilitation is more narrowly defined in some settings. For example, according to the definition currently used in the World Trade Organization (WTO) it is 'the simplification and harmonization of international trade procedures, including the activities, practices and formalities involved in collecting, presenting, communicating and processing data and other information required for the movement of goods in international trade.'[2] This definition of the scope of trade facilitation refers to administrative processes at the border and these are the focus of trade negotiations in the WTO and in various regional trading arrangements. Business commentators or survey respondents often stress the significance of those matters for their business relative to other barriers to international commerce such as tariffs. However, we present and argue for a wider definition of trade facilitation, which refers to a range of processes that affect the movement of goods, including administrative systems that are related to non-tariff barriers, and to the quality of relevant infrastructure (the 'what' question).

Matters of definition are the topic of the next section of the chapter, where we also note the different types of welfare effects associated with trade facilitation (the 'why' question). Maintaining our focus on welfare effects, we then discuss the various methods that have been used to measure the economic effects of reforms contributing to trade facilitation and we review a number of studies of the impact of reform. With this background we examine options for the implementation of trade facilitation measures, with particular attention to their treatment in regional agreements (the 'how' question). We close with some observations about institutional arrangements for the management of trade facilitation reform (the 'where' question).

II. WHAT AND WHY

The full (time and money) cost of the movement of goods across international borders depends not only on the systems for processing information about goods, but also on systems used for their physical movement.

The former relates in most cases to the application of specific border policies, such as tariffs, and much of the work on trade facilitation has concentrated on customs clearance systems, for example. However non-tariff barriers are also associated with administrative process and specific information-reporting, collection and decision-making systems, and they too should be considered. A checklist of such activities can be derived from the set of measures that traditionally were thought of as non-tariff barriers. The United Nations Conference on Trade and Development (UNCTAD) Coding System of Trade Control Measures defines over 100 measures under the classifications of:

- para-tariff measures – customs surcharges, additional taxes and charges, decreed customs valuation;
- price control measures – administrative pricing, voluntary export restraints, variable charges;
- finance measures – advance payment requirements, regulation concerning terms of payment for imports, transfer delays and queuing;
- quantity control measures – non-automatic licensing, quotas, prohibitions, export restraint arrangements, enterprise-specific restrictions;
- monopolistic measures – a single channel for imports, compulsory national services; and
- technical measures – technical regulations, pre-shipment inspection, special customs formalities.

To this list, as noted, we would add the conditions affecting the physical movement of goods. The time and cost of movements also matter. Those variables will be related to the quality of the infrastructure associated with border movements, such as port and road capacity and the cost of intermodal transfers. Included in this category might also be inspections undertaken for security purposes (PECC, 2005).

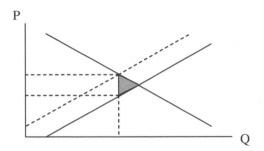

Figure 3.1a   Rent-creating non-tariff barriers

The degree to which trade is facilitated therefore depends on a range of features of the trading system. These features are associated with both rent-creating and cost-creating effects. The rent-creating effects, which arise from limiting entry, are familiar. Measures which have these effects are akin to taxes, or tariffs and quotas. Some other features of the trading system are cost-creating, and this may be in addition to their effects on rents. For example, cargo inspections slow down the movement of goods.[3] Compliance costs also increase the cost of delivery (for example, compliance with technical measures). Further, administrative procedures associated with the application of 'rent-creating' quantity controls or other charges can add to the full cost of delivery of goods (for example, the time and money costs of applying for an import licence). Different measures or features of the trading system can therefore add to both rents and costs to different degrees.

The welfare and distributional effects of various measures are illustrated in Figure 3.1. Liberalization of rent-creating measures will yield 'triangle gains' in producer and consumer surplus associated with improvements in allocative efficiency (the shaded area in Figure 3.1a), but would also have redistributive effects associated with the elimination of rents to incumbents.[4] Alternatively, liberalization of cost-escalating measures, which create the same vertical shift in the supply curve, would be equivalent to a productivity improvement (saving in real resources), and yield 'roughly rectangle' gains associated with a downward shift in supply curves (the shaded area in Figure 3.1b). This could increase returns for the incumbent service providers, as well as lowering costs for users elsewhere in the economy.

The distinction between these effects is critical, for a number of reasons. The aggregate welfare effect of measures which are cost-creating (for the same movement in the supply curve) will be greater than rent-creating measures, that is, the rectangle gains are likely to exceed triangle gains by a significant margin. This suggests priority attention to cost-creating

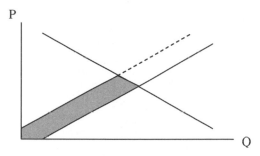

Figure 3.1b   Cost-escalating non-tariff barriers

measures in a setting of unilateral or non-discriminatory multilateral reform programmes. In the context of preferential trade agreements, the danger of net welfare losses from net trade diversion arises only if the relevant barriers are rent-creating (see also Baldwin, 1994). Furthermore, the differential effects on incumbent suppliers suggests the political economy of reform programmes will differ for cost-escalating measures compared to those which added to rents.

In summary, a wide range of measures affect the full cost of movement of goods between countries. All such measures fall within the scope of 'trade facilitation'. However, these measures affect costs and rents to varying degrees and this distinction is important in the design and implementation of policy reform. Empirical work would ideally be able to make this distinction and measure the difference.

In the following sections we outline methods for achieving these goals and then review relevant empirical work. We begin with a review of work on the impact of non-tariff barriers (NTBs), for two reasons: (1) the administration of NTBs is an important element of the set of trade facilitation issues, and (2) the same methodology applied to measure the impact of NTBs, we argue, is relevant to work on the wider set of trade facilitation measures. In this review, however, we also pay particular attention to the links between infrastructure and trade.

III.   HOW TO MEASURE ECONOMIC EFFECTS

Measuring the economic effects of non-tariff barriers requires a counterfactual – a representation of how economic performance would differ if the non-tariff barriers were not in place. Measurement techniques have followed one of two strategies for obtaining a measure of the counterfactual, depending on whether the traded good or service can be seen as homogeneous across different markets (Figure 3.2).

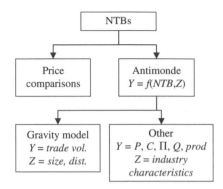

Figure 3.2   Measurement methods

If the good or service is homogeneous, the counterfactual can be obtained by observing the characteristics (typically the price) of that good or service in some other market where non-tariff barriers do not apply. Often this involves price comparisons between domestic and foreign markets. Sometimes it involves price comparisons of similar goods within a domestic market. Deardorff and Stern (1997) give the most detailed description of this approach. Recent applications are by Ando (2005), Bradford (2005), Dean et al. (2005) and Yoo (2005). Homogeneity ensures that the relevant counterfactual is directly observable.

If no similar good or service can be found, then the counterfactual cannot be observed – it needs to be constructed. Econometric methods are used to estimate the effects of some measure of non-tariff barriers (NTB) on some measure of economic performance (Y) in a market, controlling for all the other factors (Z) that affect economic performance in that market. The estimated model is then used to construct the value Y' that would obtain in that market if there were no non-tariff barriers (normally, if NTB took a zero value). This is often called the *antimonde*.

One particular application of this second approach is the well-known gravity model. In that model, the measure of economic performance Y is bilateral trade volumes, and the control variables Z include the sizes of the trading partner economies and the distance between them. Recent applications of the gravity model framework to quantifying the effects of trade facilitation include Estevadeordal and Suominen (2005), Wilson et al. (2005), Otsuki et al. (2001), Guasch and Spiller (1999), Moenius (1999) and Swann et al. (1996). We review some of these studies in more detail in a later section.

Another application of the antimonde approach is measurement of regulatory barriers to services trade. Since services are highly differentiated to the needs to individual consumers, non-homogeneity is acute. Further, the regulatory barriers operate behind the border. So the measures of economic performance are typically behind-the-border measures of price (P), cost (C), profit (Π), or productivity, while the controls are other industry characteristics. Dee (2005a) gives a brief survey of the recent literature.[5]

The Antimonde Approach

While the antimonde approach does not require an observable measure of the counterfactual, it does require a quantifiable measure of the non-tariff barrier. Unlike tariffs, these do not come with a ready number attached. There have been a number of approaches to this problem.

An early approach was to avoid quantifying *NTB* directly, but to attribute the residuals from a regression of outcomes Y on controls Z to the presence or absence of non-tariff barriers. This was the approach taken in the gravity model estimation by Francois and Hoekman (1999), for example, in their early work on quantifying services trade barriers. A number of writers (for example, Whalley, 2004) have criticized this indirect approach as risking misattribution of the effects of other omitted variables to non-trade barriers, and of leading to paradoxical results, such as negative impacts of non-tariff barriers.

A second approach has been to use frequency counts of non-tariff measures as quantifiable regressors. For example, Swann et al. (1996) used simple counts of the stocks of idiosyncratic or international standards in the UK and Germany in their study of the effects of standards on trade volumes. Frequency measures have featured in previous surveys of non-tariff quantification (Bora et al., 2002; Deardorff and Stern, 1997) as measures of economic effects in their own right, and have been rightly criticized as measuring prevalence, rather than economic significance. But they can play a vital role as explicit measures of policy in an antimonde estimation, where the estimation process is the extra step that establishes economic significance.

Recently a more sophisticated frequency count approach has been used to quantify the presence of NTBs. This involves compiling an index measure, taking account of the severity of non-tariff barriers as well as their prevalence. Index measures can be compiled to capture a single dimension of policy. For example, in measuring the policy determinants of port efficiency, Clark et al. (2004) included an index measure, ranging from 1 to 7, that measures the absence of organized crime. Data on this were taken from the Global Competitiveness Report, based on surveys of representative firms about whether organized crime did not impose significant costs on business and was not a burden.

Alternatively, to conserve degrees of freedom, an index can be compiled that weights together more than one dimension of policy. This requires judgements, not just about the relative severity of each policy, but also about the relative severity of the different policies against each other. For example, Kalirajan et al. (2000) use an index measure of policy barriers to trade in banking services that weights together licensing restrictions, foreign equity limits, restrictions on lending, restrictions on raising funds, prohibitions on other lines of business (for example, insurance, securities), limits on the number of banking outlets and restrictions on the temporary movement of people.

In some cases, the different dimensions of policy are weighted together using judgemental weights assigned by the researcher. In other cases, factor analysis is used to determine linear combinations of individual policies that best 'span' (in the technical, mathematical sense) the total policy space. Neither approach is entirely satisfactory. The quality of judgemental weights depends on the extent to which the researcher has specialist knowledge of the industry under study. Factor analysis confuses in-sample variation with economic significance. Better than either approach is to enter indices of each policy dimension separately into the antimonde estimation. Using principal components here, rather than factor analysis in a prior step, could help to conserve degrees of freedom, while showing which combinations of policy measures best 'spanned' the economic outcome space – a truer measure of economic significance.

The quality of the measures derived using antimonde estimation also depends on the quality and comprehensiveness of the control variables Z. There has been a recent revival of interest in the theoretical foundations of the gravity model, which determine the control variables in that context (for example, Baier and Bergstrand, 2001; Deardorff, 1998; Evenett and Keller, 2002; Feenstra et al., 2001). Anderson and van Wincoop (2003) have shown that many empirical implementations have strayed from the theoretically derived reduced form, by omitting measures of relative trade resistance. Harrigan (2004) shows how the effects of relative trade resistance (or relative distance, in his interpretation) can be controlled for using country fixed effects.

In the services trade literature, the empirical models of sectoral performance have typically been drawn from the industrial organization literature on structure, conduct and performance, and the relevant control variables Z have varied widely from one sector to the next. For example, in banking they have included interest rate volatility and measures of the extent of prudential regulation (Barth et al., 2004; Kalirajan et al., 2000), in telecommunications they have included household density and the length of waiting lists for a fixed line connection (Warren, 2000), while in electricity generation they have included the proportion of electricity generated from hydro or nuclear sources (Steiner, 2000). Recent empirical support for the structure–conduct–performance approach has been provided by Slade (2004). Some authors have used a plethora of fixed effects in lieu of structural controls (for example, Moenius, 1999).

As will be seen, when estimates of non-tariff barriers are used in modelling exercises of trade liberalization, the question discussed earlier of whether they are rent-creating or cost-escalating is often argued by assertion. But the antimonde estimation can provide some guidance. Estimation that uses price cost margins as a performance measure can identify whether barriers are rent-creating. Estimation that uses cost or productivity as a performance measure can identify whether barriers are cost-escalating. Ideally, more than one performance measure should be used.[6]

The aim of antimonde estimation is to measure the extent to which non-tariff barriers cause a vertical shift in the supply or demand curve.[7] So, ideally, the econometric models of sectoral performance should be both developed and estimated at the structural level – that is, supply and demand side influences should be separately identified and estimated. In practice, some models are developed structurally but then estimated in reduced form, as in the model of financial intermediation used by Kalirajan et al. (2000). Other models are both developed and estimated in reduced form, as with the model of electricity prices used by Steiner (2000). Hence it is not always clear that the estimated price or cost wedge corresponds to a vertical shift in the supply or demand curve. On this score, the direct effects of non-tariff barriers may be underestimated.

Price Comparisons

Price comparisons rely on the assumption of homogeneity for a directly observable measure of the counterfactual, and do not require a quantifiable measure of the non-tariff barrier. But for that reason, they do not provide information about which particular non-tariff barriers are responsible for the price gap. As noted, Deardorff and Stern (1997) give a thorough overview of this approach, so the focus here is on recent developments.

When the prices being compared are at different stages in the distribution chain, corrections have to be made to account for transport and other distribution costs (perhaps including tariffs) between the two stages. Bradford (2005) makes this correction using direct data on distribution margins, transport costs and indirect taxes from input–output sources, as well as direct tariff data. Dean et al. (2005) use econometric techniques to control for the influence of transport costs and wholesale and retail margins, using proxy measures of these variables.

Ando (2005) also mixes price comparisons with antimonde estimation techniques. She uses price comparisons (net of tariff levels) to estimate overall tariff equivalents of non-tariff barriers, and then econometrically estimates a relationship between these tariff equivalents and by-type frequency ratios (with other control variables), to decompose the tariff equivalents into price effects by type of measure. Thus several recent applications of price comparisons have used the same econometric techniques as in the antimonde literature, both to control for other factors, and to attribute economic effects to particular policies.

IV. WITH WHAT RESULT – THE GAINS FROM REFORM[8]

The recent empirical literature has confirmed the significance of a variety of measures that facilitate trade. We begin with studies that focus on policies related to infrastructure services.

Infrastructure and Trade

A number of papers that examine links between infrastructure and transport or logistics services and trade are summarized in Table 3.1. Generally, these papers find that infrastructure quality can have a significant effect on trade, and relatively significant effects compared to reductions in other impediments.

The studies in Table 3.1 generally try to explain variations in trade volumes. For example, Wilson et al. (2005) examine the effects of four different dimensions of trade facilitation – port efficiency (both water and air), the customs environment (prevalence of hidden import barriers and bribes), the regulatory environment (transparency and control of corruption) and what they call services sector infrastructure (Internet access and use). Using simulations based on their gravity model, they find the total gain in trade flow in manufacturing goods from trade facilitation improvements in all four areas is estimated to be US$377 billion: all regions gain in imports and exports. Further, the most important ingredient in achieving these gains, particular in the Organisation for Economic Co-operation and Development (OECD) market, is a country's own trade facilitation efforts.

Clark et al. (2004) is the exception in the table, since they try to explain variations in trade costs. They find that improving port efficiency from the twenty-fifth to the seventy-fifth percentile can reduce shipping costs by 12 per cent. They find port inefficiency is linked to excessive regulation, the prevalence of organized crime and the general condition of the country's

Table 3.1 Summary of studies of infrastructure, transport and logistics services

Paper	Empirical model	Dependent variable	Data	Key variables	Main findings
Berthelon and Freund (2004)	Regression of trade growth on distance	Trade growth	Four-digit data from the COMTRADE database for periods 1985–89, 1990–94, 1995–2000	Distance	The effect of distance is decomposed into the composition effect (trade shift towards more distance sensitive industries) and distance sensitivity effect (industries have moved towards distance sensitive practices). The empirical evidence favours the increase of distance sensitivity across industries instead of a compositional shift of trade towards more distance sensitive industries
Clark et al. (2004)	IV regression equation on maritime charges	Charges per unit of weight	US Import Waterborne Databank (US Department of Transportation) for years 1996, 1998 and 2000	Distance, level of containerization, trade imbalance, port efficiency	Doubling in distance generates an 18% increase in transport costs. Level of containerization presents a significant negative effect on transport costs and improvement of port efficiency from the 25th percentile to 75th percentile reduces transport costs by 12%

Table 3.1 (continued)

Paper	Empirical model	Dependent variable	Data	Key variables	Main findings
Djankov et al. (2006)	Difference gravity models	ln(Exports_jk/ Exports_hk)	World Bank data on the days it takes to move standard cargo from the factory gate to the ship in 126 countries	Added export time in the gravity equation	10% saving in exporting time increases exports by 4% or each additional day delayed reduces trade by 1%
Freund and Weinhold (2004)	Panel gravity model and cross-section gravity model	Export growth/ exports	Constructed from various sources	Internet domain host counts	Evidence supporting the theory that Internet growth reduces trade cost and hence increases trade
Hanson and Xiang (2002)	Difference in difference gravity model	Ratio of high mark-up good export over Ratio of low mark-up good export	World Trade Database for 1990 for bilateral trade flows for three- or four-digit SITC revision 2 product classes.	Ratio of two countries' GDP to detect home market effect	The home market effect is strongest in the high transportation cost industries
Hausman et al. (2005)	Augmented gravity models	Total bilateral exports	Compiled by World Bank in 2005 containing detailed country-level data on the time and cost of	Added various measures of logistic friction, later constructed a logistics index	Logistics performance significantly affects the level of trade

| Nordas and Piermartini (2004) | Gravity models | Imports | ... moving a typical 20-foot FCL container from the port of entry to a firm in the most populous city.

Tariff data are derived from TRAINS (Trade Analysis and Information System), Bilateral trade flows are extracted from COMTRADE (Commodity and Trade Database), Trade cost indicators are derived from various World Bank data sources all in year 2000 | ... to replace individual measures

Applied tariff rate and infrastructure quality measures | 10% reduction in tariff increases trade by 12.5%, quality of infrastructure has significant and large impact on trade, especially for port efficiency, 10% improvement in port efficiency increases bilateral trade by 6% |

Table 3.1 (continued)

Paper	Empirical model	Dependent variable	Data	Key variables	Main findings
Nordas et al. (2006)	Gravity/probit	Probability that a firm in country i will export to country j	A panel of 192 countries exporting intermediate inputs, clothing and electronics to Australia, Japan and UK in 1996–2004	GDP, relative distance (GDP weighted), relative time	Support for scale effect (indicated by GDP), time is important factor on market entry, even taking away some influence from distance, which remains important
Shepherd and Wilson (2007)	Gravity model with importer and exporter fixed effects	ln(Export)	Constructed from various sources	A set of trade costs determinant variables	Trade flows may be more sensitive to upgrades of infrastructure than to reductions of tariff barriers.
Wilson et al. (2005)	Gravity model	Exports	Trade flow data from COMTRADE of UN Statistics Division for 2000–01 in the manufactured goods sector	Tariff and trade facilitation measures (port efficiency, regulatory environment, service sector infrastructure)	1% reduction in ad valorem tariff will increase the trade flow by 1.1%, similar to the effect of distance. Improvement of port efficiency, customs improvement, improving regulatory environment and improving service sector infrastructure all improve trade

infrastructure, so improvements in these areas would help to generate the reductions in shipping costs.

Other Regulatory Barriers

In this section, we review empirical work on other regulatory barriers, such as rules of origin, anti-dumping and standards. We also comment briefly on work on barriers to trade in services.

Estevadeordal and Suominen (2005) draw the following conclusions from their gravity model analysis of the impact of rules of origin: restrictive product-specific rules of origin undermine aggregate trade; regimes that allow flexibility in the application of product-specific rules boost trade; high levels of sectoral selectivity in rules of origin undermine trade; and the restrictiveness of rules of origin in final goods encourages trade in intermediate products.

Chu and Prusa (2005) document the rapid rise in anti-dumping cases filed against People's Republic of China (PRC) exporters, the high probability that anti-dumping duties are imposed and the high rates that are imposed. They note that as FDI has flowed into PRC from the four East Asian Tigers, PRC-sourced exports have replaced exports from the parent company home markets. They speculate that anti-dumping filing against PRC may be replacing filings against those countries. They use econometric analysis to confirm a positive association between anti-dumping cases filed on PRC exports and inward FDI flows to the PRC, although they are unable to fully explore the 'anti-dumping triangle' hypothesis. They also cite evidence of low concentration ratios on PRC industries that have contributed to the competitive price and low profit margins. Their review of anti-dumping filings against the PRC confirms that anti-dumping practice can be a very convenient and effective tool to deter trade.

Moenius (1999) finds that bilaterally shared standards are favourable to trade – a 1 per cent increase in bilaterally shared standards between the USA and its trading partners could increase US trade volumes by about US$6 billion. But Moenius does not find country-specific standards to be a barrier. While country-specific standards of importers reduce imports for non-manufactured goods, they promote trade in the manufacturing sector. Information costs explain this latter finding. If goods have to be adapted to a foreign market, then country-specific standards of the importing country offer valuable information for adapting the product to that market.

Kalirajan et al. (2000) find that the barriers to trade in banking services that prevailed in 1997 may have raised the price of banking services by around 5 per cent in economies such as Argentina, Canada, the European Union (EU) and Switzerland, by 15 per cent in Japan, by over 30 per cent in Chile, Korea, Singapore and Thailand, and by up to 60 per cent in Malaysia. Extending the methodology of Kalirajan (2000) and others, Copenhagen Economics (2005) find that the EU's proposed Directive on Services in the Internal Market could more than halve the burden of non-tariff regulatory measures in accountancy, information technology (IT) services and wholesale and retail trade. For example, the total price burden on foreign accountancy services would be reduced from 22.8 per cent to 8.1 per cent, partly because costs would be reduced, and partly because markups would be squeezed.

Rents v. Costs

While these results confirm that non-tariff barriers can have significant direct effects, they do not always give clear guidance on policy priorities. With tariffs, the height of the tariff barrier already conveys a great deal about the likely welfare effects of tariff removal, subject to a number of qualifications about tariff dispersion, intersectoral linkages, trade shares of gross domestic product (GDP), and so on. But with non-tariff barriers, measures that imply similar vertical movements in supply curves can have vastly different welfare effects, as Figures 3.1a and 3.1b demonstrate. So a proper evaluation of the economic effects of non-tariff reform requires that measures of their direct effects be used in a modelling framework that can take into account whether they are rent-creating or cost-escalating.

As noted, some of the literature on trade facilitation seems to *define* trade facilitation measures as those that eliminate cost-escalating barriers (Elek, 2006). In this view, the trade facilitation agenda can deliver 'gains all round', with few of the problems of trade diversion or other awkward redistributive effects that can sometimes beset tariff liberalization. But Walkenhorst and Yasui (2005) argue that even with the measures generally agreed to be at the core of this more narrow trade facilitation agenda, the assessment is not straightforward. They argue that indirect trade transactions costs, such as longer border waiting times, are best thought of as being cost-escalating. But the direct trade transaction costs, such as form-filling, while being a cost to the exporter or importer, are a source of income for the form processors. These costs are best modelled as being tax-like, recognizing that they have a large transfer component rather than a wastage component. They argue that previous modelling assessments of the effects of trade facilitation may be overstated, by treating all measures as cost-escalating. And according to their analysis, the biggest policy impact would come from reducing *indirect* trade transaction costs.

Bradford (2005) instead assumes that all non-tariff barriers are tax-like, rather than creating waste or adding to the real resource cost of doing business. Not surprisingly, he finds that reform of non-tariff barriers has similar effects to tariff reform. Across the eight countries in his modelling analysis,[9] the correlation between the height of non-tariff barriers and the welfare gains from their unilateral removal (expressed as a percentage of GDP) is 0.83. The correlation between the height of total (tariff plus non-tariff) barriers and the welfare gains from their removal is very similar, at 0.81. Further, he finds that non-tariff barriers are about as high as tariff barriers in Canada, but up to eight times higher in Japan. The gains from reform of non-tariff barriers tend to exceed the gains from tariff reform accordingly.

By contrast, Hertel et al. (2001) consider three elements of the 'new age' agreement between Japan and Singapore – customs automation, security and harmonization measures in e-commerce, and liberalization of trade in business and construction services – and assume that all would remove barriers that create waste and add to real resource costs, rather than being tax-like. They find the new age measures to be virtually the sole source of gains from agreement, because they do not produce trade diversion in the way that the preferential tariff cuts do. This follows directly from their treatment of the non-tariff barriers as being cost-escalating.

This modelling evidence suggests that possibly the single biggest determinant of the projected gains from removing non-tariff barriers is whether they are modelled as being rent-creating or cost-escalating. This 'treatment' effect can dominate the estimated 'height' of the trade barrier, and play a crucial role in determining the apparent policy priorities.

There is very little modelling literature to date that has evaluated the effects of removing non-tariff barriers, while taking seriously the available empirical or theoretical evidence about whether they are rent-creating or cost-escalating. One of the few examples is Walkenhorst and Yasui (2005). Another is Andriamananjara et al. (2005). They model non-tariff barriers in three different ways – as import tax wedges in footwear, as export tax wedges in apparel and as what they call 'sand in the wheels' (or waste) in food processing. This treatment is based on careful consideration of the types of non-tariff measures applying in each sector. Although the height of the barriers in processed food is lower than in footwear, the global welfare gains from liberalization are greater, in part because of the difference in treatment. The gains from liberalizing non-tariff barriers in apparel swamp both, however, because of the much greater prevalence of barriers in this sector around the world.

Another modelling example that takes into account whether non-tariff barriers are rent-creating or cost-escalating is the study of the EU's proposed services directive by Copenhagen Economics (2005). Their modelling results suggest that total consumption in the European Union could increase by approximately 0.6 per cent, or 37 billion euros, both because markups would be squeezed and real costs reduced.

Finally, Dee (2005b) uses the available evidence on the nature of barriers to services trade to look at the effects of various East Asian economic integration initiatives. She finds that the biggest gains would be achieved from reforming on a unilateral basis those behind-the-border restrictions on competition that affect both foreigners and domestic new entrants equally. Such initiatives would provide economic gains of more than five times those that might be available through an East Asian preferential trade agreement.

V. HOW ARE TRADE FACILITATION MEASURES IMPLEMENTED?[10]

Trade facilitation is explicitly included in the Doha Development Round negotiations and it is a common topic in preferential trade negotiations. In this part, we summarize the treatment of trade facilitation in these negotiations, in the latter case with reference to the Association of South East Asian Nations (ASEAN), the Pacific Agreement for Closer Economic Relations (PACER) and the Economic Cooperation Organization (ECO). All these negotiations focus on the subset of border related measures. We also compare the treatment of trade facilitation in the Asia-Pacific Economic Cooperation (APEC) process.

The scope of the World Trade Organization (WTO) treatment of trade facilitation is limited to the relevant aspects of the General Agreement on Tariffs and Trade, in particular Articles X (transparency), VIII (fees and formalities) and V (goods in transit). The main transparency issues concern publication and availability of information, the time period between publication and implementation of rules, allowance for consultation and comment on new or amended rules, advance rulings, appeal procedures, and measures to enhance impartiality and non-discrimination. The fees and formalities associated with importing and exporting, simplified release and clearance of goods, and tariff classification are all relevant. Disciplines on goods in transit include simplification and standardization of fees, formalities and documentation required for goods in transit, as well as limitation of inspections and controls. Other topics in the WTO include technical assistance and capacity-building and special and differential treatment for low-income countries.[11]

The ASEAN, the oldest regional trading arrangement in the Asia-Pacific region, has made progress, especially since 2002, in trade facilitation areas such as customs co-operation and standards harmonization and mutual recognition. In 2002 the ASEAN leaders, acknowledging the importance of trade facilitation, made an ASEAN Customs Partnership a high priority. A guiding principle is to take the Revised Kyoto Convention on customs processes, procedures and practices as the basis for ASEAN countries' customs legislation. The ASEAN introduced a harmonized tariff nomenclature in 2004, which increases consistency and transparency in tariff application. A customs valuation guide introduced in 2003 is intended to ensure progressive adoption of the WTO Agreement on Customs Valuation into ASEAN customs procedures. Work is under way to simplify, improve and standardize customs forms. In 2005 a majority of ASEAN members adopted the ASEAN Customs Declaration Document, which contains 48 information parameters and which was developed on the basis of the Single Administrative Document recommended by the World Customs Organization.

The ASEAN Single Window (ASW) Agreement was signed at the December 2005 summit.[12] By having a single point for the submission and processing of information and for making all decisions relevant to customs clearance, the ASW aims to cut customs clearance time for any single transaction to 30 minutes by 2010, from the current three to four hours average. Initial implementation is, however, on a bilateral basis.

The Pacific Agreement for Closer Economic Relations, signed in Nauru in 2001, is a framework agreement envisaging creation of a reciprocal free trade area between the 16 Pacific Island Forum countries. The initial focus is the development of co-operation on trade facilitation, with a current work programme in the areas of customs, quarantine, and standards and conformance. Australia and New Zealand agreed to partially fund a trade facilitation programme, and all signatories agreed that their national programmes should be consistent with other regional and international agreements. It allows for periodic revision of national trade facilitation programmes but it also contains a very general opt-out clause giving any signatory the option of not participating in a trade facilitation programme which they consider to be 'disadvantageous'.

The Central Asian countries are all landlocked states.[13] Unpredictable changes in official policies (such as imposition of temporary tariffs or other levies, temporary border closure, and changing requirements about bonds or the need for transiting trucks to travel in convoy), innumerable documents and approvals required at border crossing (which are often an excuse for unofficial charges), and frequent delays and fees while transiting a country have been features of the relations between them. Regional agreements among these economies, such as the Economic Cooperation Organization, have failed to address transit issues. One explanation is that too many individuals see personal gains from the current system and national governments are unable or unwilling to curtail the activities of these rent-seekers. Alternatively, the national governments themselves view transit as an opportunity to tax foreigners to the hilt.

At some stage in the history of most developed economies, the central government imposed law and order to protect traders from unnecessary and unpredictable delays or taxes by local officials or highway robbers. An example of such a goal being achieved bilaterally, with external assistance, is the Almaty–Bishkek road agreement signed by the governments of Kazakhstan and the Kyrgyz Republic in order to obtain funding from the Asian Development Bank for upgrading the road between the largest cities in the two countries. Transiting Kazakhstan in the late 1990s was notoriously expensive; a common estimate was that it cost a truck from the Kyrgyz Republic an average of US$1700 to cross Kazakhstan, and this made previously flourishing sales of Kyrgyz vegetables to Russia unprofitable.[14] The ADB (2000: 11–12) estimated that in the Almaty–Bishkek corridor roadside checks alone increased transport costs in 2000 by US$2 million due to delays and by US$16 million in bribes. The loan for the road was made conditional on the two governments' collaboration in facilitating passage through the border post on the road and also reducing the behind-the-border costs due to specious fines or unofficial levies.[15]

With respect to negotiations in progress, many announcements of trade facilitating measures remain paper measures as the actual practice at the border continues to inhibit trade. Some trade costs require bilateral attention, such as co-ordination of opening times of border crossings, but the implementation of many border measures related to trade facilitation may be non-preferential. Reductions in behind-the-border costs or increases in customs clearance efficiency should facilitate all trade. In practice, however, there may be discrimination for technical reasons, for example, if Thai customs expand the electronic clearance facility this may benefit Malaysian exporters to Thailand but not be feasible for Lao exporters to Thailand who do not have computers. The only explicitly preferential aspect of recent regional trade agreements' impact on trade facilitation is the US position on fast-tracking container clearance, which is limited to trading partners with whom the USA has a trade agreement; a container from Singapore does not require the individual inspection legislated post-9/11 as long as it has been certified and sealed in Singapore, but a container from Indonesia will not be exempted from inspection.

Trade facilitation is one of the three pillars of APEC along with liberalization and economic and technical co-operation. The principles espoused in APEC documents on trade facilitation are transparency, efficiency, simplification, non-discrimination, procedural fairness, co-operation and capacity-building.[16]

In 2001, at the Shanghai summit, the APEC Committee on Trade and Investment was mandated to reduce transactions costs on trade by 5 per cent by 2006. Starting in 2002 each APEC member was expected to submit annual Trade Facilitation Action Plans (TFAPs), which would achieve the 5 per cent target, and report on their progress. Since 2002, 1400 items had been selected in individual countries' TFAPs, mainly in the sub-category of customs procedures, and 62 per cent of these have been completed and a further quarter are in progress (Elek et al., 2006). Customs measures have the highest completion rate (69 per cent), followed by business mobility (60 per cent), standards (52 per cent) and e-commerce (47 per cent). Ministers from APEC declared the 2006 target met by members and asked for another 5 per cent reduction in transactions costs by 2010.[17]

In June 2005 APEC trade ministers agreed to develop model measures on trade facilitation for free trade agreements. There had always been some overlap of membership between APEC and regional trading arrangements. Seven ASEAN members are in APEC (not Lao PDR, Cambodia and Myanmar), and other APEC signatories are in the North American Free Trade Agreement (NAFTA) or the Closer Economic Relations (CER). The issue has become more acute since the turn of the century, with over half of APEC's members having negotiated bilateral and plurilateral preferential trading arrangements, and an increased potential for spaghetti bowl effects, including conflicting trade facilitation arrangements.[18]

In summary:

- Important progress is being made in the Doha Round negotiations to refine the ambit of WTO commitments on trade facilitation. However, the scope of these negotiations under the banner of trade facilitation in the WTO is limited and does not meet our criterion for a desirable scope. On the other hand many measures being examined elsewhere in the WTO, in the services negotiations for example, are also relevant, although this linkage of services reform and trade facilitation is not often made.
- In regional or bilateral agreements, trade facilitating measures generally remain propositions on paper, as the actual practice at the border continues to inhibit trade. One explanation of slow progress may be the presence of significant elements of rents in current arrangements.
- Since 2001, APEC has had a more structured trade facilitation programme, with well specified timetables, and the ASEAN countries have gone further in pushing for co-ordinated trade facilitation measures, but there is a significant variation in implementation.

VI.   WHERE SHOULD TRADE FACILITATION BE MANAGED?

Trade facilitation is popular in international negotiations – do they help? Dee and Sidorenko (2006) argue that when the impacts of reform are on costs and resource savings there is less case for reciprocity, for the purpose of mobilizing countervailing political interests to offset the resistance to reform. Trade facilitation in this case is more likely to be manageable within a domestic reform agenda. The contribution of international commitments and co-operation continues to be significant, for example, as a device to demonstrate the commitment to reform, to benchmark domestic policy and to receive guidance on paths of reform.

The conditions identified by Dee and Sidorenko (2006) do not always apply, since some measures have both rent and cost effects, as noted above and as illustrated in some of the experiences reported in Central Asia. The presence of the rent effects complicates the implementation of trade facilitation agenda. Does this increase the value of embedding the reform agenda within a formal set of negotiations with foreign trading partners? Not necessarily.

The political economy issues to be resolved in dealing with the origins of trade facilitation problems (by improving infrastructure quality, for example) may not be so much to do with domestic versus foreign interests, but rather incumbent versus new entrant interests. With respect to the use of preferential trade agreements to deal with trade facilitation matters, which is a popular argument for signing such agreements, Dee (2005b) argues that for reasons of political economy 'new age' trade agreements tend to be limited to measures that can be liberalized on a preferential basis, and tend to target only those provisions that explicitly discriminate against foreigners. But the available empirical evidence is that these types of provisions tend to be rent-creating rather than cost-escalating. So the gains from even the 'new age' trade agreements are trivial, compared with the gains from comprehensive reform of non-discriminatory impediments to competition, as part of a thoroughgoing programme of unilateral domestic regulatory reform. It is the latter which is more likely to deal with the issues of trade facilitation.

Further, a focus on the terms of foreign entry into these protected sectors may lead to a redistribution of existing rents, including transfers offshore to the detriment of domestic welfare, rather than their reduction and increases in efficiency. For example, suppose in infrastructure services a licensing scheme is used to manage access to the market. An allocation of an additional licence to a foreign entrant, rather than opening the sector more widely to competition, would have this effect.

Finally, much of the debate about trade facilitation concerns actions of governments and the ways in which they add to costs in the trading system, but sometimes what matters more is what governments are not doing, rather than what governments are doing. This concern is especially relevant to matters related to infrastructure services. It is also relevant to enforcing the rule of law (to restrain unofficial levies) or to enforcing co-ordination among government agencies (for example customs, quarantine, border guards, tax authorities) in order to simplify border-crossing procedures. Competition might be introduced in that example by separation of the bottleneck facility from the rights to operate in that facility, via an access regime. The absence of effective competition policy regimes to constrain monopoly power and remove barriers to entry lead to higher-price services, lower volumes of transactions (of domestic and foreign origins) and reductions in welfare.

To conclude:

- Dealing with trade facilitation, trade negotiations about foreign entry are either not required (for cost-increasing measures) or risk inefficient results (for rent-creating measures).
- What matters is a comprehensive reform of non-discriminatory impediments to competition, as part of a thoroughgoing programme of unilateral domestic regulatory reform. This programme may require correction of lack of action, rather than a reform of current action.
- International co-operation on trade facilitation makes a contribution to domestic reform by documenting and making transparent the results, demonstrating commitment and preventing backsliding, and benchmarking domestic policy and providing a guide for reform.

NOTES

1. The authors thank Shengjun Guo for assistance in compiling and reviewing empirical studies of trade facilitation. Earlier drafts of sections of this chapter were presented at the LAEBA Annual Meeting on 'Regional integration and regional cooperation in Asia and Latin America' in November 2006 and prepared for a project on 'A comparative analysis of trade facilitation in regional integration agreements' undertaken by the Institute of International Trade at the University of Adelaide for UNESCAP ARTNet (United Nations Economic and Social Commission for Asia and the Pacific Asia-Pacific Research and Training Network on Trade). Support of those organizations for this work is gratefully acknowledged by the authors. All errors are their own.
2. See www.oecd.org/document/13/0,2340,en_2649_34665_35305549_1_1_1_1,00.html.
3. Costs include those of the lack of reliability, or variations in delivery times, associated with these measures.
4. It is also possible that the rent-creating barriers lead to a tragedy of the anti-commons whereby uncoordinated rent-seekers destroy trade so that all the gains are forgone (not just the triangle) – see the Kyrgyz example below (p. 46).
5. See also Bagai and Wilson (2006).

6. See Dee (2005a) for a summary of the performance measures used in the context of estimating barriers to services trade.
7. Quantity effects can be turned into price effects using an estimate of the elasticity of demand (for example, Warren, 2000).
8. Parts of this section draw on Dee and Ferrantino (2005).
9. The countries are Australia, Canada, Germany, Italy, Japan, the Netherlands, the UK and the USA.
10. Material in this section was originally drafted for a project on 'A comparative analysis of trade facilitation in regional integration agreements' undertaken by the Institute of International Trade at the University of Adelaide for UNESCAP ARTNet.
11. There are also proposals for special and differential treatment for countries whose mother tongue is not a WTO official language and for landlocked economies, although the usual assumption is that such treatment is of most significance for poor countries with these characteristics. For an update on WTO negotiations, see www.wto.org/English/tratop_e/tradfa_e/tradfa_negoti_docs_e.htm.
12. This followed seven years of ad hoc initiatives sponsored by the ASEAN Secretariat but implemented unilaterally (for example, the Gold Card Program in Indonesia, the Super Green Lane in the Philippines and the Single Window in Singapore), which reduced customs clearance times from several days to several hours.
13. At the United Nations, constraints on transit in developing countries were the subject of General Assembly Resolution 56/180. This resulted in the United Nations World International Ministerial Conference of Landlocked and Transit Developing Countries being held in Almaty (Kazakhstan) in August 2003, which resulted in the 'Almaty Declaration' highlighting transit issues.
14. This was an example of the tragedy of the anticommons. Each official with power to levy unofficial charges along the road did so, but the cumulative effect was that trucks stopped plying the trade and everybody lost out.
15. The two countries were moving in this direction but there was much inertia. The ADB was able to facilitate the trade facilitation process.
16. Several of these principles are already part of WTO obligations (for example, Article X requires transparency in trade regulations, Article VII covers customs valuation procedures, Article VIII requires minimization of complexity of fees and formalities associated with trade).
17. See the Eighteenth APEC Ministerial Meeting Joint Statement at www.apec2006.vn/article/77.
18. Scollay and Gilbert (2001) have highlighted the cost-increasing potential of the spaghetti bowl effects which were popularized by Jagdish Bhagwati in the 1990s. Spaghetti bowl diagrams of the regional and bilateral trade agreements in the Asia-Pacific region can be found in Feridhanustyawan (2005: 10–11).

REFERENCES

Anderson, J. and E. van Wincoop (2003), 'Gravity with gravitas: a solution to the border puzzle', *American Economic Review*, **93** (1), 170–92.
Ando, M. (2005), 'Estimating tariff equivalents of core and non-core non-tariff measures in the APEC member economies', in P. Dee and M. Ferrantino (eds), *Quantitative Methods for Assessing the Effects of Non-tariff Measures and Trade Facilitation*, Singapore: APEC Secretariat and World Scientific, pp. 235–87.
Andriamananjara, S., M. Ferrantino and M. Tsigas (2005), 'Alternative approaches in estimating the economic effects of non-tariff measures: results from newly quantified measures', in P. Dee and M. Ferrantino (eds), *Quantitative Methods*

for Assessing the Effects of Non-tariff Measures and Trade Facilitation, Singapore: APEC Secretariat and World Scientific, pp. 525–40.

Asian Development Bank (ADB) (2000), *Transport Policy Issues for Regional Cooperation in the Central Asian Region*, Final Report, August.

Bagai, S. and J. Wilson (2006), 'The data chase: what's out there on trade costs and nontariff barriers?', *World Bank Policy Research Working Paper*, 3899, Washington, DC: World Bank.

Baier, S.L. and J.H. Bergstrand (2001), 'The growth of world trade: tariffs, transport costs and income similarity', *Journal of International Economics*, **53** (1), 1–27.

Baldwin, R. (1994), *Towards an Integrated Europe*, London: Centre for Economic Policy Research.

Barth, J., G. Caprio and R. Levine (2004), 'Bank regulation and supervision: what works best?', *Journal of Financial Intermediation*, **13**, 205–48.

Berthelon, M. and C. Freund (2004), 'On the conservation of distance in international trade', *World Bank Policy Research Working Paper*, 3293, Washington, DC: World Bank.

Bora, B., A. Kuwahara and S. Laird (2002), 'Quantification of non-tariff measures', UNCTAD Policy Issues in International Trade and Commodities Study Series No. 18, United Nations, New York and Geneva.

Bradford, S. (2005), 'The extent and impact of final goods non-tariff barriers in rich countries', in P. Dee and M. Ferrantino (eds), *Quantitative Methods for Assessing the Effects of Non-tariff Measures and Trade Facilitation*, Singapore: APEC Secretariat and World Scientific, pp. 435–81.

Chu, T. and T. Prusa (2005), 'The reasons for and the impact of antidumping protection: the case of People's Republic of China', in P. Dee and M. Ferrantino (eds), *Quantitative Methods for Assessing the Effects of Non-tariff Measures and Trade Facilitation*, Singapore: APEC Secretariat and World Scientific, pp. 411–33.

Clark, X., D. Dollar and A. Micco (2004), 'Port efficiency, maritime transport costs, and bilateral trade', *Journal of Development Economics*, **75** (2), 417–50.

Copenhagen Economics (2005), 'Economic assessment of the barriers to the internal market for services', Copenhagen Economics, Copenhagen.

Dean, J., R. Feinberg and M. Ferrantino (2005), 'Estimating the tariff-equivalent of NTMs', in P. Dee and M. Ferrantino (eds), *Quantitative Methods for Assessing the Effects of Non-tariff Measures and Trade Facilitation*, Singapore: APEC Secretariat and World Scientific, pp. 289–309.

Deardorff, A.V. (1998), 'Determinants of bilateral trade flows: does gravity work in a neoclassical world', in J.A. Frankel (ed.), *The Regionalization of the World Economy*, Chicago and London: University of Chicago Press, pp. 23–8.

Deardorff, A.V. and R.M. Stern (1997), 'Measurement of non-tariff barriers', Economics Department Working Papers No. 179, OCDE/GD(97)129, OECD, Paris.

Dee, P. (2005a), 'Measuring and modelling barriers to services trade: Australia's experience', in P. Dee and M. Ferrantino (eds), *Quantitative Methods for Assessing the Effects of Non-tariff Measures and Trade Facilitation*, Singapore: APEC Secretariat and World Scientific, pp. 71–105.

Dee, P. (2005b), 'East Asian economic integration and its impact on future growth', Pacific Economic Papers No. 350, Australia-Japan Research Centre and the Asia Pacific School of Economics and Government.

Dee, P. and M. Ferrantino (2005), 'Introduction', in P. Dee and M. Ferrantino (eds), *Quantitative Methods for Assessing the Effects of Non-tariff Measures and Trade Facilitation*, Singapore: APEC Secretariat and World Scientific, pp. 1–12.

Dee, P. and A. Sidorenko (2006), 'The rise of services trade: regional initiatives and challenges for the WTO', in H. Soesastro and C. Findlay (eds), *Reshaping the Pacific Economic Order*, London and New York: Routledge.

Djankov, S., C. Freund and C. Pham (2006), 'Trading on time', *World Bank Policy Research Working Paper*, 3909, Washington, DC.

Elek, A. (2006), 'APEC in the emerging international economic order: lame duck or catalyst', in H. Soesastro and C. Findlay (eds), *Reshaping the Pacific Economic Order*, London and New York: Routledge.

Elek, A., N.A. Nguyen and Y.P. Woo (2006), 'Final Review of APEC's Trade Facilitation Action Plan (2001–2006) and Suggestions for Future Initiatives', paper presented to the APEC Public-Private Dialogue on Trade Facilitation, Ho Chi Minh City, May.

Estevadeordal, A. and K. Suominen (2005), 'Rules of origin in the world trading system and proposals for multilateral harmonisation', in P. Dee and M. Ferrantino (eds), *Quantitative Methods for Assessing the Effects of Non-tariff Measures and Trade Facilitation*, Singapore: APEC Secretariat and World Scientific, pp. 337–409.

Evenett, S.J. and W. Keller (2002), 'On theories explaining the success of the gravity equation', *Journal of Political Economy*, **110** (2), 281–316.

Feenstra, R.C., J.R. Markusen and A.K. Rose (2001), 'Using the gravity equation to differentiate among alternative theories of trade', *Canadian Journal of Economics*, **34** (2), 430–47.

Feridhanustyawan, T. (2005), 'Preferential trade agreements in the Asia-Pacific region', *IMF Working Paper 05/149*, July.

Francois, J. and B. Hoekman (1999), 'Market access in the services sectors', Tinbergen Institute, manuscript, cited in B. Hoekman (2000), 'The next round of services negotiations: identifying priorities and options', *Federal Reserve Bank of St Louis Review*, **82** (4), 31–47.

Freund, C. and D. Weinhold (2004), 'The effect of the internet on international trade', *Journal of International Economics*, **62**, 171–89.

Guasch, J.L. and P. Spiller (1999), *Managing the Regulatory Process: Design, Concepts, Issues, and the Latin American and Caribbean Story*, Washington, DC: World Bank.

Hanson, G. and C. Xiang (2002), 'The home market effect and bilateral trade patterns', NBER Working Paper Series, Working Paper 9076, Cambridge, MA.

Harrigan, J. (2004), 'Specialization and the volume of trade: do the data obey the laws?', in E.K. Choi and J. Harrigan (eds), *Handbook of International Trade, Volume 1*, Oxford: Blackwell.

Hausman, W., H.L. Lee and U. Subramanian (2005), 'Global logistics indicators, supply chain metrics, and bilateral trade patterns', *World Bank Policy Research Working Paper*, 3773, Washington DC.

Hertel, T., T. Walmsley and K. Itakura (2001), 'Dynamic effects of the "new age" free trade agreement between Japan and Singapore', *Journal of Economic Integration*, **16** (4), 446–84.

Kalirajan, K. (2000), *Restrictions on Trade in Distribution Services*, Productivity Commission Staff Research Paper, Ausinfo, Canberra.

Kalirajan, K., G. McGuire, D. Nguyen-Hong and M. Schuele (2000), 'The price impact of restrictions on banking services', in C. Findlay and T. Warren (eds), *Impediments to Trade in Services: Measurement and Policy Implications*, London and New York: Routledge, pp. 215–30.

Moenius, J. (1999), 'Information versus product adaption: the role of standards in trade', mimeo, University of California, San Diego.

Nordas, H. and R. Piermartini (2004), 'Infrastructure and trade', WTO Economic Research and Statistics Division Staff Working Paper ERSD-2004-04, WTO, Geneva.

Nordas, H., E. Pinali and M. Grosso (2006), 'Logistics and time as a trade barrier', OECD Trade Policy Working Paper No. 35, Paris.

Otsuki, T., J.S. Wilson and M. Sewadeh (2001), 'What price precaution? European harmonisation of aflatoxin regulations and African groundnut exports', *European Review of Agricultural Economics*, **28** (2), 263–83.

Pacific Economic Cooperation Council (PECC) (2005), 'Study on the mutually supportive advancement of APEC's trade facilitation and secure trade goals post September 11', PECC, Singapore, available at www.pecc.org/publications/papers/secure-trade-summary-report.pdf.

Scollay, R. and J. Gilbert (2001), *New Regional Trade Arrangements in the Asia-Pacific?* Washington, DC: Institute for International Economics.

Shepherd, B. and J.S. Wilson (2007), 'Trade, Infrastructure, and Roadways in Europe and Central Asia: New Empirical Evidence', *Journal of Economic Integration*, **22** (4), 723–47.

Slade, M. (2004), 'Competing models of firm profitability', *International Journal of Industrial Organisation*, **22** (3), 289–308.

Steiner, F. (2000), *Regulation, Industry Structure and Performance in the Electricity Supply Industry*, Working Paper No. 238, ECO/WKP(2000)11, Economics Department, OECD, Paris, 12 April.

Swann, P., P. Temple and M. Shurmer (1996), 'Standards and trade performance: the UK experience', *The Economic Journal*, **106** (438), 1297–313.

Walkenhorst, P. and T. Yasui (2005), 'Benefits of trade facilitation: a quantitative assessment', in P. Dee and M. Ferrantino (eds), *Quantitative Methods for Assessing the Effects of Non-tariff Measures and Trade Facilitation*, Singapore: APEC Secretariat and World Scientific, pp. 161–92.

Warren, T. (2000), 'The impact on output of impediments to trade and investment in telecommunications services', in C. Findlay and T. Warren (eds), *Impediments to Trade in Services: Measurement and Policy Implications*, London and New York: Routledge, pp. 85–100.

Whalley, J. (2004), 'Assessing the benefits to developing countries of liberalisation in services trade', *World Economy*, **27** (8), 1223–53.

Wilson, J.S., C.L. Mann and T. Otsuki (2005), 'Assessing the potential benefit of trade facilitation: a global perspective', in P. Dee and M. Ferrantino (eds), *Quantitative Methods for Assessing the Effects of Non-tariff Measures and Trade Facilitation*, Singapore: APEC Secretariat and World Scientific, pp. 121–60.

Yoo, J. (2005), 'Estimation of nominal and effective rates of protection', in P. Dee and M. Ferrantino (eds), *Quantitative Methods for Assessing the Effects of Non-tariff Measures and Trade Facilitation*, Singapore: APEC Secretariat and World Scientific, pp. 311–35.

4. Regional co-operation, governance, soft infrastructure and trading costs

Haider A. Khan[1]

INTRODUCTION

The main purpose of this chapter is to clarify some important links between regional co-operation, (soft) infrastructure and trading costs, and to suggest some hypotheses for further investigation. Khan and Weiss (2006) discuss the issue of both hard and soft infrastructure in this context. This chapter is a continuation of Khan and Weiss (2006) but in the specific context of soft infrastructure, and particularly governance, including corporate governance. As Khan and Weiss (2006) point out, conceptually such discussions can be seen as a part of the analysis of the 'New Regionalism'. The key idea here is co-operation through preferential trade and investment agreements that aim to strengthen structural economic reform, aid economic transformation, attract foreign investment and generally raise the international competitiveness of participating countries (IDB, 2002).

In this chapter, the focus is on co-operation in various aspects of soft infrastructure (for example, social networks, legal frameworks). However, such regional co-operation in soft infrastructure will also have an impact on growth, efficiency and equity of hard infrastructure (for example, ports, roads, telecoms, and so on). In particular, I examine the implications of regional co-operation in soft infrastructure for trading costs within the region.

It should be mentioned that, at the Asian Development Bank in particular, several other aspects of regional co-operation have also been examined. These include:

1. formal agreements on trade and investment (free trade agreements, investment agreements);
2. monetary co-operation (currency swaps, exchange rate pegs, currency unions); and
3. regional public goods (health and environmental protection).

Many of these have been examined extensively elsewhere (for example, see Bhattacharya, 2006; Kawai, 2005). The issue I discuss in this chapter is how and why soft infrastructure can assist in this process. Clearly, regional co-operation and co-ordination, and operation of economic activity regionally, require infrastructure. However, the following discussion is intended to clarify more sharply why this might be so, particularly for soft infrastructure. The aim is to offer a tentative framework for subsequent empirical analysis of where policy interventions might be most effective in promoting inclusive growth.

MOTIVATING FUTURE WORK ON REGIONAL CO-OPERATION AND SOFT INFRASTRUCTURE: AN EXAMPLE OF EMPIRICAL WORK AND THE NEED FOR REFINING THE IDEA OF SOFT INFRASTRUCTURE

In a pioneering study, K.C. Fung, Alicia Garcia-Herrero, Hitomi Iizaka and Alan Siu (Fung et al., 2005) examine the impact of soft infrastructure reform in the PRC on FDI inflow to various regions within the PRC.

Their basic regression model has the following form:

$$\begin{aligned}
\ln(FDI_{i,t}) = \alpha_i &+ \beta_1 \ln(GDP) + \beta_2 \ln(LAGWAGE_{i,(t-1)}) \\
&+ \beta_3 \ln(HE_{i,t}) + \beta_4 \ln(RAIL_{i,t}) + \beta_5 \ln(HIGHROAD_{i,t}) \\
&+ \beta_6 \ln(POLICY_{i,t}) + \beta_7 \ln(REFORM_{i,t}) \, FDI_{i,t}
\end{aligned}$$

where the subscripts i and t stand for China's region i and period t and the variables used in this analysis are given below.

$FDI_{i,t}$: FDI from the USA, Japan, Hong Kong, China, Taipei,China and Korea to region i at time t.

$GDP_{i,t}$: GDP of region i at time t.

$LAGWAGE_{i,(t-1)}$: average wage of region i at time $t-1$.

$HE_{i,t}$: the ratio of the number of students enrolled in higher education in region i to its population at time t.

$RAIL_{i,t}$: kilometres of railway in region i per square kilometre of land at time t.

$HIGH\ ROAD_{i,t}$: kilometres of high-quality roads in region i per square kilometre of land mass at time t.

$POLICY_{i,t}$: the number of Special Economic Zones in region i, the number of Open Coastal Cities in region i and the number of the Economic and Technological Development Zones in region i at time t.

$REFORM_{j,t}$: the proportion of manufacturing output produced by state-owned enterprises (SOEs) in region i at time t.

Their focus is to compare the effects of hard infrastructure (as proxied by *RAIL* and *HIGHROAD*) and soft infrastructure (as proxied by *REFORM*), after controlling for other standard determinants.

The hypothesis that well-developed regions with better hard infrastructure such as superior transportation facilities are more attractive to foreign firms is examined by including the proxy, density of railway and high quality roadway. They use the variable '*REFORM*' to represent soft infrastructure. '*REFORM*' is included to test the degree of internal reforms. It is constructed by calculating the share of the SOEs in manufacturing output in each region in each year. China's economic reform has transformed the economy from a centrally planned economy dominated by the state sector to an increasingly market-orientated economy. A larger proportion of state-owned output should indicate a less transparent legal system, more corruption and less market-orientated institutions.

The results show that the higher degree of domination by SOEs in the industrial sector impedes the flow of direct investment from all five countries. The coefficient is found to be negatively significant at 1 per cent level for all countries except Korea, whose level of significance is 5 per cent. A large share of output by SOEs signals to the foreign investors that economic reforms are still far from complete and foreign investors should expect to face difficult political and economic challenges in that region. They explain:

> Furthermore, in attracting FDI from the US, Japan, Hong Kong and Taipei,China, soft infrastructure is more important than hard infrastructure. Korea is the only exception in the analysis. Among five countries, there is a wide variation in the size of the influence of soft infrastructure is the most important determinant. The coefficient of 'REFORM' IS -0.89 and -0.97 for the US and Japan regressions, respectively, which is larger than any other variables examined in the analysis for both countries. On the other hand, the negative influence of the variable on Hong Kong and Taipei,China FDI is much smaller -0.73 and -0.61, respectively. Korea is positioned between the two groups. One potential explanation may be that the firms from Hong Kong and Taipei,China have an advantage of being familiar with the investment conditions due to the longer association with China than the US, Japan, or Korea. Geography as well as linguistic affinity may strengthen the network effect among investors from Hong Kong and Taipei,China on one hand and mainland Chinese businessmen on the other. In general, our empirical studies show that soft infrastructure is more important than hard infrastructure in attracting FDI. (Fung et al., 2005: 412)

This type of empirical work obviously can be refined further. The importance of various specific types of soft infrastructure will need to be underpinned and tested for both their joint and separate effects. This motivates the main concern of this chapter to refine the idea of soft infrastructure. Clearly, such a refinement can be used to study a broad array of problems of regional co-operation and infrastructure. As an initial foray into possible future empirical work in the context of regional co-operation, I aim to relate this relatively more refined conceptualization of soft infrastructure to trading costs and further trade creation in Asia.

THE ROLE OF INSTITUTIONS AND SOFT INFRASTRUCTURE IN THE CONTEXT OF REGIONAL CO-OPERATION

The discussion in Khan and Weiss (2006) focused on both hard and soft infrastructure, drawing on the framework of trade costs and their impact on protection and prices. As noted there, soft infrastructure can be defined much more broadly and below I discuss the wider implications of soft infrastructure for regional co-operation, including co-operation in building, operating and maintaining hard infrastructure. This forms the main body of the chapter after a preliminary discussion of trading costs below.

This section discusses the key elements of soft infrastructure with a view to answering several important policy questions. These questions range from the nature of soft infrastructure institutions to what is the best policy package for soft infrastructure reforms so that regional co-operation can be optimized and trade costs reduced. Although a broader view of soft infrastructure reforms is possible, we deliberately confine ourselves to the narrower issue of soft infrastructure reforms as they relate to trade costs and regional co-operation. Therefore, we do not attempt an exhaustive survey of issues or the large literature that exists. Estache (2006) is a good survey of both hard infrastructure and corruption. Soft infrastructure is defined here as all the institutional facilities used to deliver both hard infrastructure such as energy, water and sanitation, telecommunication and transport services, and generally to provide means to enhance economic well-being through both market and non-market economic, social and political interactions. In this sense, soft infrastructure is the institutional means to enable citizens as producers and consumers to get the most out of their economic activities, including, but not limited to, the economic activities in the hard infrastructure sectors. In Sen's terms, soft infrastructure together with the hard infrastructure can work to enhance the capabilities of citizens. At the end of our discussion I attempt to provide a rough blueprint for a research agenda on soft infrastructure in order to overcome the knowledge gap for the policy-makers in this vital area. Clearly, regional co-operation in overcoming this knowledge gap is itself an important item in the policy agenda of the governments, international non-governmental organizations (INGOs) and the non-governmental organizations (NGOs) in the region.

I discuss soft infrastructure mainly under three distinct but related categories. These are: governance in general, corporate governance and corruption. I discuss the issue of privatization of infrastructures in these contexts where it seems appropriate to do so. But, first, there must be a clear understanding of the nature of trading costs and the relationship between infrastructure and trading costs.

'TRADING COST', INFRASTRUCTURE AND REGIONAL CO-OPERATION[2]

As Weiss (2006) and Khan and Weiss (2006) point out, trading costs are often defined as the range of costs involved in moving a product from a point of production to a market and can refer to both national and cross-border transactions. They draw upon the work on trade intensity indices from the very detailed work of Ng and Yeats (2003) on East Asia to argue that lowering trade costs can significantly increase trade. They also point to some results from gravity-type models (for example, De, 2006; Limao and Venables, 2001) that provide indirect evidence for a negative relation between trading costs and volume of trade.

Much more work remains to be done in quantifying accurately the trade cost to be used in these models, but provided the proxies applied there are broadly reasonable the results indicate a fairly strong elasticity of trade to declines in trade cost. Hence there are further potential benefits from infrastructure investment or intervention in these areas to lower trade cost barriers to trade.

As with any other form of cost, an increase in trade costs of all types will be expected to impact on the incentive to invest. This is reflected in the responses typically found in 'investment climate' surveys that poor quality hard infrastructure that provides poor road and air communications, unreliable power supplies and congested ports is a major disincentive to investment (World Bank, 2005).[3] I now turn to a discussion of specific types of soft infrastructure and their relations to trading costs.

SOFT INFRASTRUCTURE COMPONENTS

As mentioned before, I discuss soft infrastructure mainly under three distinct but related categories. These are: governance in general, corporate governance and corruption. I also discuss the issue of privatization of infrastructures in these contexts where it seems appropriate to do so.

Soft Infrastructure: Governance, Trade Costs and Regional Co-operation

'Governance' refers to institutions and processes by which we make collective decisions and solve collective problems. It has become the dominant term in discussing issues such as the role of the state as various pressures converged in the 1980s to force researchers and leaders of governments and multilateral organizations to shift attention from government to governance. These pressures included demands to reduce the size of government, frustration with inefficient and corrupt government bureaucracies, and recognition that the formulation and implementation of public policy appropriately included non-government actors. Public officials must now co-ordinate and co-operate with partners in vertical, authority-based and horizontal, negotiation-based systems responsible for provision of public goods. Clearly, these developments have significant implications for the supply and management of infrastructure.

In the past ten years, the World Bank has taken the lead in operationalizing the concept of governance. According to the research there, governance has several measurable dimensions related to:

- process whereby *governments* are selected, monitored, replaced
  - voice and accountability; civil and political rights; freedom of media
  - political instability and violence;
- capacity of *government* to effectively formulate and implement sound policies
  - definition of role – which public goods to provide?
  - commitment to policies, capacity of civil service, independence of civil service, quality of public service provision
  - regulatory burden; and
- respect of citizens and the state for institutions that govern economic and social interactions between them
  - rule of law
  - graft and corruption.

In a recent summary of the governance literature, ('Governance matters V: aggregate and individual governance indicators for 1996–2005'), Daniel Kaufmann, Aart Kraay and Massimo Mastruzzi (Kaufmann et al., 2006) report on the latest version of the worldwide governance indicators, covering 213 countries and territories and measuring six dimensions of governance since 1996 until the end of 2005: voice and accountability, political stability and absence of violence, government effectiveness, regulatory quality, rule of law and control of corruption. The indicators are based on several hundred individual variables measuring perceptions of governance, drawn from 31 separate data sources constructed by 25 different organizations. Using these extensive data sources, Kaufmann et al. construct indicators of the following six dimensions of governance:

1. *Voice and accountability*, the extent to which a country's citizens are able to participate in selecting their government, as well as freedom of expression, freedom of association and free media;
2. *Political stability and absence of violence*, perceptions of the likelihood that the government will be destabilized or overthrown by unconstitutional or violent means, including political violence and terrorism;
3. *Government effectiveness* (GE), the quality of public services, the quality of the civil service and the degree of its independence from political pressures, the quality of policy formulation and implementation, and the credibility of the government's commitment to such policies;
4. *Regulatory quality* (RQ), the ability of the government to formulate and implement sound policies and regulations that permit and promote private sector development;
5. *Rule of law*, the extent to which agents have confidence in and abide by the rules of society, and in particular the quality of contract enforcement, the police, and the courts, as well as the likelihood of crime and violence; and
6. *Control of corruption*, the extent to which public power is exercised for private gain, including both petty and grand forms of corruption, as well as 'capture' of the state by elites and private interests.

We discuss corruption under a separate heading later. In this section we focus on the possible relations between trade costs and the other dimensions of governance in the context of regional co-operation. If we look at illustrations of trade cost and infrastructure interventions, we find that already several areas of governance reform leading to trade cost reductions are indicated. In fact, it could be argued that almost all areas except direct transportation costs can be affected by desirable governance reforms. In particular, unofficial payments could cease or be reduced drastically as government effectiveness – that is the quality of public services, the quality of the civil service and the degree of its independence from political pressures, the quality of policy formulation and implementation, and the credibility of the government's commitment to such policies – increases with appropriate reforms. Furthermore, if the reforms are carried out on a co-ordinated basis within the region, the benefits will be reaped by all the parties regardless of their country of origin.

Another area where co-ordinated governance reforms can reduce trade costs is customs delays. The informal anecdotal evidence indicates that there are substantial losses from such delays. Clearly, even unilateral reform by one country can improve the situation for that country and its trading partners; but a co-ordinated reform package will provide incentives for cross-border co-operation among exporters, importers and other allied interest groups including consumers, which can lead to significant cuts in trading costs. For example, the harmonization of customs procedures, a regional co-operation issue par excellence, can save each party involved considerable sums. It can also lead to the creation of goodwill and operational procedures that can ease the way for future gainful co-operation in other areas.

A third area where governance reforms can (at least indirectly) affect trading costs is insurance regulation. Regulatory quality, the ability of the government to formulate and implement sound policies and regulations that permit and promote private sector development. If governance reforms lead to an improvement in RQ, then freight insurance and related regulations can lead to significant lowering of costs.

These are probably the most obvious areas in which cross-border co-ordination together with governance reforms will have significant impact on lowering trading costs. In addition an increasingly general tendency to follow the rule of law will undoubtedly make regional co-operation and lowering of trade costs more feasible. The lowering of information costs through such co-operation and an improvement of the quality of information can also improve the investment climate as well.

Much of the recent research in governance has focused on defining and measuring various indicators of governance. Operational work has relied largely on survey-based statistical techniques. It is still too early to say how useful the current set of measurement techniques will be in the area of measuring the impact of soft infrastructure reforms on trading costs and other factors related to regional co-operation. But the value added from doing such work can potentially be great (see also the section on corruption). We now turn to a brief discussion of corporate governance, particularly as it may relate to the public–private partnership idea in the area of infrastructure provision and regional co-operation, and its possible impact on trading costs.

Corporate Governance, Regional Co-operation and Infrastructure Management

Corporate governance in a narrow sense addresses the fundamental micro-economic issue of how the managers of a firm are induced by banks, equity markets or other mechanisms to act in the best interests of its shareholders and hence to maximize the discounted present value of the firm. In a wider sense, corporate governance can or should address a whole host of issues for multiple stakeholders – ranging from efficiency and equity to the promotion of economic and political freedom.

By now there is an extensive literature on corporate governance. The interested reader is referred to Khan (2004b) for a relevant survey of literature. Here the focus is on particular types of corporate governance in Asia, their possible reform and their impact on trading costs.

Khan (1999; 2004b) develops the idea of a family-based corporate governance system (FBS) and contrasts this with the bank-led system (BLS) and equity-market based system (EMS). Both BLS and EMS are closely associated with the dominant mode of corporate finance by banks and equity markets respectively. In the case of FBS, the financing can come from three different sources. Initially, family business is financed largely by internal funds. As the enterprise grows over time, the role of banks and outside equity becomes more prominent. However, the key difference between FBS as a governance system and BLS and EMS lies in the fact that neither the banks nor the equity markets ultimately control the family business groups. The control resides with the family groups in the final analysis. This may not be without economic rationale, but ultimately FBS can run into trouble as well. Since many developing economies are characterized by FBS, it is important to analyse the role of FBS in infrastructure delivery and management. In addition, the role of BLS and EMS in infrastructure delivery and management needs also to be considered.

According to the theory developed in Khan (1999; 2004b) it is possible to analyse the FBS type of governance by considering five essential aspects: (1) the extent of family controlled corporations in the specific regions, for example, in East Asia or Latin America; (2) the dominant modes of financing; (3) the key information asymmetries and agency conflicts; (4) problems of monitoring family businesses; and (5) investment and capital accumulation. For infrastructure delivery and management all five aspects are important, but information asymmetry, monitoring and investment issues are of particular salience.

It is fair to say that work on the role of corporate governance in ensuring efficiency and equity in infrastructure delivery and management is yet to begin. But this is likely to be a research area with particularly high pay-off. Infrastructure projects are typically large, involve external financing including foreign financing, and have many informational asymmetries arising from many sources, particularly the specialized nature of many projects. In view of the popularity and potential of the public–private partnership (PPP) in infrastructure delivery and management, it is imperative that we try to understand the issues related to corporate governance in this area. Public–private partnership can lead to the desired outcome only when many of these informational and agency issues have been sorted out and proper corporate governance with an efficiently functioning board of directors is in place.

With respect to trading costs in particular, to the extent a well-governed corporation is able to deliver infrastructure at or close to the minimum average cost, the direct transportation cost itself can be lower. In addition, a well-governed insurance industry will deliver insurance products at lower costs as well. Cross-border co-ordination of corporate governance reforms by instituting best practices in several countries can lead to substantial lowering of trade costs among these countries and between the region and the rest of the world. Some particular hypotheses to test in this context can flow from the relationship between factors that concern the relations between outside members of the board, independent auditing committees and remuneration committees, on the one hand, and trading costs, on the other. For example, one could test the hypothesis that an independent auditing committee can lower trading costs (via an improvement of the delivery of services by decreasing the incentive to overcharge, follow dilatory practices, and so on).

Corruption: How Significant a Problem?

Our last broad research theme emerging from this quick survey of soft infrastructure, trading costs and regional co-operation may be the most complex one. In the final analysis, corruption is really about accountability for governance failures as the subsection on governance already indicated. Our major concern here, as in the last two sections, is with how corruption increases trading costs. We suggest research strategies for determining these links and policies for improving regional co-operation through fighting cross-border corruption such as smuggling.

Although 'unofficial payments' may be the most obvious and perhaps the most widespread type of corruption with regard to trading costs, there are clearly many aspects of regulatory environment that are affected by corruption.[4] The impact of corruption in the financial sector is particularly important to understand. It would appear that most trade costs are likely to increase because of corruption.

The usual explanation of the existence of corruption in public sector infrastructure delivery and management relies on the phenomenon of low wages in the public sector. There are at least two other important features of infrastructure that can account for the higher than average risks of corruption in these sectors. First, on average, projects tend to be much bigger than in other sectors. Second, firms delivering services in infrastructure are often allowed a monopoly on delivery.

The existence of widespread corruption among public monopolies in the infrastructure sectors was often one of the arguments used to advocate privatization. This was supported by the theoretical modelling of corruption.[5] Assuming that it is easier for corrupt politicians to control public firms than private firms, these researchers argued that privatization could reduce the control government has over the rent offered by full control of the sector by making political interference more costly or more visible.[6]

However, as Estache (2006: 20) correctly observes:

> Most of the evidence offered by these surveys is however anecdotal and indirect. There is no real systematic measurement of the level of corruption in the sector. With the exception of a database compiled by Clarke and Xu (2004) for Eastern Europe and some sense of the ranking of utilities among corrupt institutions from the *Global Corruption Report* (2004), the annual *Global Competitiveness Report* provides the only comparable, quantitative, multi-country (59 developing countries) overview of corruption in infrastructure sectors, ranking countries according to the perceived degree of corruption (based on interviews with private firms) among many other criteria.

What can be done to reduce corruption in infrastructure? Four main directions have been suggested. These are: (1) privatization, (2) regulation and related processes, (3) increased decentralization, and (4) adoption of participatory process in the selection, implementation and supervision of projects. In each of these areas cross-border co-operation can significantly improve efficiency and reduce costs, including trading costs.

If we wish to attain more precision in future research on corruption in infrastructure and its impact, some preliminary work needs to be done first. In this effort, there are at least two areas in which basic work is likely to pay off significantly. The first is data collection, refinement and organization according to some given theoretical framework. There is a significant body of theoretical work in micreconomic theory, corporate governance and related areas that can be used as a starting point for this. Second, and at least equally important, is the empirical effort that will also be necessary. Empirically, the measurement of corruption levels in the infrastructure sector is still generally approximated by the level of corruption in the country. More direct data are needed.

The assessment of the effectiveness of the policy instruments for the infrastructure sector depends on refining data in ways described above. Once such data are available, accurate estimates of the impact of corruption on trading (and other) costs can be computed by using state-of-the-art econometric methods.

We concur with Estache (2006: 26) with regard to the assessment of theoretical work in this area and the need for empirical evidence:

The main message of this discussion of the effectiveness of theoretical solutions may be that there is not enough evidence to get a sense of how much and under what circumstances each one of them really matters. When evidence is available, it is too narrow or not robust enough. This defines an important research agenda for the sector. Finding out more about the actual effectiveness of the theoretical recommendations on how to deal with corruption in the sector should be a higher priority.

Therefore, estimating the impact of corruption on trading costs empirically looms as an important research task. At our present state of knowledge, one could begin with some existing (unrefined) index of corruption as a right-hand side variable and run regressions on a cross-sectional basis to see what the impact of corruption (*ceteris paribus*) on trading costs may be. Even at this level, a rather extensive cross-section data-set on a number of variables including governance, corporate governance and industry-specific indicators will be necessary. But the pay-off is likely to be large since the existing state is one of theoretical deductions of limited applicability at best, or following one's prejudices with a few anecdotes for support at worst. As mentioned earlier, more refined data on corruption in infrastructure in particular will lead to more accurate empirical estimates of its impact, and hence, one hopes, to better – or at least better informed – policies.

SOFT INFRASTRUCTURE, TRADING COSTS AND REGIONAL CO-OPERATION: A FINAL OBSERVATION

All three related areas of soft infrastructure discussed so far can lead to a significant reduction in trading costs. Once the relevant data are available this plausible hypothesis can be specified econometrically. With further testing we will be in a position to assess existing policies in the area of soft infrastructure reforms. Turning to trading costs in particular, we saw that trade costs were thought to be more important than policy barriers to trade. We could test whether this was true particularly for soft infrastructural factors related to trading costs, thus providing a deeper explanation for Anderson and van Wincoop's (2004: 693) claim that 'inferred border costs appear on average to dwarf the effect of tariff and non-tariff barriers'.[7] Regional co-operation in the soft infrastructure as a broader policy area could also be assessed for effectiveness econometrically. Furthermore, there are also economy-wide modelling approaches that can be used for these and other purposes, including assessing the impact of regional co-operation in infrastructure on poverty reduction.

INFRASTRUCTURE REFORMS, TRADE COSTS AND POVERTY REDUCTION: CGE MODELLING

We also wish to emphasize that soft and hard infrastructure reforms and the consequent reduction of trading costs do not happen in a vacuum but that they also have an impact on the poor through their impact on other markets (such as the labour market and investment savings market) that matter to the poor. These feedback effects are potentially significant for poverty reduction. Models that can carry out counterfactual policy experiments and estimate their impact on poverty, making possible an economy-wide analysis, are needed. Computable general equilibrium (CGE) models are increasingly becoming a useful analytical response to these needs. At the ADBI, we have carried out such modelling exercises with respect to trade liberalization and its impact on poverty (Khan, 2004a and b; 2005; 2006).

In general, through a simultaneous and recursive equations system structure, the CGE models can simulate economic and social impacts of reforms and are based on the socio-economic structure of a social accounting matrix (SAM), with its multi-sectoral disaggregation. As illustrated in Khan (2004a and b), for example,[8] the basic idea behind a SAM is to identify the linkages in an economic system. The basic elements when constructing a SAM are input–output tables combined with government accounts, labour force and household surveys. The household surveys are crucial for performing impact analysis on welfare and poverty. How deep the analysis can go depends on data availability. The CGE literature on the effects of public infrastructure service reform is rather modest: Adam and Bevans (2004) for Uganda, Boccanfusso et al. (2006) for Senegal, Chisari and his colleagues (1999; 2003) and Navajas (2000) for Argentina, and Andersen and Faris (2002) for natural gas in Bolivia. Their main contribution is to show the importance of infrastructure for achieving the MDGs and to show that good regulation can be redistributive and progressive. Multi-country CGE models for particular regions can also capture the impacts of regional co-operation in hard and soft infrastructure areas.

SUMMARY AND CONCLUSIONS

This chapter has attempted to provide a framework for considering how soft infrastructure can contribute to the process of regional co-operation in various parts of Asia. Following Weiss (2006) and Khan and Weiss (2006), it has drawn on the familiar formulation of the effective rate of protection – developed decades ago when tariffs and quotas were serious barriers to trade – and argued that this concept can be modified to quantify the empirical significance of broader trade cost barriers. The effective rate of protection concept is flexible enough to allow the effect of a range of potential trade costs to be addressed. Soft infrastructure interventions can be interpreted as instruments to lower trade costs and hence are a means of stimulating closer trading links.

In this chapter I have emphasized specifically the relationship between soft infrastructure and trade costs. Clearly, much work remains to be done to quantify the impact of trade costs both on domestic value added and through protection on trade flows. The basic policy point is that if we have a clear indication of the height of the barriers posed by different types of trade cost, this will give us a rough ranking of priorities in terms of soft infrastructure interventions to lower these. While a vast amount of empirical work in the 1960s and 1970s quantified the barriers to trade caused by tariffs and quotas, as yet relatively little has been done to quantify protection from these largely institutional barriers.

This chapter has identified several crucial areas of future research with potentially large value added. My general hypothesis with significant policy implications which can be elaborated and tested is that *trade costs are negatively related to the existence of and improvements in soft infrastructure*. A related hypothesis is that cross-border co-operation in building and maintaining both hard and soft infrastructure synergistically will lead to a reduction in trade costs. More specifically it will be useful to know how high are the barriers to trade created by factors like high freight costs, slow port handling, customs delays, lack of competition in the insurance sector, poor corporate governance, unofficial payments, and so forth. Some of these factors may be intrinsically difficult to quantify but the potential pay-off from policy-relevant research of this type is enormous. Optimal policies for regional co-operation in soft infrastructure will be difficult, if not impossible, to formulate in the absence of this type of research.

NOTES

1. I would like to thank Debasis Bhattacharya for valuable research assistance.
2. This section draws heavily upon Khan and Weiss (2006). See also, Weiss (2006).
3. However not all trade costs need be borne by the domestic purchaser or importer for internationally traded goods. From simple microeconomics we know that the incidence of trade costs will be determined by demand and supply elasticities. See Weiss (2006) for further details.
4. One could go further and claim that perhaps all aspects of regulatory environment are affected by corruption.
5. See, for example, Shapiro and Willig (1990), Shleifer and Vishny (1993) and Boycko et al. (1996) among others.
6. See also Estache (2006: 19) who adds insightfully: 'Favoritism, fraud, cronyism, patronage, embezzlement, bribes, and state capture are all concepts that have long been associated

with the delivery of infrastructure services in many countries.' There is an extensive literature on how to define corruption and on the semantic practices of different institutions; a
helpful recent survey is Lanyi (2004). For a recent survey on economic analysis of corruption, see Aidt (2003); on levels of corruption, see Kaufmann et al. (2003; 2006). There are
now models coming up which generate incentive structures consistent with the Latin
American stylized facts and which show that there are also cases where private ownership
can foster investment while increasing corruption. See Martimort and Straub (2006).

The focus of debate has now shifted from the interactions between public operators and
users to those between private operators and government. This can be seen in the survey
prepared for Transparency International on corruption and privatization in infrastructure
in developing countries (Boehm and Polanco, 2003; TI, 2005). There is increasing empha-
sis on this also in various publications by NGOs and Hall and Lobina (2002). Many of these
document legal proceedings that have demonstrated incidents of corruption in the sector.
Friends of the Earth (2001) and various political scientists have documented the role of corruption as a cost driver in contract negotiations and renegotiations in the sector. There is
also an increasing body of academic evidence. Flyvbjerg (2005) and Flyvbjerg et al. (2002;
2003a; 2003b) and Mitlin (2004), for instance, all document how undesirable practice fuels
cost excesses at the project level. More conceptual research is also analysing the changes in
the global market structure characterized by an increased domination of this market by a
few players. Celentani et al. (2004) develop a model consistent with the fact that an increase
in competition in international business transactions can increase corruption in the sector.

7. It may be recalled that their 'representative' international trade costs for industrialized
   countries, a combination of transport and non-transport costs, are as high as 74 per cent,
   compared with average tariffs of less than 5 per cent. Of these international trade costs,
   roughly one-third are transport related and the rest cover other types of trade cost. If
   international trade costs for inputs are below those for outputs the representative effective
   protection rate created by trade cost will be higher still.
8. See also the references cited there.

REFERENCES

Adam, C.S. and D.L. Bevan (2004), 'Aid and the supply side: public investment,
export performance and Dutch disease in low income countries', *Working Paper*,
201, Department of Economics, Oxford University.

Aidt, T.S. (2003), 'Economic analysis of corruption: a survey', *The Economic
Journal*, **113** (491), F632–F652.

Andersen, L.E. and R. Faris (2002), 'Natural gas and income distribution in
Bolivia', *Andean Competitiveness Project Working Paper*, February.

Anderson, J. and E. van Wincoop (2004), 'Trade costs', *Journal of Economic
Literature*, **42** (3) (September), 691–751.

Bhattacharya, B. (2006), 'Emergence of regional trade blocs in Asia: problems
and prospects', workshop on 'Understanding the Latest Wave of Regional
Trade and Co-operation Agreements', CESifo, Venice International University,
19–20 July.

Boccanfuso, D., A. Estache and L. Savard (2006), 'Water sector reform in Senegal:
an interpersonal and interregional distributional impact analysis', mimeo, World
Bank.

Boehm, F. and J. Polanco (2003), 'Corruption and privatization of infrastructure in
developing countries', *Transparency International*, Working Paper, 1.

Boycko, M., A. Shleifer and R.W. Vishny (1996), 'A theory of privatisation',
Economic Journal, **106** (March), 309–19.

Celentani, M., J.-J. Ganuza and J.L. Peydro (2004), 'Combating corruption in international business transactions', *Economica*, **71** (283), 417–48.

Chisari, O., A. Estache and C. Romero (1999), 'Winners and losers from the privatization and regulation of utilities: lessons from a general equilibrium model of Argentina', *The World Bank Economic Review*, **13** (2), 357–78.

Chisari, O., A. Estache and C. Waddams-Price (2003), 'Access by the poor in Latin America's utility reform: subsidies and service obligations', in C. Ugaz and C. Waddams-Price (eds), *Utility Privatization and Regulation: A Fair Deal for Consumers?*, Cheltenham, UK and Northampton, MA, USA: Edward Elgar.

Clarke, G. and C. Xu (2004), 'Privatization, competition and corruption: how characteristics of bribe takers and payers affect bribes to utilities', *Journal of Public Economics*, **88** (9–10), 2067–97.

Cororaton, C.B. (2005), 'Total factor productivity growth in the Phillippines: 1960–2000', *Asian Development Review*, **22** (1), 97–113.

De, P. (2006), 'Regional trade in Northeast Asia: why do trade costs matter?', workshop on 'Understanding the latest wave of regional trade and co-operation agreements', CESifo, Venice International University, 19–20 July.

Estache, A. (2006), 'Infrastructure: a survey of recent and upcoming issues', World Bank ABCDE Conference, Tokyo, 29–30 May.

Flyvbjerg, B. (2005), 'Policy and planning for large infrastructure projects: problems, causes and cures', *Policy Research Working Paper, 3781*, Washington, DC: World Bank.

Flyvbjerg, B., M. Skamris Holm and S. Buhl (2002), 'Cost underestimation in public works projects: error or lie?', *Journal of the American Planning Association*, **68**, 279–95.

Flyvbjerg, B., M. Skamris Holm and S. Buhl (2003a), 'How common and how large are cost overruns in transport infrastructure projects?', *Transport Reviews*, **23** (1), 71–88.

Flyvbjerg, B., N. Bruzelius and W. Rothengatter (2003b), *Megaprojects and Risk: An Anatomy of Ambition*, Cambridge: Cambridge University Press.

Friends of the Earth (2001), 'Dirty water: the environmental and social record of four multinational water companies', London, available at http://www.foe.co.uk/resource/briefings/dirty_water.pdf.

Fung, K.C., A. Garcia-Herrero, H. Iizaka and A. Siu (2005), 'Hard or soft? Institutions reforms and infrastructure spending as determinants of foreign direct investment in China', *Japanese Economic Review*, **56** (4), 408–16.

Hall, D. and E. Lobina (2002), 'Water privatization in Latin America' in K. Komives, D. Whittington and X. Wu (eds), *Infrastructure Coverage and the Poor: A Global Perspective, Policy Research Working Papers, No. 2551*, Washington, DC: World Bank.

Inter-American Development Bank (IDB) (2002), *Beyond Borders: The New Regionalism in Latin America*, Inter-American Development Bank, Economic and Social Progress in Latin America Report 2002, Washington, DC.

Kaufman, D., A. Kraay and M. Mastruzzi (2003), 'Governance matters III: Governance Indicators for 1996–2002', 30 June, draft, World Bank.

Kaufman, D., A. Kraay and M. Mastruzzi (2006), 'Governance matters V: aggregate and individual governance indicators for 1996–2005', *Policy Research Working Paper*, WPS 4012, World Bank.

Kawai, M. (2005), 'East Asian economic regionalism: progress and challenges', *Journal of Asian Economics*, **16** (1) (February), 29–55.

Khan, H.A. (1999), 'Corporate governance of family businesses in Asia: what's right and what's wrong?', ADBI paper no. 3.

Khan, H.A. (2004a), 'Using macroeconomic computable general equilibrium models for assessing poverty impact of structural adjustment policies', mimeo, ADBI.

Khan, H.A. (2004b), *Global Markets and Financial Crises in Asia: Towards a Theory for the 21st Century*, Basingstoke and New York: Palgrave Macmillan.

Khan, H.A. (2005), 'Poverty impacts of trade liberalization in a dual-dual CGE model: illustrations for South Asia', paper presented at the ADBI annual conference, Tokyo, December.

Khan, H.A. (2006), 'Trade liberalization and poverty in South Asia in a dual-dual model', in H.A. Khan and J. Weiss, *Poverty Strategies in Asia: A Growth Plus Approach*, Cheltenham, UK and Northampton, MA, USA: Edward Elgar Publishing, pp. 41–89.

Khan, H.A. and J. Weiss (2006), 'Infrastructure for regional co-operation', paper presented in the joint workshop of ADBI and IDD in Seoul, 15–17 November.

Lanyi, A. (2004), 'Measuring the economic impact of corruption', The IRIS Discussion Paper Series on Institutions and Development, University of Maryland, Paper 04/04.

Limao, N. and A. Venables (2001), 'Infrastructure, geographical disadvantage, transport costs and trade', *World Bank Economic Review*, 15, 451–79.

Martimort, D. and S. Straub (2006), 'Privatization and corruption', presentation made at the IDEI 'Conference on public services and management: designs, issues and implications for local governance', Toulouse, 12–14 January.

Mitlin, D. (2004), 'Understanding urban poverty: what the poverty reduction strategy papers tell us', International Institute of Environment and Development, Poverty Reduction in Urban Areas Series, Working Paper 13.

Navajas, F. (2000), 'El impacto distributivo de los cambios en los precios relativos en la Argentina entre 1988–1998 y los efectos de las privatizaciones y la desregulacion economica', in *La Distribucion del Ingreso en la Argentina*, Fundacion de Investigaciones Economicas Latinoamericanas, Buenos Aires: FIEL.

Ng, F. and A. Yeats (2003), 'Major trade trends in Asia: what are their implications for regional co-operation and growth?', *World Bank Policy Research Working Paper*, 3084, Washington, DC: World Bank.

Shapiro, C. and R. Willig (1990), 'Economic rationale for the scope for privatization', in E.N. Suleiman and J. Waterbury (eds), *The Political Economy of Public Sector Reform*, Boulder, CO: Westview Press.

Shleifer, A. and R. Vishny (1993), 'Corruption', *Quarterly Journal of Economics*, 108 (3) (August), 599–617.

TI (Transparency International) (2005), *Global Corruption Report*, London: Pluto Press.

Weiss, J. (2006), 'Hard infrastructure and regional cooperation', paper presented at ADBI annual symposium, Tokyo, 8 December.

World Bank (2005), *World Development Report 2005*, Washington, DC: World Bank.

5. Empirical estimates of trade costs for Asia[1]

Prabir De

I. INTRODUCTION

Trade costs have become a key area for reform in regional and multilateral context mainly due to the rise in volume and complexity of international trade. Trade costs include all costs incurred in getting a good to a final user other than the marginal cost of producing the good itself, such as transportation costs (both freight costs and time costs), policy barriers (tariffs and non-tariff barriers), information costs, contract enforcement costs, costs associated with the use of different currencies, legal and regulatory costs, and local distribution costs (wholesale and retail). Components of trade costs form a potentially important barrier to trade, and some of these are provided in Table 5.1.

Why do we need to give special attention to trade costs? One compelling argument is that countries will not fully realize the gains from trade liberalization unless they also initiate adequate infrastructure interventions in order to reduce costs of doing trade across borders. For example, reductions in tariff levels – at home and abroad – will offer fewer benefits to economies whose international trading infrastructures are ill-equipped to handle increased imports or clear exports quickly enough.

Therefore, higher trade costs is an obstacle to trade and it impedes the realization of gains from trade liberalization.[2] Studies show that integration is the result of reduced costs of transportation in particular and other infrastructure services in general.[3] Direct evidence on border costs shows that tariff barriers are now low in most countries, on average (trade-weighted or arithmetic) less than 5 per cent for rich countries, and with a few exceptions are on average between 10 to 20 per cent for developing countries (Anderson and van Wincoop, 2004). While, on the one hand, the world has witnessed a drastic fall in tariffs over the past two decades, a whole lot of barriers, on the other, remain and do penalise trade, among which some are seen as policy barriers, such as tariff and non-tariff barriers (NTBs), and others as barriers relating to environment, such as

71

Concepts and measurement issues

Table 5.1   Trade costs and infrastructure interventions

Type of trade costs	Type of barriers	Infrastructure intervention
Transport cost	Hard/visible	Port, shipping, road, rail, aviation
Time in transit	Hard/visible	Port, shipping, road, rail, aviation
Freight insurance	Soft/invisible	Insurance regulation
Customs delays	Soft/invisible	Harmonization of customs procedures
Unofficial payments	Soft/invisible	Governance reform
Information search	Soft/invisible	Investment climate
Currency changes (cost of hedging)	Soft/invisible	Financial sector regulation
Management of supply chain	Hard/visible and soft/invisible	Telecommunications, investment climate, regulatory environment
Excess inventories	Hard/visible and soft/invisible	Port, shipping, road, rail, aviation, harmonization of customs procedures

Source: Adapted from Khan and Weiss (2006).

infrastructure quality.[4] In policy formulation, one set of such policy barriers (soft barriers) are dealt with through measures in trade and business facilitation, whereas the set of barriers relating to the environment (hard barriers) is managed through transport facilitation measures. Improvements in infrastructure can lower these barriers and, thus, declines in such costs make goods more cost competitive and raise the return on investment (Khan and Weiss, 2006).

Therefore, today's trade strategy goes beyond the traditional mechanisms of tariffs and quotas, and includes 'behind-the-border' issues, such as the role of infrastructure and governance in supporting a well-functioning trading economy. Attention is now focused on lowering trade costs through facilitation of merchandise and services trade logistics, both inbound and outbound.[5] Given this awareness, trade costs are cited as an important determinant of the volume of international trade and specialization. Indeed, the more countries progress forward economically, and commit to remove barriers to trade, as has happened in some parts of the European Union (EU), assessing the size and shape of trade costs will help countries to strengthen the economic integration process. Therefore, trade costs play a crucial role in policy formation as the optimality of preferential trade arrangements depends on the size and shape of 'natural' trade barriers (Krugman, 1991).

Trade volume in Asia has been rising fast. To date, 51 per cent of Asia's exports are conducted within the region (Table 5.2), and 27 per cent of world exports come from Asia, compared with 18 per cent when China

Table 5.2   Intra- and inter-regional merchandise trade in 2005

Origin	Destination							
	North America	South and Central America	Europe	CIS*	Africa	Middle East	Asia	World
Value (US$billion)								
Asia	608	51	498	37	54	89	1424	2779
World	2093	301	4398	224	240	321	2443	10159
Share of inter-regional trade flows in each region's total merchandise exports (%)								
Asia	21.9	1.9	17.9	1.3	1.9	3.2	51.2	100.0
World	20.6	3.0	43.3	2.2	2.4	3.2	24.0	100.0
Share of regional trade flows in world merchandise exports								
Asia	6.0	0.5	4.9	0.4	0.5	0.9	14.0	27.4
World	20.6	3.0	43.3	2.2	2.4	3.2	24.0	100.0

Notes: * Commonwealth of Independent States

Source: WTO (2006).

started liberalizing her economy in 1978 and 26 per cent when India adopted a liberal trade regime in 1991. The composition of trade in Asia is also changing fast. Asia is gradually specializing in trade in intermediate and finished products. Fifty-four per cent of world exports of electronic data processing and office equipment come from Asia (in 2005), compared with 48 per cent in 2000, and 66 per cent of world exports in integrated circuits are contributed by Asian countries (Table 5.3). These are the high-end products where cost of international trade appeared to be high, if barriers at both ends are counted (De, 2007).

Considering the rise in trade interdependence in Asia, the need for a pan-Asian free trade agreement (FTA) in the region has also gained high momentum in recent years. This has been reflected in a growing number of studies conducted in the past few years aiming to find out the feasibility of an FTA in Asia.[6] On the demand side, the noticeable development is that, as a result of trade liberalization, the tariff level in Asia has become low. However, on the supply side, the question remains whether or not Asia as a region witnesses a decline in 'trade costs'. Despite technological advancement, cost of movement of goods across countries has not fallen.[7] Venables (2006: 62) commented: 'technical change in shipping is no longer faster than technical change in goods shipped, so freight rates relative to shipment value are no longer falling'.

Since the countries in Asia are planning to intensify regional co-operation through FTAs,[8] these countries should display smaller trade

Table 5.3   Merchandise exports of Asia by product

Product	Share in exports of Asia (%)		Share in world exports (%)	
	2000	2005	2000	2005
Total merchandise exports	100.0	100.0	26.4	27.4
Agricultural products	6.1	5.6	18.3	18.1
Fuels and mining products	7.6	9.1	14.5	14.4
Manufactures	86.3	85.2	29.7	31.6
Iron and steel	2.2	3.0	24.9	26.5
Chemicals	6.1	7.4	17.3	18.5
Pharmaceuticals	0.5	0.6	8.1	6.2
Other chemicals	5.6	6.7	19.4	22.5
Other semi-manufactures	5.6	5.8	20.5	22.8
Machinery and transport equipment	51.2	48.6	32.2	35.1
Office and telecom equipment	27.5	25.2	47.2	54.9
EDP and office equipment	10.7	9.0	47.7	53.9
Telecommunications equipment	6.2	8.0	35.8	47.7
Integrated circuits	10.6	8.2	57.2	66.0
Transport equipment	10.2	10.2	20.3	21.9
Automotive products	6.9	7.0	19.8	21.3
Other transport equipment	3.3	3.2	21.3	23.2
Other machinery	13.4	13.2	26.7	28.7
Textiles	4.2	3.4	44.2	46.7
Clothing	5.5	4.7	46.4	47.7
Other manufactures	9.5	10.1	29.6	33.0
Personal and household goods	2.2	2.3	31.4	36.2
Scientific and controlling instruments	1.6	2.5	22.4	32.7
Miscellaneous manufactures	5.8	5.3	31.8	31.9

Source: WTO (2006).

costs. Free trade agreements are expected to put added competitive pressure on Asian economies, particularly on trade and through investments. To gain anything from a liberalized trade regime in Asia, there is an urgent need to control trade costs. A decline in trade costs will not only multiply the welfare emanating from the liberalized trade environment but also strengthen the trade capacity of the region. Therefore, gaining a fair idea about the factors that contribute to trade costs will help Asian countries to make more accurate and appropriate infrastructure interventions.

Asian countries' performance in controlling trade costs, relative to the EU, has not progressed well. Despite a fall in absolute base ocean freight,

Table 5.4 Trends in ocean freight in selected Asian countries[1] (US$ per TEU)

Origin	Destination	Base ocean freight		Auxiliary charges[2]		Total	
		2003	2005	2003	2005	2003	2005
Japan	China	250	275	178	223	428	498
Japan	Korea	300	275	238	289	538	564
Japan	Hong Kong	196	200	419	425	615	625
Japan	Malaysia	366	375	244	296	610	671
Japan	Singapore	312	325	307	321	619	646
Japan	India	1546	1600	489	523	2035	2123
Japan	Thailand	312	275	232	258	544	533
China	Japan	900	800	162	366	1062	1166
China	Korea	300	500	190	240	490	740
China	Hong Kong	412	400	331	345	743	745
China	Malaysia	620	600	213	217	833	817
China	Singapore	410	400	240	241	650	641
China	India	2109	2000	288	302	2397	2302
China	Thailand	608	600	166	180	774	780
Korea	Japan	300	400	218	262	518	662
Korea	China	250	350	203	220	453	570
Korea	Hong Kong	444	450	419	422	863	872
Korea	Malaysia	388	400	267	282	655	682
Korea	Singapore	398	400	309	318	707	718
Korea	India	2010	1950	517	528	2527	2478
Korea	Thailand	395	400	251	255	646	655

Notes:
1 Rates are collected for shipment of a 20 ft container (TEU) among country's major ports. Rates are averaged for the year 2005.
2 Including container handling charges, documentation fees, government taxes and levies, etc. of both the trading partners.

Source: De (2007).

auxiliary shipping charges are increasingly becoming critical to trade in Asia.[9] Table 5.4 indicates that while ocean freight for movement of vessels from three Northeast Asian countries to selected Asian countries has been reduced during the period 2003 and 2005, auxiliary shipping charges have witnessed a steep rise.

To a great extent, auxiliary shipping charges often overtake base ocean freight (see Figure 5.1). These auxiliary charges are nothing but outcome

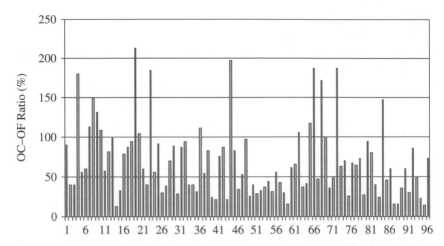

Note: Total number of observations is 97, taken in bilateral pairs. OF and OC refer ocean freight (base) and other charges (auxiliary), respectively, for a shipment of a container (TEU) in bilateral trading pair in ten selected Asian countries for the year 2005.

Source: Calculated based on freight rates, provided by Maersk Sealand (2006).

Figure 5.1   Variations in shipping rates in selected Asian countries in 2005

of market imperfections, and obviously have negative effect on trade. While some auxiliary charges are market driven, such as terminal handling charges, imposition of government duties and levies on ocean freight (similar to tariffs) is very much ad hoc and offers less 'economic rationale'. Size and the level of duties and levies also differ across countries. On an average, 3 per cent was imposed as government duties and levies on ocean freight in 2005. The rates of government duties and levies are relatively more on the freight between Japan and countries in Northeast and Southeast Asia, where the volume of two-way trade is also high.

Expectedly, the rise in auxiliary shipping charges is thus not only offsetting the gains arising from tariff liberalization, but also making the entire trade costlier. A major part of these auxiliary shipping charges like documentation fees, government taxes and levies, and so on, are the 'soft' barriers to trade and very much implicit in the system, on which shippers (exporters and importers) have less control. Countries that cannot or will not control auxiliary shipping charges, may lose their export markets to rivals. This provides opportunities for cross-border co-operation, which ultimately leads to a reduction in trade costs.

In view of above, this chapter attempts to assess the relative importance of trade costs in the context of selected Asian countries. The remainder of the chapter is organized as follows. Section II offers a quick overview of theoretical discourse on trade costs, particularly in the context of new trade theory. This discussion is relevant here since we attempt to assess the impact of trade barriers on trade flows. Data and methodology are covered in section III. An assessment of the relative importance of trade costs is done in section IV. Finally, conclusions are briefed in section V.

II. TRADE COSTS AND NEW TRADE THEORY

In traditional trade theory, it is customarily assumed that trade takes place between countries which have no spatial dimensions.[10] The neoclassical trade theory completely ignores the transport costs, and considers some assumptions which have comparatively less relevance in today's complex trade issues. For example, in the factor abundance model, which is popularly known as the Heckscher, Ohlin and Samuelson (HOS) model, comparative advantage is determined by cross-country differences in relative abundance of factor endowments. The HOS model uses some assumptions such as perfect competition, homogeneous goods, production with constant returns to scale, no transport costs, and mobility of factors between industries and not between countries. In new trade theory, transport cost is incorporated as a factor of determinant, where trade is analysed in models in a world of increasing returns to scale, and monopolistic competition (Dixit and Stiglitz, 1977).[11] Therefore, one of the implications of the new trade theory is growing interdependence between countries through increased trade and/or increased factor mobility where transport costs play a pivotal role in integrating the countries and/or factors.

However, to a great extent, the foundation of new trade theory was laid down by Samuelson (1952) when he introduced the concept of iceberg transport costs.[12] The whole set of literature on new trade theory introduces the importance of transport costs in explaining cross-country trade and movement of factors, the most notable of which are Krugman and Venables (1990) and Krugman (1991). They show how an increase in the degree of economic integration (using a fall in transport costs as a proxy) affects the countries engaged in trade. Figure 5.2 shows how it occurs. In a two-country model, Krugman and Venables show that in autarky (when high transportation costs prohibit trade) both countries have a share in the manufacturing sector equal to their share in world endowments.[13] The difference in endowments is given in segments A and B in Figure 5.2. It turns out that for an intermediate range of transport costs, economic

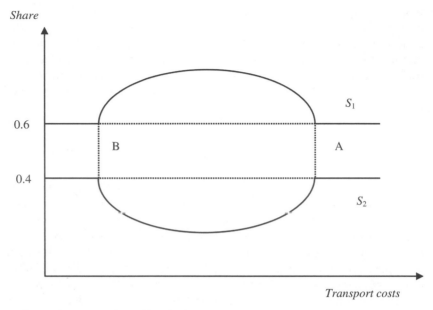

Source: Krugman and Venables (1990).

Figure 5.2   Share of world production in manufactures

integration strengthens country 1. As shown in Figure 5.2, country 1's
share of world industry, S_1, gets larger than its share of world endowments, and vice versa for country 2 ($S_2 < 0.4$). As a result, given the larger
market size and minimization of transport costs, new firms prefer country
1 even though wages are higher. As transport costs continue to fall,
country 1's share of world industry eventually starts to decrease again. At
very low transport costs, the advantage of producing in the country with
the larger market (here, country 1) becomes small, which combined with
the stiffer labour market competition in country 1 implies that new firms
find it profitable to start production in country 2 where wages are lower.
At the extreme zero transport costs, wages will be equal and each country's
share of manufactures will return to its share in world endowments. There
is thus a non-linear relationship between a country's share in world industry and transport costs in which the shares always sum to one.

   Trade costs are reported in terms of their *ad valorem* tax equivalent. In
Anderson and van Wincoop's (2004) term: the 170 per cent 'representative'
trade costs in industrialized countries breaks down into 21 per cent transportation costs, 44 per cent border related trade barriers and 55 per cent
retail and wholesale distribution costs (Figure 5.3).[14]

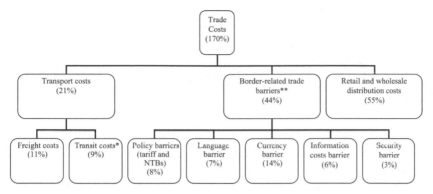

Notes:
* Tax equivalent of the time value of goods in transit. Both are based on estimates for US data.
** The combination of direct observation and inferred costs, which, according to author, is an extremely rough breakdown.

Source: Drawn from Anderson and van Wincoop (2004).

Figure 5.3   Representative trade costs of industrial countries

In general, an exporter or importer incurs trade costs in all the phases of the export or import process, starting from obtaining information about market conditions in any given foreign market and ending with receipt of final payment. One part of the trade cost is trader specific and depends upon his or her operational efficiency. The magnitude of this trade cost diminishes with an increase in the efficiency level of the trader, under the prevailing framework of any economy.

The other part of trade costs is specific to the trading environment and is incurred by the traders due to inbuilt inefficiencies in the trading environment. It includes institutional bottlenecks (transport, regulatory and other logistics infrastructure), information asymmetry and administrative power that give rise to rent-seeking activities by government officials at various steps of transaction. This may cost traders (or the country) time and money, including demurrage charges, making transactions more expensive.

Trade costs are large, even aside from trade policy barriers and even between apparently highly integrated economies. In explaining trade costs, Anderson and van Wincoop (2004) referred to the example of Mattel's Barbie doll, discussed in Feenstra (1998), indicated that the production costs for the doll were US$1, while it sold for about US$10 in the United States. The cost of transportation, marketing, wholesaling and retailing represent an *ad valorem* tax equivalent of 900 per cent. Anderson and van Wincoop (2004: 692) commented:

Tax equivalent of representative trade costs for rich countries is 170 percent. This includes all transport, border-related and local distribution costs from foreign producer to final user in the domestic country. Trade costs are richly linked to economic policy. Direct policy instruments (tariffs, the tariff equivalents of quotas and trade barriers associated with the exchange rate system) are less important than other policies (transport infrastructure investment, law enforcement and related property rights institutions, informational institutions, regulation, language).

Direct transport costs include freight charges and insurance, which is customarily added to the freight charge. Indirect transport user costs include holding cost for the goods in transit, inventory cost due to buffering the variability of delivery dates, preparation costs associated with shipment size (full container load v. partial loads) and the like. Indirect costs must be inferred. Alongside tariffs and NTBs, transport costs look to be comparable in average magnitude and in variability across countries, commodities and time.

Trade costs have large welfare implications. Current policy-related costs are often worth more than 10 per cent of national income (Anderson and van Wincoop, 2002). Obstfeld and Rogoff (2000) commented that all the major puzzles of international macroeconomics hang on trade costs. Some of the studies, for example, APEC (2002), OECD (2003), and Francois et al. (2005), estimate that for each 1 per cent reduction of trade transaction costs, world income could increase by US$30–40 billion.

Some studies have indicated that the cost of trade, specifically trade documentation and procedures, is high – between 4 and 7 per cent of the value of goods shipped. In 1996, APEC conducted a study that highlighted the gain from effective trade facilitation. For example, the gains from streamlining customs procedures exceeded those resulting from trade liberalization, such as tariff reduction. Gains from effective trade facilitation accounted for about 0.26 per cent of real GDP of APEC members (about US$45 billion), while the gains from trade liberalization would be 0.14 per cent of real GDP (US$23 billion).[15] According to the World Bank, raising performance across the region to halfway up to the level of the APEC average could result in a 10 per cent increase in intra-APEC exports, worth roughly US$280 billion (World Bank, 2002).

Details of trade costs also matter to economic geography. For example, the home market effect hypothesis (big countries produce more of goods with scale economies) hangs on differentiated goods with scale economies having greater trade costs than homogeneous goods (Davis, 1998). The cross-commodity structure of policy barriers is important to welfare (for example, Anderson, 1994).

In dealing with cross-country trade, influenced by new trade theory, several studies have explicitly considered transport costs such as Bergstrand

(1985; 1989), Krugman (1991), Davis (1998), Deardorff (1998), Limao and Venables (2001), Fink et al. (2002), Clark et al. (2004), Redding and Venables (2004), Hummels (1999a; 1999b; 2000), Wilson et al. (2003), De (2006a; 2006b; 2007), to mention a few.

Poor institutions and poor infrastructure penalize trade differentially across countries. While dealing with barriers to trade, there are some studies which have explicitly emphasized the quality of infrastructure (as a proxy of trade costs), associated with cross-country trade. The country's infrastructure plays a vital role in carrying trade. For example, by incorporating transport infrastructure in a two-country Ricardian framework, Bougheas et al. (1999) have shown the circumstances under which it affects trade volumes. According to Francois and Manchin (2006), transport and communication infrastructure and institutional quality are significant determinants not only for a country's export levels, but also for the likelihood of exports. Nordås and Piermartini (2004) showed that the quality of infrastructure is an important determinant of trade performance wherein port efficiency alone has the largest impact on trade among all indicators of infrastructure. De (2005) provided evidence that transaction cost is an important determinant in explaining variation in trade in Asia. In addition, this author also found that port efficiency and infrastructure quality are two important determinants of trade costs in the context of selected Asian countries. De (2006b) found a negative non-linear relationship between transaction costs and imports in the context of 15 Asian economies for the year 2004 (see Figure 5.4). This relationship clearly points to the fact that transaction costs do influence trade. In another study, De (2007) showed that the propensity to increase trade in the context of selected Asian countries is higher with the reduction of transport costs, rather than tariff reduction.[16]

The infrastructure variables have explanatory power in predicting trade volume. Limao and Venables (2001) emphasized the dependence of trade costs on infrastructure, where infrastructure is measured as an average of the density of the road network, the paved road network, the rail network and the number of telephone main lines per person. A deterioration of infrastructure from the median to the seventy-fifth percentile of destinations raises transport costs by 12 per cent. The median landlocked country has transport costs which are 55 per cent higher than the median coastal economy.[17] Inescapably, understanding trade costs and their role in determining international trade volumes must incorporate the internal geography of countries and the associated interior trade costs.

Many commentators indicate that the success of trade liberalization will always be suboptimal if transport cost is not controlled. The World Trade Organization (WTO, 2004: 114) commented: 'the effective rate of protection provided by transport costs in many cases is higher than that provided

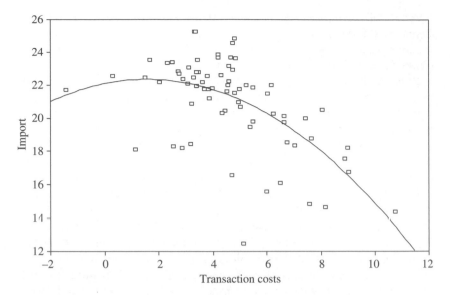

Note: Import and transaction costs are based on pooled bilateral trading pairs for
15 Asian economies for the year 2004.

Source: De (2006b).

Figure 5.4   Relative importance of trade transaction costs in Asia

by tariffs'. According to the World Bank (2001), for 168 out of 216 trading
partners of the USA, transport cost barriers outweighed tariff barriers. It
is estimated by Hummels (1999b) that doubling distance increases overall
freight rates by between 20 and 30 per cent. Djankov et al. (2006) showed
that, on average, each additional day that a product is delayed prior to
being shipped reduces trade by at least 1 per cent.[18] Therefore, what follows
is that countries will not fully realize the gains from trade unless they also
prioritize facilitation of trade and transport.

III.   DATA AND METHODOLOGY

This study is undertaken in two stages. First, we provide some estimates of
sector-wise trade costs for ten Asian countries at disaggregated (four-digit
Harmonized System of Product Categories [HS]) level.[19] We stress that the
specification of the gravity equation, together with the choice of the distance measure, is crucial for evaluating the size of the barriers. Second, we
estimate the impact of trade costs on selected sectors, following which,

policy conclusions are drawn. In this study, we deal with selected components of trade costs which are imposed by both policy (tariff) as well as
environment (transport and others). In particular, we consider tariffs,
transport costs, and infrastructure quality in bilateral pairs in this chapter,
thereby including barriers relating to both policy and the country's environment in the model.

Measuring Sector-wise Transport Costs

Importing countries report the value of imports from partner countries
inclusive of transportation charges, and exporting countries report their
value exclusive of transportation charges, which measures the cost of the
imports and all charges incurred in placing the merchandise aboard a
carrier in the exporting port. The ratio of import and export prices provides
the measure of transport costs on trade between each pair of countries. As
an alternative, using the freight rate, we arrive at variation in transport costs
across countries.

In this chapter, to estimate bilateral transport costs, two methods have
been used interchangeably: (1) the difference of *ad valorem* trade-weighted
freight rate,[20] and (2) the differences of inter-country costs of transportation using shipping rate, collected from shipping companies.[21]

Let, t_{ij} represent costs of transportation between country i and j. We use
two separate methods to estimate t_{ij}.[22] Method I is trade-weighted transport costs, derived from using export and import prices, whereas the
Method II represents trade-weighted costs of transportation, estimated
using cross-country shipping rates. While both the methods have been
widely used to estimate transport costs, there is an explicit methodological
difference between the two. The trade-weighted transport cost in Method I
for commodity k is as follows:

$$t_{ij}^k = \left(\frac{IM_{ij}^k}{EX_{ji}^k} - 1 \right) S_i^k \qquad (5.1)$$

where IM_{ij}^k stands for import price of country i from country j for the
commodity k, EX_{ji}^k denotes export price of country j to country i for
the commodity k, and S_i^k is the value-share of commodity k in country i
in the bilateral trade (here at the four-digit HS). In terms of the data, we
use CIF values to represent IM_{ij}^k, and FOB values for EX_{ji}^k. As pointed out
by Limao and Venables (2001), CIF/FOB data does contain information
about the cross-sectional variation in transport costs, and results from
using this data are consistent with those obtained from the shipping costs
data.[23]

The trade-weighted transport costs in Method II is derived using:

$$t_{ij}^k = \frac{Q_{ij}^k f_{ji}^k}{Q_{ij}} \qquad (5.2)$$

where Q_{ij}^k stands for import in quantity of country i from country j for the commodity k, f_{ji}^k stands for shipping costs of per unit of import of commodity k by country i from country j, and Q_{ij} is country i's total import from country j.

Measuring Quality of Infrastructure[24]

For country characteristics, we have focused on infrastructure measures – the country's ability to enhance the movement of merchandise. Here we treat infrastructure as a proxy of those costs, which are equally responsible for movement of goods across and within countries. Infrastructure facilities, arising from differential factor endowments within a country, are responsible for movement of goods. To assess impact of infrastructure facilities on bilateral trade, we have constructed an infrastructure index (II), comprising nine infrastructure variables for each individual country. The II is designed to measure the costs of travel across a country. In theory, the export and import prices are border prices and thus it would seem that own and trading partner infrastructures, as defined here, should not affect these rates. It is possible that there are interactions between the variables. The simplest example is that an increase in land distance should increase the cost of going through a given infrastructure. The II was constructed based on principal component analysis (PCA),[25] and it measures the relative position of a country considering a set of observables. Briefly, the II is a linear combination of the unit free values of the individual facilities such that:

$$II_{ij} = \sum W_{kj} X_{kij} \qquad (5.3)$$

where II_{ij} is infrastructure development index of the i-th country in j-th time, W_{kj} is weight of the k-th facility in j-th time, and X_{kij} = unit free value of the k-th facility for the i-th country in j-th time point.

While indexing the infrastructure stocks of the countries, we have considered following nine variables which are directly involved in moving the merchandise among countries: (1) railway length density (km per 1000 sq. km of surface area), (2) road length density (km per 1000 sq. km of surface area), (3) air transport freight (million tons per km), (4) air transport, passengers carried (percentage of population), (5) aircraft departures (percentage of population), (6) country's percentage share in world fleet, (7) container port traffic (TEUs per terminal), (8) fixed line and mobile phone subscribers (per 1000 people) and (9) electric power consumption (kWh per capita). The weights of these variables, and the index, derived from the PCA, are given in Appendix Tables 5A.1 and 5A.2.

The Augmented Gravity Model

In order to explore the impact of trade costs on sector-wise trade flows, our empirical analysis has considered an augmented gravity model, since it is one of the popular partial equilibrium models known in explaining the variation of trade flows. The gravity model provides the main link between trade barriers and trade flows. The gravity equation proposed here is a sort of reduced form of an intra-industry trade model. Following Anderson and van Wincoop (2003), the baseline equation is as follows:

$$X_{ij} = \frac{Y_i Y_j}{Y_w} \left(T_{ij} \Big/ P_i P_j \right)^{1-\sigma} \tag{5.4}$$

where, Y_i, Y_j and Y_w denote the aggregate size of countries i, j and the world, respectively; T_{ij} accounts for trade costs and other trade barriers; P_i and P_j reflect the implicit aggregate equilibrium prices; and σ is the constant elasticity of substitution (CES) between all goods in the consumption utility function.[26]

We assume from equation (5.4) that T_{ij} may be divided into several components, namely, infrastructure quality, tariff barriers, transport costs, distance, difference in language, and other border effects. Assuming monopolistically competitive market, the term $(1-\sigma)$ should be negatively related to volume of trade.

In order to carry out the estimations, following Head (2003), and Anderson and van Wincoop (2003), we assume the implicit aggregate equilibrium prices P_i and P_j are basically resistance term or remoteness (trade weighted average distances from the rest of the world).[27] Here, we derive remoteness (R_i), as a proxy of implicit aggregate equilibrium prices, through following equation:

$$R_i = \sum_{m \neq j} \left(d_{im} \Big/ Y_m \right) \tag{5.5}$$

where R_i reflects the average distance of country i from all trading partners other than j, d_{im} is the distance between countries i and m, Y_m is the GDP of country m.

Therefore, final estimable gravity equation takes following shape.

$$\ln IM_{ij}^k = \alpha_0 + \alpha_i + \beta_1 \ln Y_i Y_j + \beta_2 \ln II_i + \beta_3 \ln II_j$$
$$+ \beta_4 \ln TC_{ij}^k + \beta_5 \ln T_{ij}^k + \beta_6 \ln R_i + \beta_7 \ln R_j$$
$$+ \beta_8 \ln D_{ij} + \beta_9 d_1 + \beta_{10} d_2 + \beta_{11} d_3 + \varepsilon_{ij} \qquad (5.6)$$

where i and j are importing and exporting country respectively, and k is trade sector. IM_{ij} represents import by country i from country j, taken at constant US\$, Y_i and Y_j denote gross domestic products, taken at constant US\$, of countries i and j, respectively, II represents country's infrastructure quality, measured through an index, TC_{ij} stands for transport costs for bilateral trade between countries i and j for sector k, T_{ij} stands for bilateral tariff (weighted average) between country i and j for sector k, R_i and R_j denote average remoteness of countries i and j, D_{ij} is the distance between countries i and j. Dummies 1, 2 and 3 in equation (5.6) refer to PTA (Preferential Trade Agreement)/FTA in force, adjacency and language, respectively. To capture country effects, we use country specific dummy, α_i. The parameters to be estimated are denoted by β, and ε_{ij} is the error term.

The augmented gravity model explains bilateral trade flows as a function of the trading partners' market sizes and their bilateral barriers to trade. As indicated in Nordås and Piermartini (2004), a number of them are standard variables in the empirical literature to capture trade barriers: (1) transport costs are generally captured by distance and island, landlocked and border dummies to reflect that transport costs increase with distance – they are higher for landlocked countries and islands and lower for neighbouring countries; (2) information costs are generally captured by a dummy for common language; (3) tariff barriers are generally neglected. However, data on tariff barriers show that there is a high degree of variability in cross-country bilateral applied tariffs. Since neglecting tariffs may be a source of an omitted variable bias, we, therefore, include bilateral tariffs in our estimations.

The augmented gravity model considered here uses data for the year 2004 for ten Asian countries, namely, China, Hong Kong, India, Indonesia, Japan, Korea, Malaysia, Singapore, Taipei,China and Thailand, for eight commodity groups (sectors) such as food, chemicals, textiles and clothing, machinery, electronics, auto components, steel and metal, and transport equipment. The corresponding codes of these commodity groups at HS 2 are provided in Appendix Table 5A.3. By taken tariffs, transport costs and infrastructure quality, we cover a major portion of trade costs. Trade, transportation costs and tariffs are taken at HS 4 level for the year 2004.[28]

The major sources of secondary data are collected from the International Monetary Fund (IMF), the United Nations Statistical Division and the United Nations Conference on Trade and Development (UNCTAD). Appendix Table 5A.5 provides the data-specific sources.

IV.   RELATIVE IMPORTANCE OF TRADE COSTS: ESTIMATION RESULTS

In this chapter we have considered eight sectors, among which six sectors, namely, electronics, automobile, machinery, textiles and clothing, steel and metal, and chemicals, share the larger pie in trade of Asia. These six industries constitute three-quarters of Korea's and Japan's exports, and two-thirds of China's exports in intra-regional trade. Except food, China (including Hong Kong and Taipei,China) has a higher share in intra-regional imports of the remaining seven sectors, compared with others (Table 5.5). To a great extent, Asia's trade is not evenly distributed and is mostly driven by China.

The barriers to trade in eight sectors, namely, food, chemicals, textiles and clothing, machinery, electronics, auto components, steel and metal, and transport equipment, are estimated through equation (5.6). Tables 5.6 to 5.13 show the estimation results of equation (5.6) for two scenarios: one using equation (5.1) and another using equation (5.2). The explanatory variables of interest are II, TC and T in equation (5.6). We expect that the TC, T and II are negatively correlated with the volume of imports, respectively.[29]

The gravity model performs well as most of the variables do have expected signs. Variables being in natural logarithms, estimated coefficients show elasticity. Given large cross-section nature of the data at four-digit HS for the year 2004, estimated gravity model explains 52 to 80 per cent of the variations in direction of trade flows. The volume of imports is increasing in GDP and decreasing in the distance. The most interesting result is the strong influence that transport costs had on trade in all the sectors: the higher the transport costs between each pair of partners, the less they trade. Significance of transport costs using equation (5.2) is always found to be higher than that estimated by equation (5.1) for most of the sectors. It also indicates that trade-weighted transport costs using ocean freight through equation (5.2) seems to be a better method compared to the conventional way to estimate transport costs using equation (5.1) in our case. The results also indicate that the exporting countries' infrastructure is more important than the importing countries'. As seen from Tables 5.6 to 5.13, coefficients of transport costs in most of the cases are statistically significant at the 1 per cent level and always negative. The sign of country effects is a reflection

Table 5.5   Country-wise shares in intra-regional imports in 2005 (%)

Country	Auto components	Chemicals	Electronics	Food
China, Mainland	28.17	35.71	25.66	3.54
China, Hong Kong	5.75	11.34	22.48	11.48
India	2.09	2.92	1.39	0.43
Indonesia	8.58	4.05	0.45	5.23
Japan	10.43	10.12	13.27	50.49
Korea	5.13	9.68	7.93	8.77
Malaysia	9.00	5.14	5.92	6.68
Singapore	9.49	4.56	11.68	6.20
Taipei,China	9.74	10.36	7.60	4.20
Thailand	11.62	6.12	3.63	2.99
Total	100.00	100.00	100.00	100.00

Country	Machinery	Steel & metal	Textiles & clothing	Transport equipment
China, Mainland	34.08	28.63	17.24	14.51
China, Hong Kong	8.39	9.09	34.88	6.12
India	2.47	1.88	1.72	18.87
Indonesia	4.36	3.03	1.12	5.30
Japan	7.77	12.53	28.02	2.59
Korea	10.66	15.38	6.16	12.23
Malaysia	4.92	6.24	2.05	18.27
Singapore	6.44	5.35	3.28	6.82
Taipei,China	13.29	9.52	3.12	10.86
Thailand	7.63	8.35	2.40	4.43
Total	100.00	100.00	100.00	100.00

Note: Intra-regional sector-wise imports consider trade at HS 4 among ten countries in Asia.

Source: Calculated based on IMF (2006).

of the current trade situation. In many cases country effects have also appeared to be significant.

Food

With 1609 observations at four-digit HS in the food sector, we found variables representing trade costs like tariff, infrastructure and transport costs are significant in both the models in Table 5.6. The estimated coefficients indicate that a reduction in tariff and transport costs by 10 per cent each would increase bilateral trade in the food sector by about 3.2 and 1.2 per

Table 5.6   OLS results at four-digit HS for the year 2004: food

	Model 1		Model 2	
	Coefficients	t-values	Coefficients	t-values
GDP of importing countries	0.054	0.496	0.011	0.111
GDP of exporting countries	0.088	1.009	0.074	0.903
Infrastructure of importing countries	0.213*	1.294	0.221*	1.448
Infrastructure of exporting countries	−0.372***	−4.142	−0.241**	−2.886
Tariff	−0.257***	−5.604	−0.318***	−7.458
Trade-weighted transport costs$	−0.026	−1.031		
Trade-weighted transport costs#			−0.116***	−12.811
Remoteness of importing countries	−0.093	−0.806	−0.050	−0.470
Remoteness of exporting countries	−0.188*	−2.037	−0.136*	−1.586
Distance	−0.545***	−6.511	−0.467***	−6.011
FTA dummy	0.459***	3.781	0.281**	2.483
Adjacency dummy	0.230*	1.367	0.199*	1.273
Language dummy	0.222*	1.497	0.246*	1.784
Country effect				
China	−0.973**	−3.484	−0.607**	−2.337
Hong Kong	0.983**	3.542	1.045***	4.056
India	−2.183***	−9.136	−2.104***	−9.506
Indonesia	−0.457**	−2.218	−0.403*	−2.132
Japan	1.270**	3.508	0.914**	2.714
Korea	−0.190	−0.794	−0.405*	−1.870
Malaysia	0.087	0.413	0.194	1.014
Singapore	0.194	0.643	0.379*	1.359
Thailand	−2.018***	−9.689	−1.899***	−9.851
No. of observations	1609		1609	
Adjusted R²	0.568		0.752	

Notes:
$ Estimated following equation (5.1).
# Estimated following equation (5.2).
* Significant at the 10 per cent level.
** Significant at the 5 per cent level.
*** Significant at the 1 per cent level.
OLS regressions excluding all missing, negative or zero transport costs.

cent respectively (in Model 2). The significant and negative signs of exporting countries' infrastructure quality indicate that the present state of infrastructure facilities is penalising trade in the food sector. In other words, an improvement of current state of infrastructure by 10 per cent in exporting countries will lead to rise in exports by 2.4 per cent.

The interesting result is that the FTA among the countries considered in this study has positively influenced the trade in food products. Countries like Hong Kong and Japan show positive and significant country effect, whereas China, India, Indonesia and Thailand have negative but significant country effect in the food sector. The reason is that small countries import large amounts of food products (due to domestic resource constraints) and, thus, they show comparatively lower trade frictions as they are equipped with improved infrastructure. With a 50 per cent share in total imports, Japan is the largest importer of food and food products in Asia (see Table 5.5). Hong Kong shares about 12 per cent of total imports of food and food products in Asia. These countries have improved infrastructure facilities, and offer negligible tariffs. Singapore has also shown a positive country effect but this is statistically insignificant. Larger or medium-sized countries, which are producers/exporters of food items, like China, India, Indonesia and Thailand, are still not able to get much benefit due to presence of comparatively higher trade barriers such as higher tariffs and transport costs. Interestingly, both the coefficients are statistically significant and carry negative signs. Since exporters of food products figure large in the group, exporting countries' infrastructure quality does matter in raising trade in food products in Asia.

Estimated coefficients of all three dummies are significant in both the models. We can conclude that the FTA environment among the countries in Asia has positively influenced the trade in food products. In the present context, trade in food products is also influenced by geographical contiguity as the adjacency dummy carries a positive sign and is statistically significant. Language similarity does influence trade in food products as reflected in an estimated positive and statistically significant coefficient.

Chemicals

Table 5.7 reports the estimated results for the chemical sector. Except for China, the rest of the Asian countries share about 2 to 12 per cent of intra-regional trade in the chemical sector (Table 5.5). However, China alone shares 36 per cent of trade conducted in the chemical sector. Hong Kong, Japan and Taipei,China come next. With observations of 7907, the Model 2 in Table 5.7 explains about 69 per cent of the variations in direction of trade flows in the chemical sector. At the same time, we observe variations in the significance level of transport costs. The transport cost in Model 1 shows positive sign but statistically insignificant, while the same, calculated using equation (5.2) in Model 2, has appeared as highly significant (at the 1 per cent level) and also carries the correct (negative) sign.

Table 5.7 OLS results at four-digit HS for the year 2004: chemicals

	Model 1		Model 2	
	Coefficients	t-values	Coefficients	t-values
GDP of importing countries	0.320***	11.683	0.222***	8.758
GDP of exporting countries	0.397**	2.529	0.503***	3.472
Infrastructure of importing countries	−0.058	−1.019	0.058	1.100
Infrastructure of exporting countries	−0.159***	−3.893	−0.075*	−1.981
Tariff	−0.323***	−11.457	−0.338***	−12.996
Trade-weighted transport costs$	0.002	0.111		
Trade-weighted transport costs#			−0.119***	−11.634
Remoteness of importing countries	Insignificant			
Remoteness of exporting countries	−0.279*	−1.682	−0.088	−0.579
Distance	−0.534***	−12.781	−0.435***	−11.258
FTA dummy	0.144**	2.408	0.090*	1.637
Adjacency dummy	0.141*	1.699	0.074	0.973
Language dummy	0.205**	2.880	0.243***	3.698
Country effect				
China	0.279**	2.631	0.054	0.551
Hong Kong	0.686***	7.046	0.527***	5.870
India	−1.338***	−11.183	−1.169***	−10.582
Indonesia	−0.400***	−4.295	−0.363***	−4.228
Japan	Insignificant			
Korea	−0.527***	−5.684	−0.564***	−6.593
Malaysia	0.082	0.915	0.282***	3.414
Singapore	Insignificant			
Thailand	−0.653***	−7.035	−0.682***	−7.954
No. of observations	7907		7907	
Adjusted R^2	0.521		0.686	

Notes:
$ Estimated following equation (5.1).
# Estimated following equation (5.2).
* Significant at the 10 per cent level.
** Significant at the 5 per cent level.
*** Significant at the 1 per cent level.
OLS regressions excluding all missing, negative or zero transport costs.

Estimated coefficients in Model 2 indicate that tariff, transport costs and the quality of the exporting countries' infrastructure are significant barriers to trade. However, infrastructure quality as a barrier to trade has appeared to be less significant except in Model 1 for exporting countries.

Estimated coefficients show that a reduction in tariff and transport costs by 10 per cent each would increase bilateral trade in the chemical sector by about 3.4 and 1.2 per cent respectively (in Model 2), and an improvement in the current state of infrastructure by 10 per cent in exporting countries will lead to a rise in exports of 1 per cent.

From the country effects, it may be said that China, being the largest importer in the chemical sector, does play an influential role in trade in that sector, and thus its effect is correctly captured in the country-specific dummy. All the three dummies are significant in Model 1, while except for the adjacency dummy, the other two dummies are found as significant in Model 2. Significant coefficient of the FTA dummy tells us that trade in the chemical sector has benefited from the FTA in Asia. Language similarity is found to be an important determinant of trade in the chemical sector, whereas adjacency of countries does not have much influence. In general, developing countries in the region show negative and significant country effect, thereby indicating low exploitation of trade potentiality and the high presence of trade barriers. Nevertheless, findings provide sufficient indications of presence of trade barriers in the chemical sector in Asia.

Textiles and Clothing

Asian countries are major exporters in the textile and clothing sector. Within Asia, shares of Japan, Hong Kong and China in intra-regional imports of textiles and clothing are on the higher side. The results in Table 5.8 indicate that trade in textiles and clothing is also associated with considerably higher trade costs. All the trade costs components have expected signs, and are statistically significant.

With 8370 observations at HS 4 level, Model 2 in Table 5.8 confirms that 10 per cent savings in tariff and transport costs each will lead to 3 and 1.5 per cent rise in trade in the textile and clothing sector when geographical contiguity (significant adjacency dummy) positively influences the trade. Estimated coefficients in Model 2 in the textile and clothing sector indicate that tariff, transport costs and quality of exporting countries' infrastructure are significant barriers to trade. The exporting country's infrastructure quality is the most significant determinant; an improvement of the current state of infrastructure quality by 10 per cent in exporting countries will lead to a rise in exports of 4 per cent. Unlike previous cases, here, except for Hong Kong, the remaining countries show a significant negative country effect. This is likely the result of multicolinearity. Language and FTA dummies are also significant and carry positive signs.

Table 5.8   OLS results at four-digit HS for the year 2004: textiles and clothing

| | Model 2 | |
	Coefficients	t-values
GDP of importing countries	0.313***	12.840
GDP of exporting countries	−1.462***	−10.380
Infrastructure of importing countries	0.327***	6.320
Infrastructure of exporting countries	−0.402***	−10.360
Tariff	−0.295***	−13.290
Trade-weighted transport costs#	−0.148***	−12.650
Remoteness of importing countries	Insignificant	
Remoteness of exporting countries	−2.072***	−14.000
Distance	−0.453***	−11.850
FTA dummy	0.094*	1.720
Adjacency dummy	0.191**	2.540
Language dummy	0.078*	1.220
Country effect		
China	−0.272**	−2.970
Hong Kong	0.799***	9.630
India	−1.515***	−15.640
Indonesia	−0.596***	−6.720
Japan	Insignificant	
Korea	−0.717***	−9.190
Malaysia	−0.438***	−5.160
Singapore	Insignificant	
Thailand	−1.166***	−13.360
No. of observations	8370	
Adjusted R²	0.725	

Notes:
Model 1 is omitted due to insignificant results.
Estimated following equation (5.2).
*, ** and *** imply estimated coefficients are significant at 10, 5 and 1 per cent level, respectively.
OLS regressions exclude all missing, negative or zero transport costs.

Machinery

The import of machinery sector (as indicated in Table 5.5) is most unevenly distributed across the countries selected in this study. China has the highest share in total imports in the machinery sector (34 per cent). Expectedly, its dummy effect on import is positive and significant (at the 1 per cent level). Imports and exports in the machinery sector are

Table 5.9   OLS results at four-digit HS for the year 2004: machinery

	Model 2	
	Coefficients	t-values
GDP of importing countries	0.092*	1.307
GDP of exporting countries	0.393***	6.885
Infrastructure of importing countries	0.262*	2.412
Infrastructure of exporting countries	0.050	0.923
Tariff	−0.171***	−3.938
Trade-weighted transport costs#	−0.101***	−14.299
Remoteness of importing countries	−0.092*	−1.240
Remoteness of exporting countries	−0.511***	−8.457
Distance	−0.757***	−13.814
FTA dummy	−0.103*	−1.345
Adjacency dummy	−0.009	−0.081
Language dummy	0.198*	2.107
Country effect		
China	1.004***	5.621
Hong Kong	0.197	1.072
India	−0.253*	−1.603
Indonesia	0.447**	3.520
Japan	0.229	0.953
Korea	−0.745***	−4.856
Malaysia	0.396**	2.934
Singapore	0.059	0.297
Thailand	0.044	0.326
No. of observations	1965	
Adjusted R^2	0.789	

Notes:
Model 1 is omitted due to insignificant results.
Estimated following equation (5.2).
*, ** and *** imply estimated coefficients are significant at 10, 5 and 1 per cent level,
respectively.
OLS regressions exclude all missing, negative or zero transport costs.

dominated by developing countries and, unlike previous cases, developed
countries have relatively less influence (for example, Japan with an
insignificant dummy effect). Model 2 in Table 5.9 explains 79 per cent of
the variations in the direction of trade flows, whereas the estimated
coefficients show that tariff and transport costs have a negative effect on
trade in the machinery sector.

Electronics

In trade in the electronics sector, China and Hong Kong have over 20 per cent of the share of intra-regional imports. With a 13 per cent share, Japan comes next (see Table 5.5). In general, China relies on Japan for intermediate goods in the electronics sector (and for raw materials and technology) and for marketing their finished products. This has been reflected in a positive country effect for China and Hong Kong in both models in Table 5.10. Geographical adjacency has played a positive role in enhancing regional trade in electronics (t = 4.065 in Model 1 and t = 3.893 in Model 2). Both the models explain 56–76 per cent of the variations in direction of trade flows.

Nevertheless, trade in the electronics sector is highly influenced by trade costs components. Estimated coefficients in both the models indicate that tariff, transport costs and quality of infrastructure (for both countries) are significant barriers to trade. Estimated elasticities in Model 2 show that an improvement in the current state of infrastructure by 10 per cent will lead to a rise in trade in the electronics sector of 3 per cent in both importing and exporting countries. With this, 10 per cent savings in tariff and transport costs each will likely increase trade in the electronics sector by 3 and 1.3 per cent, respectively, when we found significant adjacency dummy (geographical contiguity).

Auto Components

Estimated results in the case of auto components (Table 5.11) go in the same direction. China contributes 28 per cent in intra-regional imports of auto components. Thailand and Japan come next (Table 5.5). Except for India, the remaining countries considered in this study have at least a 5 per cent share in the intra-regional trade of auto components, thereby showing a greater interdependence and production network. Both the models explain 71–81 per cent of the variations in the direction of trade flows. Tariff and transport costs have appeared as significant barriers. Model 2 in Table 5.11 shows that 10 per cent savings in tariff and transport costs each will likely increase trade in the electronics sector by 4.1 and 1.2 per cent, respectively.

However, none of the dummies is statistically significant. Together with India, some of the major auto components exporting countries, like Thailand and Korea, show negative and significant country effect, whereas Japan has a positive and significant country effect in the auto component sector. Japan, being the leading automobile manufacturer, positively influences Asia's automobile and auto component sector, whereas countries

Table 5.10   OLS results at four-digit HS for the year 2004: electronics

	Model 1		Model 2	
	Coefficients	t-values	Coefficients	t-values
GDP of importing countries	0.127*	1.850	0.120*	1.781
GDP of exporting countries	0.189**	3.311	0.174**	3.100
Infrastructure of importing countries	−0.295**	−2.811	−0.269**	−2.618
Infrastructure of exporting countries	−0.256***	−4.740	−0.297***	−5.601
Tariff	−0.308***	−8.810	−0.310***	−9.051
Trade-weighted transport costs$	−0.031	−1.013		
Trade-weighted transport costs#			−0.125***	−14.125
Remoteness of importing countries	−0.147*	−2.018	−0.141*	−1.972
Remoteness of exporting countries	−0.548***	−9.081	−0.505***	−8.522
Distance	−0.669***	−12.260	−0.622***	−11.612
FTA dummy	0.016	0.210	−0.041	−0.549
Adjacency dummy	0.444***	4.065	0.417**	3.893
Language dummy	0.020	0.214	0.061	0.665
Country effect				
China	0.778***	4.429	0.846***	4.913
Hong Kong	0.381*	2.139	0.383*	2.192
India	0.179*	1.212	0.214*	1.486
Indonesia	−0.934***	−7.300	−0.954***	−7.631
Japan	0.156	0.680	0.058	0.259
Korea	−0.121	−0.828	−0.111	−0.772
Malaysia	0.223*	1.652	0.206*	1.557
Singapore	0.018	0.094	−0.007	−0.035
Thailand	−0.066	−0.480	−0.010	−0.074
No. of observations	3059		3059	
Adjusted R^2	0.563		0.764	

Notes:
$ Estimated following equation (5.1).
# Estimated following equation (5.2).
* Significant at the 10 per cent level.
** Significant at the 5 per cent level.
*** Significant at the 1 per cent level.
OLS regressions excluding all missing, negative or zero transport costs.

like India, Korea and Thailand are still not able to get adequate benefits due to the presence of comparatively higher trade barriers such as higher tariffs and transport costs.

Table 5.11   OLS results at four-digit HS for the year 2004: auto components

	Model 1		Model 2	
	Coefficients	t-values	Coefficients	t-values
GDP of importing countries	0.069	0.310	0.056	0.271
GDP of exporting countries	0.346*	1.968	0.263*	1.614
Infrastructure of importing countries	0.491*	1.414	0.439*	1.362
Infrastructure of exporting countries	−0.035	−0.193	−0.032	−0.194
Tariff	−0.460***	−4.927	−0.410***	−4.723
Trade-weighted transport costs$	0.034*	1.948		
Trade-weighted transport costs#			−0.138***	−12.007
Remoteness of importing countries	−0.084	−0.357	−0.073	−0.335
Remoteness of exporting countries	−0.479**	−2.581	−0.383*	−2.222
Distance	−0.374*	−2.197	−0.328*	−2.078
FTA dummy	0.214	0.884	0.068	0.301
Adjacency dummy	−0.273	−0.797	−0.179	−0.562
Language dummy	−0.227	−0.723	−0.269	−0.923
Country effect				
China	−0.087	−0.146	0.067	0.121
Hong Kong	0.814*	1.397	0.843*	1.558
India	1.743***	3.640	1.556***	3.499
Indonesia	0.465*	1.166	0.234	0.633
Japan	1.219*	1.603	1.011*	1.433
Korea	−1.012*	−2.073	−0.972*	−2.145
Malaysia	0.028	0.067	0.131	0.338
Singapore	0.556	0.908	0.499	0.878
Thailand	−1.128**	−2.702	−1.111*	−2.867
No. of observations	339		339	
Adjusted R²	0.711		0.806	

Notes:
$ Estimated following equation (5.1).
# Estimated following equation (5.2).
*, ** and *** imply estimated coefficients are significant at 10, 5 and 1 per cent level, respectively.
OLS regressions exclude all missing, negative or zero transport costs.

Steel and Metal

Intra-regional trade in the steel and metal sector is concentrated in China, Korea and Japan. Estimated results in Table 5.12 indicate trade in steel and metal is associated with reasonably high barriers to trade, where

Table 5.12   OLS results at four-digit HS for the year 2004: steel and metal

	Model 2	
	Coefficients	t-values
GDP of importing countries	0.100*	1.861
GDP of exporting countries	0.289***	6.707
Infrastructure of importing countries	0.151*	1.843
Infrastructure of exporting countries	−0.174***	−4.151
Tariff	−0.057**	−2.305
Trade-weighted transport costs#	−0.101***	−15.002
Remoteness of importing countries	−0.124*	−2.189
Remoteness of exporting countries	−0.382***	−8.377
Distance	−0.590***	−14.255
FTA dummy	−0.128*	−2.211
Adjacency dummy	0.087	1.055
Language dummy	0.015	0.203
Country effect		
China	0.744***	5.508
Hong Kong	0.365**	2.566
India	−0.395**	−3.477
Indonesia	−0.145*	−1.514
Japan	0.100	0.549
Korea	−0.258*	−2.238
Malaysia	−0.455***	−4.370
Singapore	0.152	1.015
Thailand	−0.223*	−2.180
No. of observations	5204	
Adjusted R^2	0.763	

Notes:
Model 1 is omitted due to insignificant results.
Estimated following equation (5.2).
*, ** and *** imply estimated coefficients are significant at 10, 5 and 1 per cent level, respectively.
OLS regressions exclude all missing, negative or zero transport costs.

estimated coefficients for tariffs, the country's infrastructure quality and transport costs are significant. The models explain 76 per cent of the variations in direction of trade flows. Model 2 in Table 5.12 shows that 10 per cent savings in tariff and transport costs each will likely increase trade in the steel and metal sector by 0.6 and 1 per cent, respectively. At the same time, a 10 per cent improvement in exporting countries' infrastructure quality will lead to a rise of 1.7 per cent of trade. Therefore, the propensity to increase the trade in steel and metal is likely to be higher with a reduction in transport costs, rather than a tariff reduction in the present context. The estimated coefficient of the FTA dummy indicates that the trade in steel and metal in Asia has benefited from the FTA. India, Indonesia, Korea and Malaysia show negative and significant country effect. One of the reasons for this could be that these countries indicate low exploitation of trade potentiality and high presence of trade barriers.

Transport Equipment

There is a slight change in direction in the case of transport equipment. The model in Table 5.13 explains 76 per cent of the variations in direction of trade flows. What is interesting is that the coefficient of the bilateral tariff is found to be insignificant with a negative sign, and the same for transport costs which carries a negative sign and is significant. It also suggests that transport equipment being project goods used for infrastructure development attracts lower tariff, and therefore the estimated coefficient has appeared insignificant. However, estimated coefficients show that a country's infrastructure quality and transport costs are significant barriers to trade in transport equipment. None of the dummies are significant. The estimated country dummy is consistent. For example, India has a 19 per cent share in total intra-regional import of transport equipment (Table 5.5) and, therefore, its country effect shows a positive and significant sign (at the 10 per cent level).

All Sectors: Pooled OLS Results

To understand whether the direction of relationship captured in individual sectors through gravity estimates has any resemblance when we consider the model with total trade in pooled framework at four-digit HS, we have found that the pooled ordinary least squares (OLS) results (in Table 5.14) show no such difference. Rather, country effects dummies have appeared with expected signs for those countries which carry more trade under the FTA environment (significant FTA dummy) and sharing borders (significant adjacency dummy). Since tariffs have been reduced heavily, the exception being agriculture and food, in a pooled framework, coefficients of tariffs have come out insignificant but have negative relationship with trade flows. This is not consistent with the results obtained in individual sectors. However, consistent with the behaviour of transport costs, the exporting country's infrastructure quality produces negative signs (and significant) with bilateral trade. Both the models explain 52 to 65 per cent of variations in trade flows. The models indicate that a 10 per cent saving in transport costs would increase trade by about 1 to 6 per

Table 5.13   OLS results at four-digit HS for the year 2004: transport equipment

	Model 2	
	Coefficients	t-values
GDP of importing countries	0.130	0.529
GDP of exporting countries	0.269*	1.548
Infrastructure of importing countries	0.286	0.764
Infrastructure of exporting countries	0.388*	2.047
Tariff	−0.014	−0.116
Trade-weighted transport costs#	−0.143***	−8.132
Remoteness of importing countries	−0.116	−0.448
Remoteness of exporting countries	−0.193	−1.051
Distance	−0.681**	−3.826
FTA dummy	0.273	1.072
Adjacency dummy	−0.191	−0.538
Language dummy	−0.078	−0.239
Country effect		
China	−0.162	−0.261
Hong Kong	1.529*	2.217
India	0.997*	1.948
Indonesia	0.110	0.261
Japan	0.262	0.306
Korea	0.077	0.149
Malaysia	0.003	0.006
Singapore	−0.411	−0.610
Thailand	−0.834*	−1.649
No. of observations	138	
Adjusted R^2	0.641	

Notes:
Model 1 is omitted due to insignificant results.
Estimated following equation (5.2).
*, ** and *** imply estimated coefficients are significant at 10, 5 and 1 per cent level, respectively.
OLS regressions exclude all missing, negative or zero transport costs.

cent in Asia. At the same time, a 10 per cent improvement in exporting countries' infrastructure quality will lead to rise of 0.6 to 1 per cent of trade.

To summarize, there is strong empirical evidence that trade costs components, namely, infrastructure quality, tariffs and transport costs, are important for international trade patterns of eight prominent sectors. A

Table 5.14   Pooled OLS estimates: all sectors

	Model 2			
	With censored t_{ij}		With replaced t_{ij}	
	Coefficients	t-values	Coefficients	t-values
GDP of importing countries	0.032	1.210	0.318***	7.460
GDP of exporting countries	0.242**	3.100	0.367***	8.740
Infrastructure of importing countries	−0.019	−0.320	−0.068	−0.500
Infrastructure of exporting countries	−0.110***	−5.200	−0.057**	−2.740
Tariff	−0.010	−0.590	−0.037	−1.080
Trade-weighted transport costs#	−0.120***	−9.120	−0.588***	−10.270
Remoteness of importing countries	0.190*	−1.900	0.106	−1.108
Remoteness of exporting countries	−0.610***	−6.840	−1.292***	−7.340
Distance	−0.520***	−8.650	−0.578***	−9.420
FTA dummy	0.080**	2.900	0.180***	7.640
Adjacency dummy	0.146***	3.750	0.151***	4.690
Language dummy	0.035*	1.560	0.022	0.103
Country effect				
China	0.399***	6.670	0.538***	7.360
Hong Kong	Insignificant		Insignificant	
India	Insignificant		Insignificant	
Indonesia	−0.076*	−1.800	−0.748***	−14.190
Japan	Insignificant		Insignificant	
Korea	0.058*	1.830	0.133**	3.880
Malaysia	0.363***	4.950	0.249***	7.080
Singapore	Insignificant		Insignificant	
Thailand	0.101*	2.240	0.207***	4.930
No. of observations	28591		60919	
Adjusted R^2	0.647		0.515	

Notes:
Estimated following equation (5.2).
* Significant at the 10 per cent level.
** Significant at the 5 per cent level.
*** Significant at the 1 per cent level.

country's infrastructure quality, tariff, and transport costs are the main three important determinants of cross-country variations of trade flows in the present context. More specifically, cross-border co-operation in building and maintaining hard and soft infrastructure will lead to a reduction in trade costs.

V. CONCLUSIONS

The analysis carried out in this chapter provides sufficient evidence to show that variations in tariffs, transport costs and infrastructure facilities have a significant influence on regional trade flows in Asia. Further, we find that tariffs have a relatively large and negative impact on trade when we consider individual sectors. Among the sectors, with the exception of transport equipment, a trade in all other sectors is influenced by tariffs, transport costs and infrastructure quality. For transport equipment, a bilateral tariff has a less significant role as trade is more demand driven.

This chapter has provided additional measures of bilateral trade restrictions in empirical estimates using the gravity model. First, the study was carried out on eight important sectors in which Asian countries have increasing trade interdependence. Second, we introduced infrastructure quality that we believe has an impact on trade. Third, we introduced bilateral tariffs, which are largely ignored in the empirical gravity literature in the context of Asia. Fourth, in order to ensure unbiased estimates, we used resistance parameters. Fifth, in order to find out the relative robustness of the transport costs, we used trade-weighted transport costs using cross-country shipping rates, which is also a new entry in the gravity literature.

Progress in lowering trade costs is uneven (World Bank, 2006c). Trading across Europe is becoming seamless but in Asia is not yet improving and, if anything, is deteriorating. Lengthy procedure and transaction at borders multiply trade costs. For example, the time taken to obtain export documentations is now less at most of the ports in Asia, but it still takes 11 to 20 days. It can average 20 days for a consignment exported from China, whereas Japan and Korea take, on average, 24 days to clear imports coming from China (Table 5.15). Generally, a consignment needs several documents, signatures and copies for final approval, for both sides, and encounters multiple transhipments, as a result of which, costs are rising day-by-day thereby often changing the composition and direction of trade. Sending a containerized cargo from China to Japan costs about US$1166 (in 2005), whereas the same from Japan to China costs only US$498.[30] Due to a favourable policy (tariff) and environment (improved infrastructure), Japan's welfare gain from her trade with Korea and China seems to be much higher than the other countries in the study.

Procedural complexities coupled with high auxiliary shipping charges work as deterrent to trade in Asia. As noted in Table 5.15, even though export facilitation (in terms of days and numbers) performances of Asian countries are comparatively better than world and Asian averages, the variability of imports facilitation between three Northeast Asian countries and

Table 5.15   Selected trade facilitation indicators in Northeast Asia in 2005

Exporter/ origin	Importer/ destination	Documents for export (number)	Time for export (days)	Shipping cost (US$ per container)[1]	Documents for import (number)	Time for import (days)
Japan	China	5	11	498.11	7	11
China	Japan	6	20	1165.90	11	24
Japan	Korea	5	11	563.68	7	11
Korea	Japan	5	12	662.25	8	12
Korea	China	5	12	570.33	8	12
China	Korea	6	20	739.86	11	24
World average[2]		7	30		11	37
Asian average[3]		7	23		10	26

Notes:
1. Cost including both the partners (taken from Table 5.7).
2. Includes 154 countries.
3. Includes ASEAN + 6 countries except Brunei and Myanmar.

Sources: World Bank (2006b); Maersk Sealand (2006).

the rest of the world and/or Asia is not very wide, thereby indicating the need for further improvement of trade facilitation performances in Asia.

Our results have important policy implications for countries seeking to expand trade at a time when tariffs tend to be lower not only in Asia but also across most of the economies in the world. Attention is being paid to trade and transport facilitation. Generally speaking, tariffs are not regarded as major barriers to trade, although high-tariff items and tariff escalation still exist for certain sensitive products. Therefore, when the tariffs have been reduced, the economies of this region could potentially benefit substantially from higher trade if improvement in quality infrastructure mitigates rising trade costs. Strengthening the chain of necessary trading infrastructure facilities, starting from the production point to the shipment point, and associated trade facilitation measures at borders, is also an important segment, which needs special attention. The challenge for Asian countries is thus to identify improvements in logistics services and related infrastructure that can be achieved in the short to medium term and that would have a significant impact on the competitiveness of these countries.

In order to better inform the policy-making process, future research may be undertaken to complement the findings of this chapter. As noted by Hummels (1999a), without knowing the CES parameter, we cannot infer the size of the trade barriers, and without knowing the size of the barrier, we cannot infer CES. So, future study should be in this direction. We should also attempt to establish the technological relationship between transportation costs and distance as we now have bigger vessels plying between Asian ports. This study has considered some direct trade costs but omitted infrastructure costs. Variability in infrastructure costs thus needs to be captured more accurately in the model. Finally, studies should be attempted to understand how the components of ocean freight costs (such as base ocean freight and auxiliary shipping charges) together with other trade barriers are affecting trade in Asia.

NOTES

1. An earlier version of this chapter was presented at the LAEBA 2006 Third Annual Conference on 'Regional integration and regional cooperation in Asia and Latin America: the role of regional infrastructure', organized by the Asian Development Bank Institute (ADBI) and Inter-American Development Bank (IDB), held at Seoul on 16–17 November 2006. The author is grateful to Bishma Raout and Tirthankar Mandal for their valuable research assistance. Insightful comments of the participants of the LAEBA 2006 Third Annual Conference were very useful in revising the chapter. The author is also grateful to John Weiss, Douglas Brooks, Yann Duval and Mia Mikic for their encouragement and co-operation. The author thanks Maersk Sealand for providing complementary access to its historical ocean freight database. The author also acknowledges ARTNeT Capacity Building Workshops on Trade Research and the ADBI research grant. The views expressed by the author are his personal views. Usual disclaimers apply.
2. A growing literature has documented the impact of trade costs on the volume of trade. Refer to Anderson and van Wincoop (2004) for the major seminal works carried out on this subject.
3. See, for example, Khan and Weiss (2006), which explains how and why infrastructure can assist the regional co-operation process.
4. In literature, policy barriers are termed 'soft' or 'invisible' barriers, while barriers relating to environment are noted as 'hard' or 'visible' barriers.
5. Trade facilitation (TF) measures are also used differently in literature dealing with the World Trade Organization (WTO) issues. Typical TF measures are very narrow in a sense to deal with the barriers to trade in goods and services. According to the World Bank, 'there is no standard definition of trade facilitation. In a narrow sense, trade facilitation simply addresses the logistics of moving goods through ports or more efficiently moving customs documentation associated with cross-border trade. In recent years, the definition has been broadened to include the environment in which trade transactions take place, including the transparency and professionalism of customs and regulatory environments, as well as harmonization of standards and conformance to international or regional regulations' (World Bank, 2006a).
6. Refer to ADB (2005; 2006).
7. By technological advancement, here, we mean, for example, bigger vessels plying between ports.
8. In 2005, about 36 bilateral agreements from Asia were notified to the WTO, of which only three involved developing Asia before 1995, whereas 46 agreements are yet to be notified to the WTO and further 42 agreements are being negotiated (ADB, 2006).
9. According to De (2007), about 60 per cent of total shipping costs for the movement of a containerized cargo in Asia in 2005 was charged by shipping lines as base ocean freight,

28 per cent as container handling charges, recovered by the terminal or port operators, and 3 per cent as government duties and taxes.

10. Correspondingly, locational problems have also been neglected in the theory of customs unions (see Balassa, 1961).

11. Refer to Krugman (1979; 1980) and Bhagwati et al. (1998).

12. Samuelson's iceberg transport cost implies that a fraction of the manufactured goods does not arrive at the destination when goods are shipped between the regions. The fraction that does not arrive represents the costs of transportation.

13. The basic assumptions of Krugman and Venables (1990) are as follows: country 1 is larger than country 2 in terms of factor endowments (capital and labour) and market size. In both countries, there are two sectors, both producing tradable goods, one perfectly competitive and the other, producing manufactures, imperfectly competitive. Country 1 has a larger number of firms in the manufacturing sector. This sector produces differentiated products under increasing returns to scale and monopolistic competition. The relative factor endowments are the same for both the countries, so there is no comparative advantage and trade is of the intra-industry type.

14. However, according to Walkenhorst and Yasui (2005), transaction cost may differ across sectors, apart from country differences.

15. Similar indications were obtained for countries in APEC (Cernat, 2001; Wilson et al., 2003; World Bank, 2002).

16. By estimating an augmented gravity model at the four-digit HS level for the year 2004, De (2007) found that a number of trade costs components, namely, infrastructure quality, tariffs, and transport costs affect international trade patterns significantly. This study shows, *inter alia*, that a reduction in tariffs and transport costs by 10 per cent each would increase bilateral trade in Asia by 2 and 6 per cent respectively.

17. Bougheas et al. (1999) estimated gravity equations for a sample limited to nine European countries. They included the product of a partner's kilometres of motorway in one specification and that of public capital stock in another, and found that these have a positive partial correlation with bilateral exports.

18. This was estimated by the authors through a structured gravity model using the newly constructed Doing Business database of the World Bank on shipment of cargo from the factory gate to the ship (vessel) in 126 countries.

19. The author has created this database with the help of ARTNeT. Interested researchers may contact ARTNeT Secretariat or the author for further use of this database.

20. Many measures have been constructed to measure transport cost. The most straightforward measure in international trade is the difference between the CIF (cost, insurance and freight) and FOB (free on board) quotations of trade. The difference between these two values is a measure of the cost of getting an item from the exporting country to the importing country. There is another source from which to obtain data for transport costs from industry or shipping firms. Limao and Venables (2001) obtained quotes from shipping firms for a standard container shipped from Baltimore to various destinations. Hummels (1999a) obtained indices of ocean shipping and air freight rates from trade journals which presumably are averages of such quotes. The most widely available (many countries and years are covered) is average *ad valorem* transport costs, which are the aggregate bilateral CIF/FOB ratios from the United Nations' (UN's) COMTRADE database, supplemented in some cases with national data sources. Nevertheless, because of their availability and the difficulty of obtaining better estimates for a wide range of countries and years, work such as Harrigan (1993) and Baier and Bergstrand (2001) used the IMF (COMTRADE) database.

21. We use ocean freight rates, collected from Maersk Sealand, a shipping company which has a presence across the world.

22. Here, methodology follows Limao and Venables (2001), which was adopted from Hummels (1999a).

23. However, CIF/FOB ratio has several drawbacks. The first is measurement error; the CIF/FOB factor is calculated for those countries that report the total value of imports at CIF and FOB values, both of which involve some measurement error. The

second concern is that the measure aggregates over all commodities imported, so it is biased if high transport cost countries systematically import lower transport cost goods. This would be particularly important if we were using exports, which tend to be concentrated in a few specific goods. It is less so for imports which are generally more diversified and vary less in composition across countries (Limao and Venables, 2001)

24. This sub-section has been adapted in part from De (2007) with due permission from ArtNeT.
25. Refer to Fruchter (1967) for further details of PCA.
26. See Anderson and van Wincoop (2003) for a compete derivation of the model. We assume, as shown in Anderson (1979) and Anderson and van Wincoop (2003), all goods are differentiated by place of origin and each country specializes in the production of only one good. Therefore, supply of each good is fixed ($n_i = 1$), but it allows preferences to vary across countries subject to the constraint of market clearing.
27. In fact, some authors tentatively estimated the model with price index variables (Baier and Bergstrand, 2001).
28. The model also suffers from data limitation when we consider equation (5.1) to estimate transport costs. On average 56 per cent of total observations for all sectors are found to be either zero or negative or missing. Theoretically t_{ij} cannot be negative or zero. This happened more due to discrepancy in data compilation. However, we get better results when we consider equation (5.2) and use shipping rates. Appendix Table 5A.4 shows the collected observations at country-level and those are with errors.
29. The usual caveat is that in our particular case, we took an inverse measure of II in the regression so that an increase in II is expected to be associated with an increase in the TC, and vice versa.
30. This refers only to textiles and clothing. Costs might go up in other industries.

REFERENCES

Anderson, J.E. (1979), 'A theoretical foundation for the gravity equation', *American Economic Review*, **69**, 106–16.

Anderson, J.E. (1994), 'The theory of protection', in D. Greenway and L.A. Winters (eds), *Surveys in International Trade*, Oxford: Blackwell, pp. 107–38.

Anderson, J.E. and E. van Wincoop (2002), 'Borders, trade and welfare', in S. Collins and D. Rodrik (eds), *Brookings Trade Forum 2001*, Washington, DC: Brookings Institution, pp. 207–44.

Anderson, J.E. and E. van Wincoop (2003), 'Gravity with gravitas: a solution to the border puzzle', *American Economic Review*, **93**, 170–92.

Anderson, J.E. and E. van Wincoop (2004), 'Trade costs', *Journal of Economic Literature*, **42** (3), 691–751.

Asia Pacific Economic Cooperation Conference (APEC) (2002), *Measuring the Impact of APEC Trade Facilitation on APEC Economies: A CGE Analysis*, Singapore: APEC.

Asian Development Bank (ADB) (2005), *Asian Economic Cooperation and Integration: Progress, Prospects, Challenges*, Manila: ADB.

Asian Development Bank (ADB) (2006), *Asian Development Outlook 2006: Routes for Asia's Trade*, Manila: ADB.

Baier, S.L. and J.F. Bergstrand (2001), 'The growth of world trade: tariffs, transport costs, and income similarity', *Journal of International Economics*, **53**, 1–27.

Balasaa, B. (1961), *The Theory of Economic Integration*, Homewood, IL: Richard D. Irwin.

Bergstrand, J.H. (1985), 'The gravity equation in international trade: some micro-economic foundations and empirical evidence', *Review of Economics and Statistics*, **67**, 474–81.

Bergstrand, J.H. (1989), 'The generalized gravity equation, monopolistic competition, and the factor-proportions theory in international trade', *Review of Economics and Statistics*, **71**, 143–53.

Bhagwati, J.N., A. Panagariya and T.N. Srinivasan (1998), *Lectures on International Trade*, 2nd edn, Cambridge: MIT Press.

Bougheas, S., P.O. Demetriades and E.L.W. Morgenrath (1999), 'Infrastructure, transport costs, and trade', *Journal of International Economics*, **47**, 169–89.

Cernat, L. (2001), *Assessing Regional Trading Arrangements: Are South-South RTAs More Trade Diverting?*, UNCTAD Policy Issues in International Trade and Commodities Study Series No. 16, UNCTAD, Geneva.

Clark, X., D. David and A. Micco (2004), *Port Efficiency, Maritime Transport Costs and Bilateral Trade*, Working Paper 10353, NBER, Cambridge.

Davis, D. (1998), 'The home market effect, trade and industrial structure', *American Economic Review*, **88** (5), 1264–76.

De, P. (2005), 'Effect of transaction costs on international integration in the Asian Economic Community', in Asian Development Bank (ed.), *Asian Economic Cooperation and Integration: Progress, Prospects, Challenges*, Manila: ADB.

De, P. (2006a), *Regional Trade in Northeast Asia: Why Trade Costs Matter?*, CESifo Working Paper No. 1809, CESifo, Munich (Version 3). Previous versions of this paper also appeared as CNAEC Research Series 06-02, Korea Institute for International Economic Policy (KIEP), Seoul (Version 1), and ARTNeT Working Paper Series No. 7, UNESCAP, Bangkok (Version 2).

De, P. (2006b), 'Trade, infrastructure and transaction costs: the imperatives for Asian Economic Cooperation', *Journal of Economic Integration*, **21** (4), 708–35.

De, P. (2007), *Impact of Trade Costs on Trade: Empirical Evidence from Asian Countries*, ARTNeT Working Paper, Trade and Investment Division, UNESCAP, Bangkok, available at www.artnetontrade.org.

Deardorff, A. (1998), 'Determinants of bilateral trade: does gravity work in a neo-classical world?', in J. Frankel (ed.), *Regionalization of the World Economy*, Chicago: University of Chicago Press.

Dixit, A. and J. Stiglitz (1977), 'Monopolistic competition and optimal product diversity', *American Economic Review*, **67**, 297–308.

Djankov, S., C. Freund and C.S. Pham (2006), *Trading on Time*, Working Paper, World Bank, Washington, DC.

Feenstra, R.C. (1998), 'Integration of trade and disintegration in production in the global economy', *Journal of Economic Perspectives*, **12** (4), 31–50.

Fink, C., A. Mattoo and I.C. Neagu (2002), 'Trade in international maritime services: how much does policy matter?', *The World Bank Economic Review*, **16**, 451–79.

Francois, J. and M. Manchin (2006), *Institutional Quality, Infrastructure, and the Propensity to Export*, London: CEPR.

Francois, J.F., H. vanMeijl and F. van Tongeren (2005), 'Trade liberalization in the Doha development round', *Economic Policy*, **20** (42), 349–91.

Fruchter, B. (1967), *Introduction to Factor Analysis*, New Delhi: Affiliated East West Press.

Harrigan, J. (1993), 'OECD imports and trade barriers in 1983', *Journal of International Economics*, **34**, 91–111.

Head, K. (2003), Gravity for beginners, mimeo, University of British Columbia, Vancouver.

Hummels, D. (1999a), *Toward a Geography of Trade* Costs, Working Paper, University of Chicago, Chicago.

Hummels, D. (1999b), *Have International Trade Costs Declined?*, Working Paper, University of Chicago Business School, Chicago.

Hummels, D. (2000), *Time as Trade Barrier*, Working Paper, Purdue University, West Lafayette.

International Monetary Fund (IMF) (2006), *Direction of Trade Statistics Year Book CD ROM 2005*, Washington, DC: IMF.

Khan, H.A. and J. Weiss (2006), 'Infrastructure for regional cooperation', paper presented at LAEBA 2006 Third Annual Conference on 'Regional integration and regional cooperation in Asia and Latin America: the role of regional infrastructure', organised by the Asian Development Bank Institute (ADBI) and Inter-American Development Bank (IDB), Seoul, 16–17 November.

Krugman, P. (1979), 'Increasing returns, monopolistic competition, and international trade', *Journal of International Economics*, **9**, 469–79.

Krugman, P. (1980), 'Scale economies, product differentiation, and the pattern of trade', *American Economic Review*, **70**, 950–59.

Krugman, P. (1991), 'Increasing returns and economic geography', *Journal of Political Economy*, **99**, 483–99.

Krugman, P. and A.J. Venables (1990), 'Integration and the competitiveness of peripheral industry', in C. Bliss and J. Braga de Macedo (eds), *Unity with Diversity in the European Economy*, Cambridge: Cambridge University Press, pp. 56–75.

Limao, N. and A.J. Venables (2001), 'Infrastructure, geographical disadvantage, transport costs, and trade', *The World Bank Economic Review*, **15**, 451–79.

Maersk Sealand (2006), Historical shipping rates database, available at www.maerskline.com.

Nordås, H.K. and R. Piermartini (2004), *Infrastructure and Trade*, Staff Working Paper ERSD-2004-04, Economic Research and Statistics Division, World Trade Organization, Geneva.

Obstfeld, M. and K. Rogoff (2000), 'The six major puzzles in international macroeconomics: is there a common cause?', in B.S. Bernanke and K. Rogoff (eds), *NBER Macroeconomics Annual 2000*, Cambridge, MA: MIT Press, pp. 339–90.

Organisation for Economic Co-operation and Development (OECD) (2003), *Quantitative Assessment of the Benefits of Trade Facilitation*, Paris: OECD.

Redding, S. and A.J. Venables (2004), 'Economic geography and international inequality', *Journal of International Economics*, **62** (1), 53–82.

Samuelson, P.A. (1952), 'The transfer problem and transport costs: the terms of trade when impediments are absent', *Economic Journal*, **62**, 278–304.

Venables, A.J. (2006), 'Shifts in economic geography and their causes', *Economic Review*, **91** (4), 61–85.

Walkenhorst, P. and T. Yasui (2005), 'Benefits of trade facilitation: a quantitative assessment', in P. Dee and M. Ferrantino (eds), *Quantitative Methods for Assessing the Effects of Non-tariff Measures and Trade Facilitation*, Singapore: APEC Secretariat.

Wilson, J.S., C.L. Mann and T. Otsuki (2003), 'Trade facilitation and economic development: a new approach to quantifying the impact', *The World Bank Economic Review*, **17** (3), 367–89.

World Bank (2001), *Global Economic Prospects and the Developing Countries 2002: Making Trade Work for the Poor*, Washington, DC: World Bank.

World Bank (2002), *The Economic Impact of Trade Facilitation Measures: A Development Perspective in the Asia Pacific*, Washington, DC: World Bank.

World Bank (2006a), *Trade Costs and Facilitation: Development Dimension*, available at http://econ.worldbank.org/WBSITE/EXTERNAL/EXTDEC/ EXTRESEARCH/EXTPROGRAMS/EXTTRADERESEARCH/EXTTRAD ECOSTANDFACILITATION/O,,contentMDK:20696563~menuPK:i743267 ~pagePK:64168182~piPK:64168060~theSitePK:1697658,00.htm.

World Bank (2006b), Doing Business database, available at www.doingbusiness.org.

World Bank (2006c), *Doing Business 2007: How to Reform*, Washington, DC: World Bank, available at www.doingbusiness.org.

World Trade Organization (WTO) (2004), *World Trade Report 2004*, Geneva: WTO, available at www.wto.org.

World Trade Organization (WTO) (2006), *International Trade Statistics 2006*, Geneva: WTO, available at www.wto.org.

APPENDIX

Table 5A.1   Estimated weights

Infrastructure indicator	Factor loadings 1	Factor loadings 2
Air transport freight (million tons per km)	0.81	0.57
Air transport, passengers carried (percentage of population)	0.88	−0.38
Aircraft departures (percentage of population)	0.91	−0.36
Country's percentage share in world fleet (percentage)	0.36	0.69
Container port traffic (TEUs per terminal)	0.53	0.69
Electric power consumption (kWh per capita)	0.90	0.10
Fixed line and mobile phone subscribers (per 1000 people)	0.93	0.02
Railway length density (km per 1000 sq. km of surface area)	0.92	−0.31
Road length density (km per 1000 sq. km of surface area)	0.90	−0.26
Expl.Var (percentage of total)	0.67	0.19

Note: Factor loadings (unrotated).

Source: Taken from De (2007).

Table 5A.2   Infrastructure index and ranks in 2004

Country	Score	Rank
Singapore	6.01	1
Hong Kong	5.60	2
Japan	4.23	3
Korea	3.22	4
China	1.92	5
Malaysia	1.74	6
Thailand	0.99	7
India	0.59	8
Philippines	0.59	9
Indonesia	0.46	10
Vietnam	0.40	11

Source: Taken from De (2007).

Table 5A.3   Trade category

Sector	Corresponding HS 2	Remarks
Food	16–23	Taken all at HS 4
Chemicals	28–40	
Textiles and clothing	41–67	
Machinery	84	Excluding HS 8415, 8418, 8471, 8473
Electronics	85, 90, 91, 92, 95,	Including HS 8415, 8418, 8471, 8473
Auto components	87	
Steel and metal	72–83	Taken all at HS 4
Transport equipment	86, 88, 89	

Table 5A.4   Discrepancy in transport costs estimation at four-digit HS

Importer	Total number of observations at HS 4	Total number of observations with positive transport costs at HS 4	Total number of observations with zero/negative/missing transport costs at HS 4
China	6 380	2 847	3 533
Hong Kong	5 734	2 626	3 108
India	5 652	2 566	3 086
Indonesia	6 213	2 916	3 297
Japan	5 582	2 548	3 034
Korea	5 705	2 599	3 106
Malaysia	6 736	2 924	3 812
Singapore	6 937	2 755	4 182
Taipei,China	5 517	2 266	3 251
Thailand	6 463	2 584	3 879
Grand total	60 919	26 631	34 288

Table 5A.5   Sources of data

Particular	Source
Bilateral trade	UN COMTRADE IMF DOTS
Bilateral tariff	WB WITS
GDP, GDP per capita, surface area, population	WB WDI 2006
Distance	Great circle distance, www.wcrl.ars.usda.gov/cec/java/lat-long.htm
Infrastructure variables: (i) railway length, (ii) road length, (iii) air transport freight, (iv) air transport passengers carried, (v) aircraft departures, (vi) container traffic, (vii) fixed line and mobile phone subscribers, (viii) internet users, and (ix) electric power consumption	WB WDI 2006
Shipping freight	Maersk Sealand, Denmark, www.maerskline.com

PART II

Implementation and Impacts of Regional
Infrastructure

6.   Roads and poverty: a general equilibrium analysis for Lao PDR[1]

Jayant Menon and Peter Warr

I.   INTRODUCTION

It is obvious that low-quality roads impose costs on people living far from market centres. In the Lao People's Democratic Republic (PDR) this is a particular problem. The country is mountainous and for historical reasons roads in many rural areas remain badly maintained or even non-existent. Because the poorest people often reside far from urban centres, these people are the most disadvantaged by the high transport costs resulting from bad roads. Over the past two decades Lao PDR has made considerable progress in reforming the legal and administrative obstacles to market-based development that were a legacy of earlier policies. But for people facing very high transport costs arising from inadequate roads, these reforms may be of limited value. For them, markets cannot be accessed except at a high cost. Bad roads are clearly an obstacle to attaining the potential benefits from market-based economic reform.

Considerable effort is being invested in the improvement of rural roads in Lao PDR. The expected benefits include reductions in the incidence of poverty within rural areas. But the quantitative relationship between road improvement and poverty reduction is not well understood. The present study focuses on this relationship. The analysis uses a general equilibrium modelling approach in which road improvement is modelled as a reduction in transport costs. The modelling framework used in the study is specially designed to analyse the manner in which transport cost reductions impact on poor people.

In Section II we describe the information available on the relationship between road improvement and transport cost. We then use this information to analyse the effects of road improvement using a general equilibrium model of the economy of Lao PDR, especially constructed for this purpose. This model is described in Section III. Three features of the model are important. First, it distinguishes four categories of households, one urban and three rural, the latter differentiated by the quality of roads which service the villages in which these rural households are located. Second, each of these four categories of households contains a hundred household sub-categories, arranged by real expenditures per household member. Third, the three rural household categories differ according to the transport costs that they face, commensurate with the quality of roads servicing them, and using the information summarized in Section II. Road improvement is then modelled as a reduction in these costs. The results of the analysis are presented in Section IV. Finally, Section V draws out the major conclusions that follow from the study.

II.   ROAD QUALITY AND TRANSPORT COSTS

The Road Network in Lao PDR: Some Basic Facts

The road system in Lao PDR, which totals just above 31 000 kilometres in length, is mostly in a bad state of disrepair. Putting aside urban and purpose-built special roads, the road network generally consists of national and local roads, with the latter subdivided into provincial, district and rural roads (Table 6.1).

Currently, less than 20 per cent of this total network is paved. The national roads, linking major towns and provincial capitals and providing connections to neighbouring countries, total 3700 kilometres in length, or 23 per cent of the road network. As a result of substantial investment by the government of Lao PDR and bilateral and multilateral donors over the last decade and a half or so, about half of this national road network is now

Table 6.1   The Lao PDR road network

Road type	Road surface							
	Paved		Gravel		Earth		All surfaces	
	km	%	km	%	km	%	km	%
National	3 771	53.0	2 244	31	1 126	16	7 141	23
Provincial	198	3.0	3 038	47	3 249	50	6 485	21
District	31	0.8	1 826	47	2 008	52	3 865	12
Rural	14	0.1	1 815	16	9 527	84	11 356	36
Urban	429	24.0	871	49	465	26	1 765	6
Special	54	9.0	304	50	249	41	607	2
Total	4 497	14.0	10 098	32	16 624	53	31 219	100

Source: MTCPC (2003).

paved, with the remainder having gravel or earth surfaces. Although this is a significant improvement in road quality, the fact remains that only about half of the best segment of the overall road network – the national roads – can be relied upon to provide all-weather connectivity.

Local roads run 21 700 kilometres in length and make up 70 per cent of the entire network, but only 4 per cent is paved. The provincial road network is 6500 kilometres in length, of which even less is paved (3 per cent). District roads are 6500 kilometres and are almost equally divided into either gravel or earth surfaces. Rural roads are the most important category in the network, and comprise more than 11 000 kilometres in length. Hardly any of it is paved, and almost 85 per cent is earth. All of this suggests that almost the entire local road network may be impassable during at least some of the wet season.

Table 6.1 does not provide any indication of the condition of the various road surfaces. The relatively small share of the network that is paved is in generally good condition, given that most is only recently upgraded. The same cannot be said about non-paved surfaces. The World Bank (2001) estimated that about 60 per cent of the district and rural road network is in either 'poor' or 'bad' condition. A more recent study, MCTPC (Ministry of Communications, Transport, Post and Construction) (2004), suggested that little had changed since the World Bank study and that only 38 per cent of the total local road network was in a 'maintainable' condition.

These facts suggest that the cost of land transport in Lao PDR is currently high, and might be reduced significantly by improving the existing network and expanding it, especially in rural areas. The need to do this is further strengthened by the fact that motorized vehicles are the dominant mode of transport, carrying 91 per cent of total freight ton-kilometres and 95 per cent of total passenger-kilometres.

All-Weather, Dry-Season and No Vehicular Access Roads

In the analysis, three types of road quality are distinguished in terms of accessibility: (1) no vehicular access; (2) dry season only access; and (3) all-weather access.

No vehicular access means that the pathways through which the village is normally reached cannot accommodate conventional motorized vehicles. It does not mean that the village is completely isolated. It may still be accessible by low-cost vehicles and carrying devices appropriate to local-level transport tasks. These are collectively called intermediate means of transport (IMTs) – intermediate, that is, between walking (with loads carried on the head, or head loading) and conventional, motorized transport (see Dawson and Barwell, 1993). Intermediate means of transport

Table 6.2   Lao PDR: numbers of rural households by road access

Road access	Code	Number of households		Percentage of households	
		LECS 2 1997–98	LECS 3 2002–03	LECS 2 1997–98	LECS 3 2002–03
No access any season	HR1	2146	2052	31.2	31.6
Dry-season access only	HR2	1934	1050	28.1	16.2
All season access	HR3	2794	3386	40.7	52.2
All rural households		6874	6488	100.0	100.0

Source: Authors' calculations from LECS 2 and LECS 3 survey data.

include simple devices to facilitate the carrying of loads by people, such as the shoulder pole and the backpack frame; human-powered vehicles such as wheelbarrows, handcarts and bicycles; animal-powered devices such as donkeys with panniers, and animal-drawn carts and sledges; and perhaps some two-wheeled motorized vehicles such as mopeds and motorcycles.

Dry-season only access roads consist predominantly of unpaved roads that are accessible to conventional motorized vehicles during the dry season but not necessarily during the wet season. During the wet season, vehicles will be forced to find alternative routes or use alternative paths along the existing road, which would facilitate passage but would result in higher transport costs due to a change in travel distance, road roughness and speeds. Depending on its condition, this covers most, but not all, earth and gravel road surfaces.

Finally, conventional motorized vehicles can use all-weather access roads during the dry and wet seasons. In other words, unlike dry season access roads, these roads would not be subject to frequent closure as a result of flooding during the wet season. This category includes almost all paved roads.

The Lao Expenditure and Consumption Survey (LECS), which has now been conducted for 1992–93 (LECS 1), 1997–98 (LECS 2) and 2002–03 (LECS 3), provides, in the cases of LECS 2 and LESC 3, a comparable classification of roads into these categories, and records the category of road servicing each village. Table 6.2 summarizes information about the importance of these three categories of rural villages, classified by road access. One point that emerges from this table is that over the five-year interval between these two surveys there was a decline in the proportion of rural households living in villages with 'dry season access only' road access and a corresponding increase in the proportion with 'all season access'. But

Table 6.3   Lao PDR: welfare of rural households by road access, 2002–03

Welfare indicator	No road access HR1	Dry season access only HR2	All season access HR3	All rural HR
Real consumption expenditures per person (thousand kip per year)	1712.6	1917.0	2280.2	2070.1
Poverty incidence	45.57	36.05	28.64	34.17
School attendance	51.90	70.48	80.67	69.41
Females (%)	47.54	67.82	80.00	67.06
Males (%)	56.27	72.98	81.37	71.72
Average expenditure on education (kip per student per month)	65152	86973	111963	96209
Proportion of persons who became ill in the last 4 weeks (%)	15.63	13.37	13.31	14.07
Of those ill, those who did not seek treatment (%)	89.80	83.16	80.69	84.35

Source: Authors' calculations from the LECS 3 database.

there was no change in the proportion having 'no access any season'. This implies that the road improvement that occurred during this interval consisted overwhelmingly of upgrading 'dry season access only' roads, making them accessible during all seasons. But no upgrading of 'no access any season' roads can be detected from these data. In 2002–03 almost one-third of all rural households lived in villages without roads that support motorized vehicle access.

The socio-economic characteristics of rural households living in these three types of villages are quite different. Table 6.3 summarizes some information on these differences, based on the LECS 3 survey for 2002–03. Villages without road access have lower mean consumption expenditures per person and higher rates of poverty incidence than households with dry season access only, which are in turn less well off by both measures than villages with all-weather access.[2] Other socio-economic indicators, relating to education and health, also support the importance of road access for the well-being of rural people. Areas with poorer roads have lower rates of school attendance for both male and female children, lower per capita expenditures on education, higher rates of sickness and lower likelihood of seeking treatment when they are ill.

Transport Costs by Road Type

Our interest is in identifying changes in transport cost associated with road improvement that changes road quality between these three categories of road access.

The most straightforward of these changes is represented by road improvement that converts a dry-season only access road to an all-weather access road. This could involve, for instance, converting a deteriorated gravel or un-engineered earth track road to a paved or asphalt surface. As mentioned above, most of the road improvement that has occurred in Lao PDR over the recent past, and particularly during the period covered by this study (between LECS 2, 1997–98, and LECS 3, 2002–03) has been of this kind. The other forms of road improvement that we study involve moving from no vehicular access to dry-season access.

In order to compute the effects of these changes, we first need to identify a base level of transport cost associated with each road type. This is most easily done for all-weather and dry-season access roads. Project performance evaluation reports of multilateral development agencies such as the ADB and the World Bank usually include such computations based on vehicle operating costs (VOCs), before and after the project.

A recent project by ADB, the Champassak Road Improvement Project (ADB, 2003), is particularly appropriate for the computation of changes in transport costs that we are interested in. This project comprised the rehabilitation and improvement of a 200-kilometre road in Lao PDR to improve transport services in the southern region. The project mainly focused on upgrading of roads to provide all-weather connectivity between Thailand and Cambodia via the Lao PDR.[3]

Transport costs are represented by VOC estimates, which are themselves based mainly on road roughness as measured by the international roughness index (IRI) and a number of other factors such as utilization rates and capital costs.[4]

Table 6.4 summarizes the VOCs for dry-season and all-weather access roads, and the percentage change in VOC associated with moving from the former to the latter, for three different categories of motorized vehicles. The base level of transport costs in dry-season access roads is represented by the VOC for roads classified in the gravel and earth category with an IRI of 15. This is the highest level of roughness in this category for which data are reported. The base level of transport costs for all-weather access roads, on the other hand, is proxied by the VOC for paved roads with an IRI of 2.2. This is the lowest level of roughness in this category for which data are reported.

Based on these base levels of transport costs, road improvement that transforms a gravel and earth dry-season access road to a paved all-weather

Table 6.4   *Vehicle operating cost estimates for all-weather and dry-season access roads*

Vehicle/IRI	VOC estimates (in US$)		Percentage change in VOC
	Gravel and earth 15	Paved 2.2	
Cars	0.297	0.141	−52.53
Light truck	0.221	0.120	−45.70
Heavy truck	0.641	0.316	−50.70
Simple average	0.386	0.192	−49.60

Source: Authors' computations based on data in ADB (2003).

access road implies a significant reduction in transport costs. The last column of Table 6.4 points to some minor variation across vehicle type, with the average reduction in VOC being about half, or 50 per cent.[5] In other words, transport costs are 2.01 times as high on dry-season only access roads as on all-weather access roads. This is the multiple that we use in conducting our simulation relating to the impact of upgrading from dry-season to all-weather access, described below.

The project performance evaluation report also presents separate estimates of changes in travel times associated with all-weather and dry-season access roads. Based on discussions with the Ministry of Communications, Transport, Post and Construction and local villagers, the average speed of vehicles before the road improvement was between 25 km/hour and 30 km/hour. After project completion, the average speed increased sharply to about 50 km/hour, amounting to a 40–50 per cent reduction in travel time. These reductions in travel times are consistent with the reductions in VOCs reported in Table 6.4.

A number of international studies lend support to these findings from the Champassak Road project. Minten and Kyle (1999), for instance, analyse the causes of food price variation in Kinshasa (the capital of the former Zaire) using survey data collected from itinerant traders. They find that transportation costs were on average two times greater on dirt roads than on paved roads. A study by Levy (1996) on the impact of converting dry-season access to all-season access roads in Morocco found that travel times, in most cases, were cut by at least 50 per cent. Other studies that focus on the link between infrastructure and trade, such as Limao and Venables (2001) also report reductions in transport costs in the same order of magnitude.

Next we consider the no vehicular access case. Identifying a base level of transport cost for this is more difficult. This is a residual category and the

Table 6.5   VOC estimates for no vehicular access, dry-season access, and all-weather roads

Tonnage	VOCs (per km per ton, US$)						
	10	50	250	500	1000	1500	2000
Motorcycle	1.2	1.15	1.15	1.15	1.15	1.15	1.15
Pickup	<1.25	<1.25	0.8	0.50	0.38	0.35	0.35
Truck	<1.25	<1.25	1.25	0.70	0.40	0.25	0.20
Percentage difference in VOCs compared with motorcycle							
Pickup	—	—	30.43	56.52	66.96	69.57	69.57
Truck	—	—	−8.70	39.13	65.22	78.26	82.61

Source: Authors' computations based on data in Starkey (2001).

surfaces that belong to this classification can vary significantly and are not as well defined as those in the all-weather and dry-season access categories. There are obvious difficulties in measuring or estimating the roughness of such 'roads' and determining the grading frequency to be applied to it in computing VOCs. Since there is no easy way of directly computing VOCs, an indirect approach is required. We draw upon some interesting work by Starkey (2001; 2006) for this purpose.

Starkey (2001) analyses how VOCs for different modes of transport change with distance and tonnage. Using his work, we proxy the type of road access by type of vehicle used. When there is no road access, we represent transport cost with the VOC for motorcycles. Dry-season access roads are proxied by pickups, on the assumption that they are better suited to navigate such roads, even during the wet season. All-weather access roads are represented by the VOC for trucks. Trucks generally carry heavier loads than pickups, and thereby require a better surface. The VOC estimates for these three modes of transportation, and how they vary with load, summarized in Table 6.5, are measured in US dollars as the cost per ton of output per kilometre travelled.

Assuming a 10-kilometre distance travelled, Starkey finds that the VOC for transport by motorcycle remains relatively unchanged at about 1.15 irrespective of tonnage. There are apparently no scale economies associated with this medium of transport. It is also unlikely that the VOC for two-wheeled vehicles such as bicycles or motorcycles will be significantly affected by the quality of roads or IRIs (see World Bank, 2005: table 6.4).

For pickups, the VOC remains above that of motorcycles for loads up to 50 tons. The fixed costs of operating a pickup need to be spread over a larger load before the VOC drops below that of motorcycles. This occurs at about the 100-ton load level. Beyond this level, the VOC drops quite sharply, reaching a low of 0.35 when the load reaches 1500 tons. This is a 70 per cent reduction in VOC compared with motorcycles, or about one-third the relative cost.

Since the fixed costs of operating trucks are higher than pickups, the VOC remains above that of pickups until the load exceeds 1000 tons. It continues to fall until the load reaches 2000 tons, where it is at a minimum of 0.2. This is an 83 per cent reduction in VOC compared with bicycles, or about one-sixth the relative cost.

For the simulations that we conduct in Section IV on the impact of reductions in transport costs, we use the VOCs associated with a load of 2000 tons because this is when they are at their minimum for all three types of vehicles.

III. A GENERAL EQUILIBRIUM MODEL OF THE ECONOMY OF LAO PDR

This section describes LaoGEM (Lao General Equilibrium Model), a 20-sector, 400-household general equilibrium model of the Lao economy, constructed specifically for the analysis of the effect of road improvement on rural poverty incidence in Lao PDR. Unless otherwise stated, the database of the model refers to the year 2002. The model's main features are as follows.

Model Structure

The theoretical structure of LaoGEM is relatively conventional. It belongs to the class of general equilibrium models that are linear in proportional changes, sometimes referred to as Johansen models. The highly influential ORANI general equilibrium model of the Australian economy (Dixon et al., 1982) also used this approach. The detailed structure of LaoGEM is based on the PARA and Wayang general equilibrium models of the Thai and Indonesian economies, respectively, described in detail in Warr (2001) and Warr (2005), respectively.[6] However, this general structure is adapted to reflect the specific objectives of the present study and important features of the Lao economy.

The microeconomic behaviour assumed within LaoGEM is competitive profit maximization on the part of all firms and competitive utility maximization on the part of consumers. Each industry has a constant returns to scale technology and there is at least one industry-specific factor present in each industry. In the simulations reported in this chapter, the markets for final outputs, intermediate goods and factors of production are all assumed to clear at prices that are determined endogenously within the model.[7] The nominal exchange rate between the Lao kip and the US dollar is fixed exogenously and its role within the model is to determine, together with international prices, the nominal domestic price level. The model is homogeneous (degree one for prices and degree zero for quantities) with respect to this exchange rate. This means that because domestic prices adjust flexibly to clear markets, a 1 per cent increase in the kip/dollar exchange rate will result in a 1 per cent increase in all nominal domestic prices, leaving all real variables unchanged.

Industries
The model contains 20 industries, listed in Appendix Table 6A.1. They include three agricultural industries: crops; livestock and poultry; and forestry and logging. Non-agricultural industries include: mining and quarrying; seven manufacturing industries; and nine services and utilities industries, one of which is transport. The transport industry will be important for the present study. Each industry produces a single output, and the set of commodities therefore coincides with the set of industries. Exports are not identical with domestically sold commodities. In each industry the two are produced by a transformation process with a constant elasticity of transformation.

The core of the production side of the model is a 20-sector input-output table for Lao PDR, estimated especially for this study. No input-output (IO) table is currently available for Lao PDR and the table constructed for the present study is thus the first publicly available input-output table for the country. It is based on information from two sources. First, there is a 20-sector input-output table for Savannaket Province of Lao PDR, relating to the year 2003, recently constructed in a detailed study by researchers at the Asian Development Bank (Secretario et al., 2005). This table is then adjusted using data from the Lao National Accounts for 2002. The method of adjustment may be understood as follows. The value-added totals for the various sectors of the Savannaket table are compared with those for Lao PDR, derived from the National Accounts. The Savannaket table is then amended using a method called RAS (row and column sum) to force the value-added totals to match those for Lao PDR.

The resulting table has a structure that reflects the industry structure of Lao PDR, as reflected in its National Accounts, but within each industry the input-output technology reflects that of Savannaket Province. The method thus assumes that the input-output technology for each industry in Lao PDR is similar to that of Savannaket, even though the relative importance of these various industries in Lao PDR is quite different from that of Savannaket. Fortuitously, Savannaket Province seems a suitable basis for this kind of exercise in that it is roughly intermediate within the provinces of Lao PDR in terms of its level of technology, neither the most nor the least advanced. The resulting table seems to make sense. When a properly constructed input-output table for Lao PDR becomes available, it should presumably replace the table constructed as above. In the mean time, this table is considered the best available. The cost structures of these 20 industries, derived from this estimated IO table, are summarized in Appendix Table 6A.2 and their sales structures are summarized in Appendix Table 6A.3.

Commodities

Although the sets of producer goods and consumer goods have the same names, the commodities themselves are not identical. Each of the 20 consumed goods consists of a composite of the domestically produced and imported version of the same commodity, where the two are imperfect substitutes. The proportions in which they are combined reflect consumer choices and depend on both (a) the relative prices of these imported and domestically produced versions of the good and (b) the (Armington) elasticity of substitution between them.

Factors of production

The mobility of factors of production is a critical feature of any general equilibrium system, where the term 'mobility' here means the capacity to move across economic activities (industries), and not necessarily the capacity to move geographically. The greater the inter-sectoral factor mobility built into the model, the greater the flexibility of the economy, as reflected in its simulated capacity to respond to changes in the economic environment. It is clearly essential that assumptions about the mobility of factors of production are consistent with the length of run that the model is intended to capture.

Labour is assumed to be fully mobile across all sectors, implying that wages must be equal in all sectors, and must move together. There are three kinds of capital: capital that is immobile across industries but mobile within industries, referred to subsequently as fixed capital; capital that is mobile among agricultural industries but not mobile between agriculture and the non-agricultural industries, referred to as agricultural mobile capital; and capital that is mobile among the non-agricultural industries but not between these industries and the agricultural industries, referred to here as non-agricultural mobile capital.

In this treatment, fixed capital in agriculture is thought of as including some land, but also some light machinery and equipment of an industry-specific kind. Mobile capital in agriculture includes some land but also machinery such as light tractors and also draught animals that can be used in the production of a range of agricultural commodities. Neither agricultural land nor agricultural capital (machinery and draught animals) is usable in the non-agricultural industries. Non-agricultural capital is thought of as including industrial machinery and buildings.

Technology
In every sector there is constant elasticity of substitution production technology with diminishing returns to scale to variable factors alone. However, there is also a sector specific fixed factor (immobile capital or land) in every sector. For convenience, we shall refer to the set of specific factors in the agricultural sectors as 'land', and to the set of those in the non-agricultural sectors as 'fixed capital', but for the reasons described above, this language is accurate only in an approximate way. The assumption of constant returns means that all factor demand functions are homogeneous of degree one in output. In each sector, there is a zero profit condition, which equates the price of output to the minimum unit cost of production. This condition can be thought of as determining the price of the fixed factor in that sector.

Factor mobility and length of run
The mobility across sectors of labour, but only partial mobility of capital, means that the analysis refers to a short-run to intermediate-run period of adjustment – not very short run, otherwise labour would not be fully mobile and capital might not be mobile at all – and not very long run, otherwise capital would be more fully mobile. The period of adjustment consistent with these assumptions is thus between two and five years.

Households
The model contains four major household categories – one urban (subsequently HU) and three rural. The three rural categories are differentiated by the quality of road access shared by the members of the village concerned. The three categories of road access are summarized in Table 6.6.

Category HR1 refers to villages not serviced by a road at all, meaning that the only access to the village is by foot or by motorcycle, along pathways, but which are not reachable by vehicles. Category HR2 refers to dirt roads that are not usable during at least some periods of the wet season. Category HR3 refers to sealed roads or well-maintained dirt or gravel roads that can be used by vehicles at all times of the year.

The incomes of each of these three household types depend on their ownership of factors of production, the returns to those factors, and their non-factor incomes, mainly consisting of transfers from others. Since our

Table 6.6   Naming of household categories

Description	Classification
Urban	HU
Rural, no road access	HR1
Rural, dry-season access	HR2
Rural, all-season access	HR3

focus is on income distribution, the sources of income of the various households are of particular interest. These differ among the four household categories. The data are extracted from the 2002–03 household income and expenditure survey, the Lao Expenditure and Consumption Survey, commonly called LECS 3.[8] The SAM is based on data from this survey, the input-output table described above, the Lao National Accounts for 2002 and Lao trade data.

Within the LAOGEM model, each of the four household categories is subdivided into a further 100 sub-categories (centile groups) each of the same population size, arranged by real consumption expenditures per capita, giving a total of 400 sub-categories.[9] The consumer demand equations for the various household types are based on a Cobb-Douglas demand system, using data on expenditure shares extracted from the LECS 3 survey. Within each of the four major categories, the 100 sub-categories thus differ according to (1) their per capita expenditures, (2) their budget shares in consumption and (3) their sources of factor and non-factor incomes.

Elasticity estimates
The elasticity estimates used in LaoGEM for the factor demand systems were taken from empirical estimates derived econometrically for a structurally similar model of the Thai economy, known as PARA. These parameters were amended to match the differences between the databases for LaoGEM and PARA so as to ensure the homogeneity properties required by economic theory. All export demand elasticities were set equal to 20. The elasticities of supply of imports to Lao PDR were assumed to be infinite and import prices were thus set exogenously. All production functions are assumed to be CES in primary factors with elasticities of substitution of 0.5 except for the paddy production industry where this elasticity is set at 0.25, reflecting the empirical observation of low elasticities of supply response in this industry. The Armington elasticities of substitution in demand between imports and domestically produced goods were set equal to 2 for all commodities.

Treatment of transport costs
The information on transport costs described in Section II, above, was used
to allocate the output of the 'transport' industry in the input-output table to
transport margins between consumer and producer prices in each of the four
household categories. The relative magnitudes of total transport costs for
each category of rural household were estimated as total tonnage of goods
transported multiplied by distance to nearest market multiplied by VOC per
ton per kilometre on this type of road. Transport costs were assumed to be
incurred primarily between the local market and the village concerned.

The distribution of total tonnage of goods transported was proxied as
the distribution of total expenditure across the household groups, calculated as mean expenditure per person estimated in the LECS 3 survey multiplied by total population of the household group. Distance to the nearest
market was proxied as distance from the village to the nearest post office,
as recorded in the LECS 3 survey. As described above, VOCs were estimated for HR2 and HR3 from an ADB study of Champassak province
(ratio HR2/HR3 = 2.01) and the ratio for HR1 to HR2 is derived using
work done by Starkey (2001) (ratio HR1/HR2 = 2.86, implying a ratio of
HR1 to HR3 of 5.75).

This gives the ratio of total transport costs for the three categories of
rural households shown in the final row of Table 6.7. These proportions
were then used to allocate the total output of the 'transport' sector of the
input–output table to transport margins in the three categories of rural
households. Transport margins thus differ across the three categories of
rural households but within each of these categories they are the same for
all households. Within each household category, the transport margins are
the same for all commodities as proportions of consumer prices.

There are two other categories of margins between consumer and producer prices defined within the model – trade and tax margins. As
Appendix Table 6A.3 shows, trade margins are even larger in total magnitude than transport margins. It is assumed in this study that trade margins
(meaning costs of warehousing, retailing and advertising) do not depend
on the type of road servicing a particular village. Trade and tax margins are
therefore assumed to be the same for all households and as proportions of
consumer prices trade margins are the same for all commodities, while tax
margins differ according to the tax rates concerned.

In summary, the estimates of the relative magnitudes of total transport
costs shown in row E of Table 6.7 are used as the basis for allocating total
transport margins among the three rural household categories defined in
the model. This is relevant for the construction of the database of the
model. The VOCs shown in row C are used as the basis for calculating the
shocks that are described below.

Table 6.7   Lao PDR: estimating total transport costs by rural household category

Household group		HR1 (No road)	HR2 (Dry season)	HR3 (All season)	HU (Urban)
Mean expenditure per capita (kip)		106 971	118 799	145 704	260 646
Population		949 698	708 054	2 197 436	1 374 542
Population share (%)		18%	14%	42%	26%
Total expenditure (million kip)	A	101 590	84 116	320 176	358 269
Distance to nearest post office (km)	B	36.67	29.61	13.47	0
Ratio to HR3		*2.64*	*1.84*	*1*	*0*
Vehicle operating cost ($/km)	C	1.104	0.386	0.192	0
Ratio to HR3		*5.75*	*2.01*	*1*	*0*
Total transport cost = A × B × C	D	4 284 121	871 736	862 553	0
Ratio to HR3	E	*4.97*	*1.16*	*1.00*	*0*

Note: Row D = Rows A × B × C.

Source: Authors' calculations based on data from National Statistical Centre, Vientiane, *Lao Expenditure and Consumption Survey, 2002–03* (LECS 3), ADB (2003) and Starkey (2001).

IV.   SIMULATING THE EFFECTS ON THE POOR OF TRANSPORT COST REDUCTIONS

The Shocks

The shocks are summarized in Table 6.8. The shocks are interpreted as changes in VOC per kilometre. Of course, upgrading a road does not change the distance it has to cover, so the shocks change only the per kilometre costs of operating vehicles on them. Four simulations are reported in this paper. The magnitudes of the shocks used draw upon the vehicle operating costs summarized in row C of Table 6.7.

Simulation S1 represents a reduction of transport costs per kilometre in households currently serviced by dry-season access only roads (HR2 households) from their current levels to the transport cost levels per kilometre of all-weather access roads (HR3 households). The simulation estimates the effects of making this change in all households currently serviced

Table 6.8   Summary of simulations

Simulation	Interpretation
Simulation S1	Reduce margin to HR2 by 50.25%
Simulation S2	Reduce margin to HR1 by 65.04%
Simulation S3	Reduce margin to HR1 by 32.57%
Simulation S4	Reduce margin to HR1 by 16.26%

by dry-season access only roads. As shown in the discussion of Table 6.2 above, this change captures the type of road improvement that has dominated in Lao PDR, at least over the five years between the LECS 2 survey period (1997–98) and the LECS 3 survey period (2002–03). Dry-season access roads have been converted to all-weather access roads. Thus, in Simulation 1 transport costs facing HR2 households are reduced by $100(0.386 - 0.192)/0.386 = 50.25$ per cent. Other households' transportation costs do not change.

In Simulation S2, the transport cost faced by household HR1 (no road access) is reduced sufficiently to make it match that of household HR2 (dry-season access), or $100(1.104 - 0.386)/1.104 = 65.04$ per cent.

As will be seen when the results are discussed, Simulation S2 produces a much larger reduction in poverty than Simulation S1. The remaining two sets of experiments, Simulation S3 and Simulation S4, thus experiment with arbitrarily smaller reductions in the transport cost facing HR1 households than is represented by S2. Simulation S3 simulates the effect of transport cost reduction half as large as S2 and S4 shows the effect of transport cost reductions one quarter of S2.

Model Closure

Since the real consumption expenditure of each household is chosen as the basis for welfare measurement, and is the basis for the calculation of poverty incidence, the macroeconomic closure must be made compatible with both this measure and with the single-period horizon of the model. This is done by ensuring that the full economic effects of the shocks to be introduced are channelled into current-period household consumption and do not 'leak' in other directions, with real-world inter-temporal welfare implications not captured by the welfare measure. The choice of macroeconomic closure may thus be seen in part as a mechanism for minimizing inconsistencies between the use of a single-period model to analyse welfare results and the multi-period reality that the model depicts.

To prevent intertemporal and other welfare leakages from occurring, the simulations are conducted with balanced trade (exogenous balance on current account). This ensures that the potential benefits from the export tax do not flow to foreigners, through a current account surplus, or that increases in domestic consumption are not achieved at the expense of borrowing from abroad, in the case of a current account deficit. For the same reason, real government spending and real investment demand for each good are each fixed exogenously. The government budget deficit is held fixed in nominal terms. This is achieved by endogenous across-the-board adjustments to personal income tax rates so as to restore the base level of the budgetary deficit.

The combined effect of these features of the closure is that the full effects of changes in policy are channelled into household consumption and not into effects not captured within the single period focus of the model.

Simulation Results

The estimated effects are summarized in Tables 6.9 to 6.11. In each case, real GDP increases and both rural poverty incidence and total poverty incidence decline. It is notable that in Simulation S2 the stimulus to GDP and the reduction in poverty incidence are both much larger than in other simulations. Shock S2 increases real GDP by 6 times as much as shock S1 (1.41 v. 0.22). But it reduces total poverty incidence by 17 times as much (1.01 v. 0.06). In other words, the poverty impact associated with providing households without any road access with dry-season access roads is 17 times higher than that associated with converting dry-season to all-weather access roads. Indeed, when the transport cost reduction represented by Simulation S2 is reduced to one-quarter of the S2 level, the reduction in poverty incidence is still four times as large as occurs under S1.

One seeming anomaly must be explained. General equilibrium models are capable of detecting small indirect effects of external shocks that might not otherwise be obvious. Transport cost reductions produce substantial benefits for the direct recipients, but there are small, indirect effects on non-recipients that can be positive or negative. For example, in Simulation S1, households in the HR2 category (dry-season access only) are the direct beneficiaries and a large reduction in poverty incidence occurs in this group. Nevertheless, there is also a small reduction in poverty in the HR1 category (no road access) while small increases occur in the HR3 (all-weather access) and HU (urban) household groups. The main reason for these effects is that the income gains for HR2 households shift the demand pattern for final consumer goods. Households that consume similar patterns of final goods to HR2 tend to incur small indirect negative effects because their costs of

Table 6.9　Simulated macroeconomic effects of road improvements (percentage change)

Simulation	S1	S2	S3	S4
Overall economy				
Gross domestic product				
Nominal (local currency)	−0.24	−1.19	−0.61	−0.31
Real	0.22	1.41	0.70	0.35
Consumer price index	−0.46	−2.60	−1.32	−0.66
GDP deflator	−0.46	−2.56	−1.30	−0.65
Wage (nominal)	−0.40	−2.15	−1.05	−0.51
Wage (real)	0.06	0.46	0.27	0.15
External sector (foreign currency)				
Export revenue	0.30	1.56	0.77	0.38
Import Bill	0.09	0.52	0.25	0.12
Government budget (local currency)				
Revenue Total revenue	0.05	0.39	0.17	0.08
Tariff revenue	0.09	0.52	0.25	0.12
Expenditure Nominal	−0.22	−1.18	−0.58	−0.29
Nominal household income				
Rural households				
HR1	−0.23	1.08	−0.03	−0.16
HR2	−0.13	−0.97	−0.52	−0.27
HR3	−0.26	−1.28	−0.66	−0.33
Total rural population	−0.243	−0.24	−1.07	−0.59
Total urban population	−0.268	−0.27	−1.34	−0.69
Total population	−0.256	−0.26	−1.26	−0.65
Total household consumption				
Nominal (local currency)	−0.26	−1.26	−0.65	−0.33
Real (CPI deflator)	0.20	1.38	0.68	0.33

living increase. In this case, this explains the, seemingly non-intuitive, small negative effects on poverty incidence among HR3 and HU households.

The results summarized above differ from those obtained from earlier econometric analysis of cross-sectional household survey data, such as those described in ADB (2005a). In particular, the econometric results suggested that the gross returns (in terms of poverty reduction) from upgrading dry-season access roads to all-weather roads, relative to the returns from upgrading no-access roads, were somewhat more substantial than those indicated by the results from the general equilibrium approach summarized here. There are two possible reasons for this difference, both of

Table 6.10 Simulated structural effects of road improvements (percentage
change)

Industry output	S1	S2	S3	S4
Crops	0.149	0.880	0.427	0.210
Livestock	0.160	0.910	0.427	0.207
Forestry	0.247	1.324	0.651	0.321
Mining	0.465	2.526	1.232	0.606
Food	0.193	1.099	0.515	0.249
Textiles	0.463	2.613	1.260	0.617
Wood and paper	0.380	1.998	0.985	0.486
Petroleum	0.669	3.702	1.794	0.880
Mineral products	0.038	0.217	0.103	0.050
Metal product	0.585	3.234	1.566	0.768
Other manufacturing	0.286	1.581	0.756	0.369
Electricity and water	0.208	1.252	0.595	0.290
Construction	0.003	0.020	0.010	0.005
Transportation	94.694	130.927	35.095	14.365
Post and telecom.	0.096	1.145	0.551	0.269
Trade	0.174	0.989	0.471	0.229
Banking	0.165	0.944	0.452	0.221
Real estate	0.263	1.639	0.768	0.371
Public administration	0.046	0.269	0.124	0.060
Other services	0.187	1.068	0.495	0.238

which relate to problems with cross-sectional econometric analysis – an
omitted variable problem and an endogeneity problem.

First, in cross-sectional econometrics, different regions differ for reasons
other than the variable of central policy interest – in this case, the type of
road that is present. In econometric analysis, multiple regression is a statistical means for overcoming this problem, but it can work properly only if
the data available include *all* relevant differences between regions other
than the policy variable of interest. If the data collected are incomplete in
this respect, and the omitted variables are correlated with the policy variable of interest, the econometric results will be biased.

Second, cross-sectional econometrics suffers from an endogeneity problem.
The data used in the analysis are not generated by a randomized controlled
experiment. The areas that receive improved roads were chosen by the road-
building agencies using some allocation criterion. For example, suppose richer
areas were chosen for road upgrading, or that a criterion was used which is positively correlated with income. The variable describing road improvement is
then not exogenous, but is endogenous to income. This will mean that, *ex ante*,

Table 6.11   Simulated distributional effects of road improvements

Simulation			S1	S2	S3	S4
Real consumption expenditures per person, deflated by household-specific CPI (Percentage change, except *ex ante* levels						
		Ex ante level		Percent change		
		(Thousand kip)	S1	S2	S3	S4
Rural households	HR1	1 712.6	0.27	15.40	7.48	3.68
	HR2	1 917.0	2.83	0.13	0.03	0.00
	HR3	2 280.2	−0.04	−0.14	−0.09	−0.05
Total rural population		2 070.1	0.47	3.05	1.51	0.75
Total urban population	HU	5 598.6	−0.13	−0.66	−0.34	−0.17
Total population		2 882.3	0.20	1.38	0.68	0.33
Poverty incidence (Level, percentage population concerned)						
		Ex ante level		Ex post level		
			S1	S2	S3	S4
Rural households	HR1	45.57	45.47	39.15	41.49	43.72
	HR2	36.05	35.37	36.07	36.07	36.06
	HR3	28.64	28.67	28.74	28.70	28.67
Total rural population		34.17	34.04	32.65	33.20	33.73
Total urban population	HU	23.64	23.76	24.05	23.95	23.80
Total population		31.40	31.34	30.39	30.77	31.12
Change in poverty incidence (Absolute change, percentage of population concerned)						
			Ex post level – Ex ante level			
			S1	S2	S3	S4
Rural households	HR1		−0.10	−6.42	−4.08	−1.85
	HR2		−0.68	0.02	0.02	0.01
	HR3		0.03	0.10	0.06	0.03
Total rural population			−0.13	−1.52	−0.97	−0.44
Total urban population	HU		0.12	0.41	0.31	0.16
Total population			−0.06	−1.01	−0.63	−0.28

areas with higher incomes will be more likely to receive improved roads. When the *ex post* econometric analysis finds that areas that received roads had higher incomes, this will not mean that the improved roads caused the higher incomes. In part, at least, it will mean the reverse. That is, causation is very difficult to sort out in this kind of econometric research and it is usually unclear how much effect this has had on the results.

The advantage of general equilibrium modelling in these respects is that the analysis is directly comparable to a fully controlled experiment. Only one variable – the exogenous variable – is changed at a time. The direction of causation is then unambiguous and the results are free of both the omitted variable problem and the endogeneity problem, both of which are a problem for econometric analysis.

Relative Costs of Road Provision and Improvement

The results presented above focus on the benefits of improving road access. Based on benefits alone, the results suggest that reducing transport costs for households without road access is highly pro-poor. This finding does not in itself imply that road improvement should be shifted away from upgrading dry-season access roads to providing road access to villages currently lacking it because we have so far not considered the costs of road-building in the two cases. These relative costs need to be taken into account in determining the most appropriate road-building strategy. It seems likely that the cost per kilometre of providing road access where there is currently none is significantly higher than the corresponding cost per kilometre of upgrading existing roads. The terrain in a significant portion of the areas where there is currently no road access is mountainous, and there could be large start-up costs associated with creating access. In addition, the average length of the required roads might be greater in the case of these areas as well, compared with the average length of existing dry-season access roads.

Unfortunately, there are no direct estimates of the cost of providing dry-season road access to areas where there is presently none relative to the cost of upgrading dry-season access to all-weather access roads. A study by the ADB (2005b) on the Northern region of Lao PDR provides estimates that capture the effect of terrain on construction costs per kilometre of road.

The ADB (2005b) provides estimates of converting earth to gravel and earth/gravel to paved roads for both flat and mountainous terrains. We proxy the cost of providing dry-season access roads to households currently without any road access (shock S2) with the cost of converting earth to gravel roads in mountainous terrain. In other words, we assume that an earth surface in a mountainous terrain is approximately equal to having no road access, and when this is converted to a gravel road, then this represents the provision of dry-season access. This is because most of the households that do not have any road access are located in mountainous regions, and often are denied such access because of the terrain. We also assume that the cost of converting earth/gravel roads to paved roads in a flat terrain is approximately equal to the cost of upgrading dry-season access to all-weather access roads (shock S1).

Although the way we proxy the cost associated with shock S1 would appear reasonable, the same level of confidence cannot be placed on the way we proxy the cost associated with shock S2. The problem with proxying costs in this way for shock S2 is that an earth surface in a mountainous terrain may not fully represent 'no road access'. There would be costs involved in converting a 'no road access' surface to an earth surface, irrespective of the terrain in which it exists. In other words, there are missing cost elements in this estimate, and these costs relate to the conversion of a 'no road access' condition to an earth road in mountainous regions. Examples of such missing elements would include various types of clearance costs associated with removing trees, rocks and (in some areas) unexploded mines contamination, cross-drainage improvements, bridge works, resettlement costs and associated compensation for affected communities, mitigation and other costs related to environmental impacts, and the like. The magnitude of these costs would be project specific and could vary significantly.

With these assumptions and caveats in mind, what can the estimates in ADB (2005b) tell us about the relative costs associated with shock S1 versus shock S2? The cost per kilometre of converting earth to gravel roads in mountainous regions is estimated at about $250 000. On the other hand, the cost per kilometre of upgrading earth/gravel roads to paved roads in flat terrain is estimated at about $110 000. These estimates suggest that the cost associated with S1 is about 2.25 times higher than that associated with S2.

This assumes, however, that in upgrading the two types of roads, the average length of the road involved is the same. Total cost will also depend on the length of the road required in each case. Fortunately, we are able to relax this assumption using data from LECS3 on the average length of the two types of roads (proxied by average distance to nearest post office; see Table 6.7, row B). The average cost per kilometre of upgrading no-road access to dry-season access needs to be multiplied by the average length of no-road access distance, 36.67. Similarly, the average cost per kilometre of upgrading dry-season access to all-weather access needs to be multiplied by the average length of these roads, 29.61. These averages suggest that required road lengths associated with shock S2 are 1.24 (36.67/29.61) times longer than S1, or 24 per cent longer, on average.

Taking into account the relative cost per kilometre and the average lengths of the two types of road improvement, the total cost associated with shock S2 is 2.79 times higher than S1 (that is, 2.25 × 1.24).

Since the costs associated with shock S2 is likely to be underestimated, as noted earlier, this ratio may also be underestimated. In an attempt to address this, we use the highest of the various cost estimates for road construction associated with shock S2 and the lowest cost estimate associated with shock S1. Furthermore, in relation to the length or road associated with shocks S1 and S2, we should emphasize that these are average distances. Some no-road access areas are very remote and the cost of upgrading them will be correspondingly large.

Recall that the poverty impact of shock S2 was 17 times higher than shock S1, while the increase in GDP was six times higher. Unless the clearing and other costs referred to earlier that are missing in our estimation of costs associated with shock S2 are extremely large, then the cost–benefit analysis clearly favours shock S2 over S1. In other words, to maximize the impact of infrastructure spending on poverty reduction and growth, the type of road improvement may have to shift away from upgrading dry-season access roads to providing road access to villages currently lacking any.

V.   CONCLUSIONS

Our analysis indicates that reducing transport costs through rural road improvement generates significant reductions in poverty incidence. It does this through improving the income earning opportunities of rural people and through reducing the costs of the goods they consume. A feature of our results is that when no vehicle access areas are provided with dirt and gravel dry-season access roads (shock S2), the reduction in poverty incidence is about 17 times the reduction that occurs when dry-season access only roads are upgraded to paved and improved gravel all-weather access (shock S1) roads. The ratio of the effect on GDP is about 6. Reducing transport costs for households without road access is more pro-poor, at the margin, than the kind of road upgrading that has characterized the recent past.

These results do not demonstrate that road improvement should be shifted away from upgrading dry-season access roads to providing road access to villages currently lacking it. Both forms of road improvement are important and both contribute to overall poverty reduction. It is important that providing inner roads, closest to markets, is a necessary condition for the provision of outer roads, more distant from markets, to be effective. Roads that lead nowhere benefit no one. The issue is the value of additional investment in roads, at the margin.

Moreover, the costs of road-building in the two cases need to be taken into account in determining the most appropriate road building strategy. Construction cost estimates of road provision and improvement from a recent study compute the cost of road provision associated with shock S2 to be about 2.25 times higher than the road improvement associated with shock S1. Even if this ratio is an underestimate of the relative costs associated with these two shocks, it is significantly lower than the corresponding relative benefits, especially in terms of the impact on poverty reduction.

Thus, there seems be a case for reconsidering the share of resources allocated towards upgrading dry-season access roads versus the provision of road access to villages currently lacking any. The relative cost–benefit ratios suggest that resources should shift from the former towards the latter, in order to maximize the impact of infrastructure spending on poverty reduction and growth. If better data on the relative costs of the different types of road improvement were available, a more comprehensive and reliable cost–benefit analysis on this issue could be undertaken. This is a significant gap in the database that needs to be overcome in order to strengthen the cost–benefit analysis. Once this data limitation is overcome, future research should revisit the issue.

NOTES

1. The authors gratefully acknowledge the assistance of Arief Anshory Yusuf in conducting the model simulations reported in this chapter, and comments received from Sharad Bhandari, Peter Broch, Philippa Dee, Kumar Kandiah, Masahiro Kawai and Paul Vallely, without implicating them in the views expressed. This work was completed while Jayant Menon was at the Asian Development Bank Institute.
2. For comparison with these data, in 2002–03 urban households had poverty incidence of 23.64 per cent and poverty incidence for the whole of the Lao PDR population was 31.4 per cent.
3. The road connects Chong Mek on the Thai border to Veun Kham on the Cambodian border via Pakse in southern Lao PDR. The works comprised pavement rehabilitation, replacement of 32 bridges, improvement of feeder roads and spur roads, and periodic maintenance of key national and provincial roads in the Lao PDR. See ADB (2003) for more details.
4. For a useful discussion on the computation of VOCs, and the relationship with the IRI, see Archondo-Callao (1999).
5. The reductions in VOC are generally consistent with other estimates for Lao PDR. World Bank (2005: table 4) reports typical unit road user costs for these categories of vehicles for different values of the IRI. Assuming a reduction in the IRI from 16 to 2, the change in road user costs for cars is about 40 per cent, for light trucks 45 per cent, and for heavy trucks 46 per cent. The average reduction is then about 44 per cent, as compared to Champassak average of about 50 per cent.
6. The structure also draws on elements of a revised version of the ORANI model of the Australian economy called ORANI-G (Horridge, 2004).
7. Variations to this assumption are possible. For example, the possibility of unemployment can be introduced by varying the closure to make either real or nominal wages exogenous, thereby allowing the level of employment to be endogenously determined by demand.
8. As noted above, the '3' in LECS 3 signifies that it is the third (and currently the most recent) such survey to be conducted. The previous two (LECS 1 and 2) were for 1992–93 and 1997–98, respectively.
9. The population sizes of the 4 major categories are not the same, but *within* each of these 4 categories the population sizes of the 100 sub-categories are the same.

REFERENCES

Archondo-Callao, R. (1999), 'Roads Economic Decision Model (RED) for economic evaluation of low volume roads', *SSATP Note No. 18*, Washington, DC: World Bank.

Asian Development Bank (ADB) (2003), 'Champassak Road Improvement Project in the Lao People's Democratic Republic, Operations Evaluation Report', Asian Development Bank, Manila.

Asian Development Bank (ADB) (2005a), *Mekong Region Economic Overview: Economic and Social Impact of Projects*, Southeast Asia Regional Department, Asian Development Bank.

Asian Development Bank (ADB) (2005b), 'Road inventory, design, and construction cost estimates', in *GMS Infrastructure Connections in Northern Lao PDR*, TA No. 6913, ch. 4.

Dawson, J. and I. Barwell (1993), *Roads Are Not Enough: New Perspectives on Rural Transport Planning in Developing Countries*, London: Intermediate Technology Publications.

Dixon, P.B., B.R. Parmenter, J. Sutton and D.P. Vincent (1982), *ORANI: A Multisectoral Model of the Australian Economy*, Amsterdam: North-Holland.

Horridge, M. (2004), 'ORANI-G: a generic single-country computable general equilibrium model', Centre of Policy Studies, Monash University, Melbourne, available at www.monash.edu.au/policy/oranig.htm (accessed 6 October 2006).

Levy, H. (1996), 'Morocco: socioeconomic impact of rural roads. Impact evaluation report', Operations Evaluation Department, World Bank, Washington, DC.

Limao, N. and A.J. Venables (2001), 'Infrastructure, geographical disadvantage and transport costs', *World Bank Economic Review*, **15**, 451–79.

MCTPC (2003), *The Road Maintenance Procedures, Sub-procedure 10: District and Village Participation*, LRD/LSRSP2, Lao PDR: Department of Roads.

MCTPC (2004), *Five Years Maintenance Plan for Local Roads in Lao PDR for the Years 2004/5 to 2008/9*, LRD/LSRSP2, Lao PDR: Department of Roads.

Minten, B. and S. Kyle (1999), 'The effect of distance and road quality on food collection, marketing margin, and traders' wages: evidence from the former Zaire', *Journal of Development Economics*, **60**, 467–95.

Secretario, F.T., A. Asra and E.B. Suan (2005), 'Development of an input-output framework: an application to Savannakhet, Lao PDR', Economics and Research Department, Asian Development Bank.

Starkey, P. (2001), 'Promoting the use of intermediate means of transport – vehicle choice, potential barriers, and criteria for success', Module 4 – Rural Transport Services and Intermediate Means of Transport, London: DFID.

Starkey, P. (2006), 'The rapid assessment of rural transport services', draft final report prepared by Practical Action Consulting for Sub-Saharan Africa Transport Policy Program (SSATP), World Bank, Washington DC.

Warr, P. (2001), 'Welfare effects of an export tax: Thailand's rice premium', *American Journal of Agricultural Economics*, **83** (November), 903–20.

Warr, P. (2005), 'Food policy and poverty in Indonesia: a general equilibrium analysis', *Australian Journal of Agricultural and Resource Economics*, **49** (December), 429–51.

World Bank (2001), *Lao People's Democratic Republic Road Maintenance Project*, Report No. 1773-LA, Transport Sector Unit, East Asia and Pacific Region, 31 January.

World Bank (2005), *Lao People's Democratic Republic Road Maintenance Project*, Implementation Completion Report No. 32642-LA, Transport Sector Unit, East Asia and Pacific Region, 30 June.

APPENDIX

Table 6A.1   The LaoGEM model: list of industries

Crops	1 CROPS
Livestock and poultry	2 LVSTK
Forestry and logging	3 FOREST
Mining and quarrying	4 MINING
Food, beverage and tobacco	5 FOOD
Textiles, garments and leather products	6 TEXTILE
Wood and paper products; printing/publishing	7 WOOD
Petroleum and chemical products	8 PETROLEUM
Non-metallic mineral products	9 MINERAL
Metal products, machinery, equipment, spare parts	10 METAL
Other manufactured goods	11 OTHMAN
Electricity and water supply	12 ELECWAT
Construction	13 CONSTR
Transportation	14 TRANSP
Post and telecommunication	15 POSTEL
Wholesale and retail trade	16 TRADE
Banking, insurance, business services	17 BANK
Real estate and ownership of dwellings	18 ESTATE
Public administration	19 GOVT
Personal, social and community services	20 OTHSERV

Table 6A.2   The LaoGEM model: cost structure of domestic industries (million kip)

Industry	1 Intermediate domestic	2 Intermediate imported	3 Margin	4 Indirect tax	5 Labour	6 Capital	7 Land	8 Production tax	9 Total costs
1 CROPS	242 954	100 077	22 661	3 719	2 745 382	1 766 305	883 152	1	5 764 251
2 LVSTK	1 386 197	150 889	120 191	15 107	844 254	1 519 619	759 808	1	4 796 067
3 FOREST	20 760	13 988	4 861	1 359	241 079	199 710	99 855	1	581 613
4 MINING	416 239	1 430 354	219 600	24 821	31 996	35 120	17 560	1	2 175 692
5 FOOD	6 426 728	264 542	457 400	86 018	885 301	1 806 187	—	1	9 926 175
6 TEXTILE	116 471	56 690	21 104	1 870	64 003	134 604	—	1	394 744
7 WOOD	418 414	140 440	88 632	29 851	30 608	72 898	—	1	780 844
8 PETROLEUM	2 879	16 105	2 392	205	261	796	—	1	22 641
9 MINERAL	49 160	53 510	16 252	1 956	37 046	70 513	—	1	228 438
10 METAL	23 424	124 715	19 445	1 476	17 235	33 163	—	1	219 459
11 OTHMAN	11 879	114 847	18 745	907	43 859	118 104	—	1	308 343
12 ELECWAT	209 009	67 005	26 488	12 016	133 952	348 218	—	1	796 690
13 CONSTR	352 785	511 014	163 392	9 271	159 856	229 981	—	1	1 426 301
14 TRANSP	72 942	116 749	21 399	2 458	465 901	463 261	—	1	1 142 711
15 POSTEL	19 644	39 002	6 172	658	54 258	84 834	—	1	204 569
16 TRADE	171 540	242 173	56 453	7 797	563 077	1 073 985	—	1	2 115 025
17 BANK	31 194	2 839	7 887	986	12 295	133 455	—	1	188 656
18 ESTATE	43 086	609	1 220	1 278	87 633	391 718	—	1	525 546
19 GOVT	252 489	123 958	32 813	6 389	510 126	1	—	1	925 777
20 OTHSERV	330 197	826 517	177 493	12 534	192 129	316 125	—	1	1 854 996
Total	10 597 991	4 396 025	1 484 601	220 675	7 120 254	8 798 596	1 760 376	20	34 378 536

Note: Some column totals vary slightly due to rounding

141

Table 6A.3   The LaoGEM model: sales structure of domestic industries and commodities (million kip)

	1 Intermediate	2 Investment	3 Households	4 Export	5 Government	6 Stocks	7 Margins	8 Total sales	9 Imports
1 CROPS	2 754 562	488 542	2 190 597	330 549	0	1	0	5 764 251	224 806
2 LVSTK	4 087 407	647 224	28 763	32 670	0	1	0	4 796 067	0
3 FOREST	456 644	66 678	29 999	28 291	0	1	0	581 613	0
4 MINING	130	695	0	2 174 866	0	1	0	2 175 693	0
5 FOOD	984 019	717 400	8 217 420	7 334	2	1	0	9 926 176	372 004
6 TEXTILE	106 344	25 497	226 109	36 793	0	1	0	394 744	238 884
7 WOOD	35 259	1 423	5 496	738 665	0	1	0	780 844	117 941
8 PETROLEUM	12 919	1	1 132	8 589	0	−1	0	22 641	2 292 650
9 MINERAL	221 442	1	5 310	1 685	0	−1	0	228 438	0
10 METAL	142 370	40 577	24 751	11 759	0	1	0	219 459	2 324 624
11 OTHMAN	180 407	16 862	78 087	32 986	0	1	0	308 343	28 193
12 ELECWAT	625 640	1	171 050	0	0	−1	0	796 690	0
13 CONSTR	67 154	1 346 019	13 127	0	0	0	0	1 426 301	0
14 TRANSP	0	1	0	0	0	−1	1 142 711	1 142 711	132 988
15 POSTEL	122 301	1	82 267	0	0	−1	0	204 569	0
16 TRADE	124 399	13 657	73 446	0	1	1	1 903 522	2 115 025	0
17 BANK	180 052	1	8 604	0	0	−1	0	188 656	0
18 ESTATE	65 233	1	460 313	0	0	−1	0	525 546	0
19 GOVT	0	1	121 949	0	803 828	−1	0	925 777	0
20 OTHSERV	431 707	1	1 423 289	0	1	−1	0	1 854 996	0
Total	10 597 991	3 364 582	13 161 709	3 404 187	803 832	2	3 046 233	34 378 540	5 732 091

Note: Total vary slightly due to rounding.

142

7. Road infrastructure and regional economic integration: evidence from the Mekong[1]

Christopher Edmonds and Manabu Fujimura

I. INTRODUCTION

As developing economies become increasingly integrated with the global economy, the role of public goods that cross borders and bring benefits that would not materialize by domestic public goods alone grows in importance. There are a variety of transnational public goods, ranging from peacekeeping, environmental protection, prevention of infectious diseases, as well as basic research and development. Regional integration initiatives involving public goods aim to generate benefits that are shared by participating countries that cannot be obtained if countries act autonomously. The effort to integrate economies requires co-operation in many areas, particularly in transport infrastructure and trade policies – including reduced tariff and non-tariff barriers – harmonization of standards and rules such as product safety rules and customs procedures. A number of regional and international institutions have been working to promote regional integration and co-operation for decades.

The analytic approach applied in this chapter draws from two broad strands of recent economic literature. First, we consider the economic geography literature, which highlights the importance of geography in explaining patterns of trade and economic development. For example, this literature notes that economies suffering multiple geographical handicaps such as landlocked status, an absence of navigable rivers and lakes, or tropical or desert ecology, tend to be among the poorest in the world (for example, Radelet and Sachs, 1998; Redding and Venables, 2004). In the context of the Greater Mekong Subregion (GMS), the relative poverty of Lao PDR has long been understood as at least a partial result of the country's landlocked status and geographic characteristics. Second, one branch of recent trade literature has focused on trade and foreign direct investment (FDI) linkages in explaining patterns of trade and, ultimately, patterns of economic development. Empirical analyses in this area have found that multinational firms can gain from intra-firm trade by integrating production processes across economies with different comparative advantages. With such gains, tendencies towards production agglomeration are reduced, and if the advantages of production integration across economies outweigh those from agglomeration, then reductions in transport costs would make FDI complementary to trade. Many researchers suggest that East Asian economies have benefited from a virtuous cycle of increased trade, economic growth and FDI through the so-called 'trade-FDI nexus'.[2]

In this chapter, we focus on the role of cross-border road infrastructure for regional economic integration in the context of the GMS.[3] Cross-border road infrastructure can reduce costs of transport across countries and lead directly to increased regional trade. Reduced transport costs can also induce regional FDI by reducing transaction costs involved in intra-firm vertical integration. Increases in such FDI, in turn, can further increase regional trade. When realized, this defines a virtuous cycle of cross-border infrastructure development, trade, and investment that fosters higher economic growth. However, despite many initiatives for economic integration – such as those supported by Asian Development Bank (ADB) in the GMS – there has been a dearth of empirical investigation on the impact of regional integration efforts, including cross-border road infrastructure. This chapter attempts to fill this gap.

The next section of the chapter discusses conceptual framework and alternative approaches to the examination of the role of transport infrastructure for regional economic integration. Section III estimates the impact of cross-border road infrastructure development in the GMS on regional trade and FDI using gravity-type models. Section IV provides an illustration from a particular road project in GMS to provide a richer interpretation of econometric results and illustrate some of the intricate issues faced in conducting benefit–cost analysis of cross-border road investments. The chapter ends with some concluding remarks.

II.   CONCEPTUAL FRAMEWORK AND ALTERNATIVE ANALYTICAL APPROACHES

In analysing the role of transport infrastructure in fostering regional integration, we would first need to define a framework in which we trace the impact of transport infrastructure in the rest of the economy and across countries. Roland-Holst (2006) provides a useful categorization of three frameworks to be considered. The first category is what he calls 'Keynesian stimulus', which refers to the impact of public expenditure on transport infrastructure on local aggregate demand and employment. Public expenditure on transport infrastructure can be targeted on geographical regions where multiplier effects are largest. He refers to the second category as 'Ricardian stimulus', which refers to the impact of reduction in transport costs primarily on trade. This could be termed a 'trade costs' framework. We leave detailed discussions on trade costs to other chapters in this volume (for example, Khan and Weiss and De), but it is clear that the immediate effect of improved transport infrastructure on the supply side would be a reduction in transport costs, which, in turn, promotes trading activities within and across national boundaries. Improved transport infrastructure reduces trade cost margins both on export and import sides, and therefore intensifies comparative advantage of trading partners, as well as improves international terms of trade (inclusive of trade costs) for every trading partner. The third category is what he calls 'neoclassical stimulus', which refers to the dynamic impact of improved transport infrastructure on the economy's total factor productivity. This could be termed an 'endogenous growth' framework, as it attempts to capture dynamic growth impacts of infrastructure development.

After deciding on the conceptual framework, we then need to decide on the analytical approach. As with any other policy analysis, we are faced with a choice from a range of alternative analytical approaches, from those modelling at the disaggregate (for example, households) to aggregate (sector or economy) level, from strictly structured quantitative to more loosely structured qualitative analyses, and from approaches based on general-equilibrium versus partial-equilibrium analysis. There are three broad alternative modelling approaches to analyse the impact of transport infrastructure on the economies concerned and regional integration: (1) applied economy-wide simulation models (for example, computable general equilibrium – CGE – models); (2) econometric analysis of historical data on trade and economic integration; (3) detailed study of particular economic integration initiatives. Within the first category, a highly structured quantitative simulation such as use of cross-country dynamic CGE models offers an approach that can capture indirect effects of changes in infrastructure variables. To the extent that disaggregated data are available to calibrate the models, it also has the advantage of allowing varied degrees of disaggregation. However, data constraints in less developed economies (LDEs) can hinder development of disaggregated CGE models – particularly multi-country CGE models involving numerous LDEs. The second category includes econometric analyses on measures of regional integration as one of the explanatory variables and selected economic outcomes as dependent variables. When trade flow is the chosen dependent variable, gravity models offer a natural framework for such analysis. This approach is advantageous in terms of the flexibility it allows in model specification and the implied economic relationships and causality between the variables. A disadvantage of the econometric approach is that it offers a less complete economic structure wherein results may be difficult to interpret and results are influenced by the availability and measurement of data. The third category can involve a number of partial equilibrium modelling approaches that attempt to account for the impact of economic integration efforts, including benefit–cost analysis. This approach is advantageous in that its data requirements are relatively modest and it can capture disaggregate impacts of transport infrastructure. However, it has a clear disadvantage in terms of its ability to capture indirect impacts.

The choice of which analytical approach to use depends on the particular questions of interest and data availability. Among the three frameworks, our preferred framework (as indicated above) is the 'trade costs' framework because our interest focuses on the linkages between geography, transport cost and regional trade. In terms of the analytical approach, the CGE approach has been carried out in other chapters in this volume (Brooks and Zhai, and Menon and Warr) and in Roland-Holst (2006). Our interest and data constraint in this chapter leaves us with the choice of trade costs framework and the use of econometric analysis and benefit–cost analysis. The following two sections pursue each of the two approaches in turn.

III.   ECONOMETRIC ANALYSIS

Our interest in this chapter is focused on the impact of 'cross-border', as opposed to general domestic, road infrastructure in the GMS. Research questions addressed here include: (i) what is the empirical relationship between the level of development of cross-border road infrastructure, and trade and FDI flows between GMS economies, (2) what is the magnitude of the marginal effects on regional trade associated with cross-border road infrastructure development; and (3) has the development of cross-border road infrastructure been associated with increased FDI flows and, if so, to what extent can trade creation be attributed to increased FDI.

Estimation Models

Our analytical approach is adapted from Limao and Venables (2001) and applies a gravity-type model to predict bilateral trade and FDI flows for each pair of GMS economies. However, departing from Limao and Venables, we omit estimation of an explicit transport cost equation due to data limitations (to be discussed below). Instead, we proceed by using an instrument for transport costs (distance) and include this directly in our trade and FDI equations.[4] Also, departing from the existing empirical literature on the trade–FDI nexus, data limitations prevented us from estimating indirect impacts that come through trade and FDI.[5]

Following the empirical approach common to gravity models of trade, our base model for the trade equation uses two specifications:

$$X_{ijt} = A\, Y_{it}^{\alpha_E}\, Y_{jt}^{\alpha_M}\, H_i^{\beta_E}\, H_j^{\beta_M}\, N_{it}^{\gamma_E}\, N_{jt}^{\gamma_M}\, D_{ij}^{\theta}(\varepsilon_{ijt} u_{ij}) \tag{7.1}$$

or

$$X_{ijt} = A(\, Y_{it} Y_{jt})^{\alpha}\, (H_i H_j)^{\beta} (N_{it} N_{jt})^{\gamma}\, D_{ij}^{\theta}\, (\varepsilon_{ijt} u_{ij}) \tag{7.2}$$

where

X_{ijt} is exports from economy i to economy j in time t,
Y_{it}, Y_{jt} are the gross domestic products of economies i and j in year t,
II_i, II_j are the geographic sizes of economies i and j,
N_{it}, N_{jt} are the populations of economies i and j in year t,
D_{ij} is the distance between (the capitals of) economies i and j,
ε_{ijt} is the regular error term,
u_{ij} is an error component specific to economy-pair i-j,
A is a constant, and
E and M indicates exporter and importer country, respectively.

In logarithmic form, we have:

$$\ln X_{ijt} = \ln A + \alpha_E \ln Y_{it} + \alpha_M \ln Y_{jt} + \beta_E \ln H_i + \beta_M \ln H_j$$
$$+ \gamma_E \ln N_{it} + \gamma_M N_{jt} + \theta \ln D_{ij} + \ln \varepsilon_{ijt} + \ln u_{ij}, \tag{7.3}$$

or

$$\ln X_{ijt} = \ln A + \alpha\, (\ln Y_{it} + \ln Y_{jt}) + \beta(\ln H_i + \ln H_j) + \gamma(\ln N_{it} + \ln N_{jt})$$
$$+ \theta \ln D_{ij} + \ln \varepsilon_{ijt} + \ln u_{ij}, \tag{7.4}$$

with the following signs generally expected for the estimation parameters: α_E, α_M, α, β_E, β_M, $\beta > 0$ and γ_E, γ_M, γ, $\theta < 0$. (The FDI equation takes the same form and is not presented here to avoid repetition.)

The first specification (equations 7.1 and 7.3) takes a Cobb–Douglas form in which the influences of each trading partner's economic size, population and geographic area are estimated separately. The second specification (equations 7.2 and 7.4) enters the characteristics of economies i and j as products, following more closely the Newtonian form of the gravity equation. The advantage of the first specification is that it allows separate examination of the effects of variables between exporting and importing economies.[6] The second specification offers a more straightforward interpretation and has the additional advantage of reducing the number of estimation parameters, which is helpful when sample size is relatively limited as in our data set. Using these specifications as our base models, we add variables for road infrastructure and obtain estimates that control for other standard variables treated in the gravity model. Gravity models are often estimated with a few other variables to characterize the geographic characteristics and proximity of economies besides distance (for example, sharing land border, landlocked status, small island status) or cultural-historical ties (for example, shared language, dominance by common colonial power); however, these variables are not included in our estimates due to insufficient degrees of freedom in our small sample of GMS economies.

Before discussing the data-set used in our analysis, some comments regarding potential problems with endogeneity between trade flows and the other variables in the model seem warranted. Endogeneity between trade flows and GDP, and between overland trade flows and the quality of road infrastructure in the border areas, in particular, are of concern in this regard. With respect to the former, we note that the widespread use of GDP as a regressor in the vast gravity model literature. Moreover, we use a measure of major goods traded over land (to be explained later) in addition to total bilateral trade as our dependent variable, which would have only a limited endogeneity problem since major goods traded over land represents a smaller share of GDP. Were it the case that cross-border road infrastructure is developed in response to increased demand by traders, then endogeneity between trade and cross-border road infrastructure would be a problem. However, the significant lead time required before a planned road is constructed and is available for transporting goods supports treating the extent of road infrastructure as an exogenous variable.

Data

Our data-set tracks trade and other variables for each pair of GMS economies over the period of 1981 to 2003. In all, 30 economy pairs can be formed across the six GMS economies. Table 7.1 summarizes descriptive statistics from the data-set together with details on the data sources and definitions of variables. In Table 7.1, 'between n' reports the number of

Table 7.1 _Descriptive statistics from the data-set used in estimates_

Variable	Units	Number observations		Mean	Std. dev.	Minimum	Maximum	Sources and notes
Economy-pair Identification code	n.a	overall between within	N n T	690 30 23	353.5	170.6	102	605	1
Year	n.a.	overall between within	N n T	690 30 23	1992	6.6	1981	2003	
Trade and trade environment								
Economy _i_'s exports to economy _j_	mil. current US$	overall between within	N n T-bar	475 29 16.4	112.75	288.84	0.00	2853.60	2, 3, 4
Major exports from economy _i_ to _j_	mil. current US$	overall between within	N n T	171 11 15.5	74.71	125.43	0.04	845.01	5, 6
Weighted average tariff rate (WATR)	expressed in fraction	overall between within	N n T-bar	525 30 17.5	0.158	0.174	0.023	1.050	7, 8
FDI flows								
Economy _i_'s FDI inflow from economy _j_	mil. current US$	overall between within	N n T-bar	231 21 11	7.0569	13.677	−9.020	97.39	9

Table 7.1 (continued)

Variable	Units	Number observations		Mean	Std. dev.	Minimum	Maximum	Sources and notes
Distance and roads								
Distance between economy i and j	kilometre	overall	N 690	802.4	344.4	217.0	1519.0	10, 11
		between	n 30					
		within	T 23					
Economy i's road infrastructure in regions bordering economy j	km/km^2	overall	N 219	0.079	0.072	0.008	0.283	12
		between	n 19					
		within	T-bar 11.5					
Economy i's road infrastructure in interior regions	km/km^2	overall	N 345	0.078	0.073	0.009	0.299	12
		between	n 30					
		within	T-bar 11.5					
Economic characteristics								
GDP	bil. current US$	overall	N 570	26.05	42.11	0.60	181.50	7
		between	n 30					
		within	T-bar 19					
PPP ratio	relative real price level btw. economies	overall	N 292	1.140	0.619	0.235	4.254	13
		between	n 20					
		within	T-bar 14.6					

Other economy characteristics

Total population	number (mil.)	overall	N	570	229.00	429.00	3.62	1290.00	7
		between	n	30					
		within	T	19					
Land area	square km (thou.)	overall	N	570	1871	3341	177	9327	13
		between	n	30					
		within	T	19					

Sources and notes:

1. Numbers 1 to 6 are assigned to Cambodia, Laos, Myanmar, Thailand, Vietnam and Yunnan Province in that order. Code number 102 indicates 'Cambodia-to-Laos', 103 'Cambodia-to-Myanmar' and so on, and finally 605 'Yunnan-to-Vietnam'.
2. IMF *Direction of Trade Statistics* (2005).
3. Yunnan statistical yearbooks (various years).
4. Yunnan exports are specific to Yunnan Province.
5. UNCOMTRADE data from Statistics Canada's Trade Analyzer database (2005).
6. Up to five commodities (HS 4 digits) were selected relying on available information on border trades in the subregion.
7. ADB Key Indicators and statistical yearbooks of GMS members (various years).
8. WATR is calculated by dividing customs revenue by imports.
9. Data for Cambodia, Laos, Myanmar, and Vietnam are approved amounts by investment approving authorities, adjusted by estimated average implementation ratios and smoothed by 5-year moving average. Data for Thailand are 'net FDI inflows' recorded by the Bank of Thailand. Data for Yunnan Province are the 'actually utilized' amount recorded in the provincial statistical yearbooks. Investments in energy are excluded.
10. Oldfield (2004).
11. Distance between capital cities was chosen, except for cases of Cambodia–Vietnam and Thailand–Vietnam where Ho Chi Minh City is used in preference to Hanoi since it represents the largest Vietnamese city near the other two countries' capitals.
12. Separate sources were used for the countries. See note 8 in the text.
13. World Bank, *World Development Indicators* (2005).

reporting economy pairs (maximum 30), 'within T(-bar)' the number of data years (maximum 23 years) and 'overall N' the total number of observations (maximum $30 \times 23 = 690$). Owing to the relatively small number of GMS economies and limited number of years for which most data are available, missing data problems were widespread and created challenges in estimating our models. In this subsection we discuss details on data collection and the measures we used for key variables.

In addition to the trade and FDI equations, we ideally would have liked to estimate the 'transport cost' equation to examine the determinants of transport cost. However, gathering reliable measures for transport costs proved difficult. The first candidate for the transport cost measure was directly observed cost such as freight charges between major markets in the GMS. We were not able to find reasonable time-series data of this sort. Then we considered using a commonly employed proxy for transport costs: the ratio of cost, insurance and freight (CIF) and free on board (FOB) prices. The CIF/FOB ratio between two economies provides a proxy for average costs of transporting goods between them weighted by the value of the goods being traded. In the case of the GMS, however, collecting panel data for CIF/FOB proved impractical because: most GMS economies record export values in FOB only and import values in CIF only; and FOB import values reported in balance of payment statistics are available only at the economy-aggregate level, but not by individual trading partner. An alternative to finding FOB import values would be to assume the FOB export values equal the FOB import values for corresponding trade partners. However, analysis of these data revealed large discrepancies between the recorded values for exporters and those for corresponding importers. Owing to these data problems with transport costs, we opt to forgo the estimation of the effects of road infrastructure in two steps – first on transport costs, and then on trade (and FDI) flows – and instead estimate the determinants of trade (and FDI) flows in one step.

For trade flows, we employ two measures: one based on total bilateral trade reported in the IMF-DOTS database (except for Yunnan Province for which data are taken from Yunnan Statistical Yearbook) and the other based on 'major exports' transported via land or river. For the latter measure, the selection of the representative commodities relied on customs data available at selected international crossing points (including river ports) in the GMS. Up to five commodities defined at the four-digit level in the UN Harmonized System of Product Categories that are considered largely transported via land (or ferry, where river transport dominates) are identified and their export values reported in the UNCOMTRADE database are summed to form the measure of major exports via land. Use of this measure is preferred to the use of total bilateral trade because cross-border road infrastructure is expected to be more important in determining the volume of overland trade flows than that of total trade, which includes ocean-bound trade and is influenced by a greater variety of factors. However, the use of the preferred measure comes at the cost of data scarcity and some unavoidable subjectivity in the selection of major goods due to sketchiness of customs data at overland points of entry. Therefore, the use of the total bilateral trade would work as a check on the sensitivity of estimates depending on the choice of the trade measures despite the presumably weaker relationship between total trade and cross-border road infrastructure. A common issue concerning the trade data in the Mekong region is the problem of undocumented trade/smuggling. The limited evidence available regarding the magnitude of smuggling suggests that a significant portion of intra-GMS trade goes unrecorded by government officials, with a broad range of 30 to 50 per cent of the value of the recorded trade.[7] However, for the purpose of this chapter, we maintain that omission of the value of unrecorded trade is unlikely to significantly influence estimates due to our focus on international crossing points – as opposed to local border crossing points – in deriving the measure of cross-border road infrastructure.[8]

Finally, we construct two separate measures for road infrastructure based on road density in GMS economies: one characterizing road density in border areas and the other characterizing road density in non-border areas.[9] In our analysis 'cross-border road infrastructure' is represented by the density of paved roads in the provinces/states containing international crossing point(s) to the corresponding GMS pair. 'Domestic road infrastructure' is represented by the density of paved roads in the provinces/states that do not border any economy. Figure 7.1 displays the GMS road network and border crossing points referenced in our data-set. For example, cross-border road infrastructure for Cambodia as an exporter and Lao PDR as an importer is represented by the road density in Stung Treng Province of Cambodia and Champassack Province of Lao PDR, respectively. Similarly the domestic road infrastructure in this case is represented by road density of all the other provinces in these economies, respectively. Road density is calculated by dividing the total road length in border (non-border) provinces by the total area of the corresponding provinces or states, with adjustments in a few cases where disaggregated road inventory data are unavailable.[10]

Estimation Procedures

Estimates are carried out using estimators suitable for the panel structure of our data. Depending on the results of Hausman and Breusch-Pagan

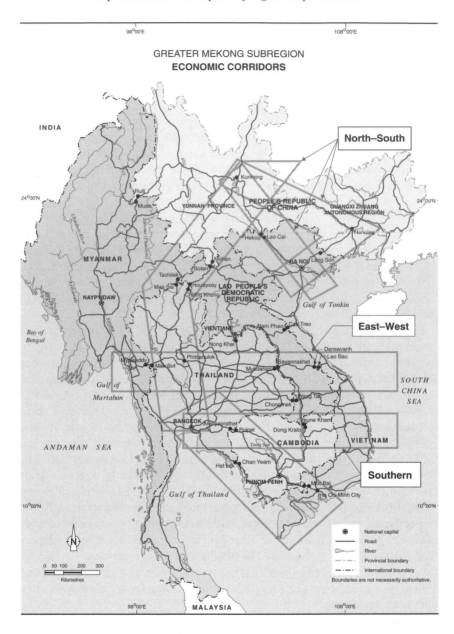

Source: Asian Development Bank (2006).

*Figure 7.1   Economic corridors, road networks and major border crossing
points in the GMS*

Lagrange Multiplier tests, either the random effects estimator or the robust ordinary least squares (OLS) estimator is applied. Robust OLS is the regular OLS estimator with a Huber-White correction, which takes into account the panel nature of the data in recalculating standard errors. The fixed effects estimator cannot be applied since key variables of concern (for example, distances, land areas) are fixed over time. The Hausman test indicates whether the fixed or random effects approach is appropriate by testing for omitted variables. A significant result from the Hausman test indicates that strong parametric assumptions of the random effects estimators are not met so this estimator is not suitable. In such cases, we use the robust OLS estimator despite its reduced efficiency. The Breusch-Pagan test evaluates the significance of random effects versus a regular OLS estimator by examining the statistical significance of economy-pair-specific error terms included in the random effects estimator. A significant result from the Breusch-Pagan test implies that the random effects estimator should be used.

Coefficient estimates in random effects estimation reflect a weighted average of the cross-sectional and time-series association between the dependent and independent variables included, with the weighting indicated by the estimation parameter rho. The statistical significance of coefficient estimates is tested using a z-test that is functionally equivalent to a standard t-test applied in OLS regression. The overall statistical significance of the estimation models is tested using the Wald chi-square test, which indicates the probability of a false rejection of the null hypotheses that the model has no explanatory power over the dependent variable. Finally, coefficient estimates in all estimation models can be interpreted as elasticities because they are estimated in logarithmic form.

Estimation Results

Table 7.2 presents estimation results on total exports between GMS economies. Seven variant specifications of the model are reported. They yield coefficient estimates that are largely consistent with expectations (for example, a negative association with distance and a positive association with economic size), and conform to gravity model results in several recent papers.[11] The overall results suggest that the gravity model approach provides a good basis upon which we can judge the marginal effect of additional variables on the level of trade. In particular, the coefficient estimates in Model 1 have the expected signs and significance, endorsing application of the gravity model to analyse trade flows in the GMS. In Model 2, cross-border road infrastructure is found to have a positive and statistically significant association with total exports on both the exporter's and

Table 7.2 Estimates of total exports between GMS countries

Estimated coefficient / Standard error of estimate / Coefficients	Total exports Model 1 (Robust OLS)	Total exports Model 2 (Robust OLS)	Total exports Model 3 (Rand.eff)	Total exports Model 4 (Robust OLS)	Total exports Model 5 (Robust OLS)	Total exports Model 6 (Robust OLS)	Total exports Model 7 (Robust OLS)
Intercept	6.778 5.665	13.488 8.229	16.663 12.363	7.311 10.200	−0.707 7.679	8.533 13.260	3.558 6.368
Distance between countries	−5.205*** 0.644	−1.052 1.108	−5.912*** 1.382	−2.471* 1.333		−2.465 1.504	−1.745** 0.667
GDP exporter [GDP exp.× GDP imp.]	1.620*** 0.179	0.839*** 0.247	1.097*** 0.302	2.145*** 0.626	1.081*** 0.259	1.204*** 0.255	0.328* 0.184
GDP importer	1.332*** 0.230			0.248 0.498			
Population exporter [Pop. exp.× Pop. imp.]	−1.327** 0.546	−0.684 0.635	−1.910** 0.797	−2.200* 1.189	−0.081 0.284	−0.896 0.563	−0.726 0.517
Population importer	−2.001*** 0.555			0.505 1.364			
Area exporter [Area exp.× Area imp.]	2.465*** 0.688	0.976 0.818	3.381*** 0.983	2.759** 1.263	0.574* 0.301	1.543** 0.681	1.367** 0.611
Area importer	3.663*** 0.701			0.260 1.269			
Cross-border roads exporter		1.705*** 0.344		0.150 0.844	0.698 0.539	0.131 0.630	
Cross-border roads importer		1.196*** 0.383		2.560*** 0.902	3.151*** 0.821	2.538*** 0.789	

	(1)	(2)	(3)	(4)	(5)	(6)	(7)
Domestic roads exporter			0.552	0.542	0.029	0.634	0.068
Domestic roads importer			0.419	0.956	0.482	0.615	0.340
Weighted average tariff rate importer			0.440	-1.921	-2.483***	-1.879***	-0.029
Value of FDI from exporter to importer			0.418	1.361	0.795	0.708	0.035
Value of FDI from importer to exporter						0.071	
Sigma_u			2.643				
Sigma_e			1.723				
Rho			0.702			0.561	
Number observations	392	156	222	131	131	128	146
Groups	29	18	26	14	14	14	16
Average years per group	13.5	8.7	8.5	9.4	9.4	9.1	9.1
R^2	0.509	0.541	0.444	0.632	0.596	0.617	0.282
F-test or Wald chi-square	20.39***	14.32***	51.10***	2954.57***	38.84***	26.80***	4.36***
Degrees of freedom	[7, 28]	[6, 17]	[6]	[12, 13]	[8, 13]	[10, 13]	[6, 15]
Hausman test	22.74**	28.34***	0.95	3.98/1	2.70***/1	9.51/1	4.70/1
Degrees of freedom	[4]	[4]	[4]	[9]	[7]	[8]	[4]
Breusch-Pagan test [1]	77.62***	24.98***	184.25***	4.23**	5.15**	3.95**	204.63***

Notes:
Statistical significance of the parameter estimates: *** 99%, ** 95% and * 90% confidence level, respectively.
Continuous variables in the models are estimated in natural logarithms.
/1 Matrix of differences between fixed and random effects variance estimates is not positive definite.

importer's sides of the border. According to this estimate, a 1 per cent increase in the stock of roads on each side of the border area are associated with 1.2 and 1.7 per cent increases in total trade for the importing and exporting economy, respectively. Model 3 adds measures of domestic road infrastructure, alone, to the base gravity model, and finds a positive but statistically insignificant association between total trade and domestic roads.

Models 4, 5 and 6 add both cross-border and domestic road infrastructure to the base gravity model estimates of total trade. Coefficient estimates for the importer's cross-border road infrastructure are all positive and statistically significant, and large in magnitude; however, those for the exporter's cross-border roads are positive but not statistically significant. In contrast, the importer's domestic roads are estimated to have a negative and statistically significant association with total trade in two of these models. Domestic road infrastructure in the exporting economies is estimated to have a positive but insignificant association with total level of trade. The magnitudes of the trade effects estimated for the importer's cross-border and domestic road infrastructure appear unreasonably large given the presumably smaller influence they would have on aggregate trade relative to their influence on major overland trade.[12] But the results could also be explained if our road measures were capturing broader policies determining trade orientation/openness. This would occur if economies more orientated towards foreign trade tended to make greater investments in cross-border infrastructure. If, as indicated by the results of Models 4 to 6, cross-border and domestic road infrastructure play non-complementary roles in promoting regional trade in the GMS, regional integration would require strategic shifts in road investments towards border areas.

Model 6 adds the average weighted tariff rate of the importer as an explanatory variable. This is found to not have a statistically significant effect on trade. Possible explanations for this are that tariff rates averaged across all goods and trading partners poorly reflect the tariff rates between particular GMS economies or that non-tariff barriers are of greater importance than tariff levels in determining trade. Model 7 adds bilateral FDI flows to the explanatory variables but finds no statistically significant relation with trade flows.[13]

Table 7.3 presents results for the determinants of the major exports over land between GMS economies, using eight variant specifications of the model. The coefficient estimates on the base variables of the gravity model, except for GDP, failed to yield expected signs and statistical significance consistently. The contrast between the results from estimates using total and major export measures could be due to the limited explanatory power of the gravity model for the latter (that is, major goods transported over land in the GMS) or to the much reduced sample available in the latter

Table 7.3 Estimates of major exports between GMS countries

Estimated coefficient / Standard error of estimate / Coefficients	Major exports Model 8 (Robust OLS)	Major exports Model 9 (Rand.eff)	Major exports Model 10 (Rand.eff)	Major exports Model 11 (Robust OLS)	Major exports Model 12 (Robust OLS)	Major exports Model 13 (Robust OLS)	Major exports Model 14 (Robust OLS)	Major exports Model 15 (Robust OLS)
Intercept	-7.724	2.378	1.273	11.006	1.483	22.255**	10.848	-3.718
	5.648	8.940	10.521	9.276	7.869	8.271	11.649	3.065
Distance between countries	3.410***	0.571	0.723	3.573**	5.210***	4.529***		-2.156
	1.078	1.241	1.504	1.403	1.304	1.006		2.994
GDP exporter (GDP exp.×)	0.231	0.323*	0.519***	0.170	0.236	-0.310	0.217	0.685
	0.219	0.195	0.136	0.206	0.212	0.285	0.301	0.142
GDP importer (GDP imp.)	0.639	0.715***						
	0.638	0.191						
Population exporter (Pop. exp.×)	1.055			0.818	1.186**	1.240*	0.869*	-0.937
	0.609			0.572	0.571	6.601	0.434	0.587
Population importer (Pop. imp.)	-0.143							
	1.669							
Area exporter (Area exp.×)	-1.389*			-1.948*	-2.591***	-3.121**	-1.141	1.906
	0.964			0.894	0.608	1.057	0.690	1.346
Area importer (Area imp.)	-0.316							
	2.193							
Cross-border roads exporter		1.087**	0.803***	1.357**	1.066**		3.402***	
		0.314	0.285	0.523	0.385		0.635	
Cross-border roads importer		0.635**	0.903***	1.210	0.800**		1.253	
		0.303	0.281	0.551	0.339		0.905	
Domestic roads exporter						1.006***	-1.744**	
						0.247	0.634	
Domestic roads importer						1.015***	-0.170	
						0.203	0.957	
Value of FDI from exporter to importer								-0.017
								0.017

Table 7.3 (continued)

Coefficients	Major exports Model 8 (Robust OLS)	Major exports Model 9 (Rand.eff.)	Major exports Model 10 (Rand.eff)	Major exports Model 11 (Robust OLS)	Major exports Model 12 (Robust OLS)	Major exports Model 13 (Robust OLS)	Major exports Model 14 (Robust OLS)	Major exports Model 15 (Robust OLS)
Value of FDI from importer to exporter								0.098
								0.010
Weighted average tariff rate importer					−0.335			
					0.366			
Sigma_u		0.977	1.266					
Sigma_e		0.485	0.488					
Rho		0.802	0.871					
Number of observations	169	78	78	78	78	102	78	70
Groups	11	9	9	9	9	11	9	8
Average years per group	15.4	8.7	8.7	8.7	8.7	9.3	8.7	8.8
$R^{2/1}$	0.470	0.589	0.487	0.717	0.741	0.667	0.725	0.684
F-test or Wald chi-square	11.79***	92.32***	90.32***	339.41***	420.5***	41.60***	296.46***	170.9
Degrees of freedom	[7, 10]	[5]	[4]	[6, 8]	[7, 8]	[6, 10]	[7, 8]	[6, 7]
Hausman test	42.71***	5.78	0.93	4.88/1	12.84*/1	−/2	5.89/1	24.46
Degrees of freedom	[4]	[5]	[4]	[4]	[5]	[4]	[6]	[4]
Breusch-Pagan Lagrange multiplier test [1]	260.79***	109.88***	129.50***	37.23***	30.96***	150.57***	14.25***	5.96

Notes:
Statistical significance of the parameter estimates: *** 99%, ** 95% and * 90% confidence level, respectively.
Continuous variables in the models are estimated in natural logarithms.
/1 Matrix of differences between fixed and random effects variance estimates is not positive definite.
/2 Model estimates fail to meet asymptotic assumptions of the Hausman test.

estimates. The distance variable shows either an insignificant or a positive influence on major exports, which is counter to the expectation from gravity model. Perhaps, distance between capitals is a poor indicator for the relevant distance in determining overland trade flows between GMS economies, which would be the case if overland trade tended to focus on markets besides the capital city (for example, regional markets closer to border areas).

When the cross-border road infrastructure variable is added separately to base variables of the gravity model (Models 9 through to 12), we find a positive and statistically significant association with trade levels for both the exporter's and the importer's sides of cross-border roads. Estimated trade elasticities with respect to cross-border roads range between 0.635 and 1.357. The coefficients are generally larger for the exporter's side (except in model 10), and relatively stable across the various model specifications estimated. The trade elasticities with respect to cross-border road infrastructure appear more reasonable in the major export estimates than in the estimate of total exports, which would follow from the expected closer relation between the road and the trade in goods selected based on their importance to overland movement, as opposed to total trade (which relies more heavily on sea shipment).

Model 13 shows that when our measure of domestic road infrastructure is added separately to the base gravity model, it alone has a significant positive association with the level of major exports – with an elasticity of about 1 for both the exporter and the importer. In parallel with our finding from the estimates of total trade, when both cross-border and domestic road infrastructure measures are included in the model (Model 14), we find that cross border roads have a positive and significant effect on major exports on the exporter's side of the border, but domestic roads in the exporting economy have negative and significant association with major exports. As discussed in reference to total export estimates, this implies that domestic road infrastructure – when separated from roads in frontier areas – mainly promotes the integration of domestic markets and diverts economic activities away from trade in major goods across GMS economies. Model 15 adds bilateral FDI flows to the base gravity model and suggests that importer-to-exporter FDI flow has a small (0.098) but statistically significant association with major exports, but that exporter-to-importer FDI flow has no significant effect. This provides some evidence of a positive trade–FDI nexus in which FDI contributes to export growth from the FDI-recipient economies, and would be consistent with the movement of export-oriented assembly and resource extraction activities.

Finally, we are also interested in examining the determinants of FDI flows between GMS economies – particularly the relationship between

FDI, trade flows and development of road infrastructure. In general, the gravity model we estimated performed poorly in explaining regional FDI flows, although, admittedly, our data-set on FDI flows was small. Few variables except GDP were found to have significant associations with FDI flows. Cross-border road infrastructure was estimated to have a positive but not statistically significant association with FDI in most models, while domestic road infrastructure was found to have a negative but again statistically insignificant association. Overall data limitation prevented us from making credible inferences about the impact of road infrastructure on FDI flows in the GMS (estimation results are not reported).

IV.   ISSUE OF BENEFIT–COST INCIDENCE: A CASE ILLUSTRATION

The above analysis provides evidence that cross-border road infrastructure has been associated with higher bilateral trade flows across the GMS economies. These would be expected to translate into positive economic benefits through forward (in the case of imports) and backward (in the case of exports) linkages to economies in the region. However, expected aggregate benefits associated with increased regional trade from the development of cross-border infrastructure are expected to be unequally distributed across involved countries. Provision of regional public goods such as cross-border roads is likely to require compensation and transfer schemes between involved countries in order to arrange financing agreeable to them. This is particularly likely in instances like the GMS, where the countries involved are disparate in economic size and in their level of economic development. The greater complexity of cross-border infrastructure projects, which require co-ordination between multiple bureaucracies, cost-sharing between affected countries and synchronizing project work across different countries and contractors, can make them riskier than projects based in a single country. Participating countries face different political and economic circumstances and cycles, and often have starkly contrasting abilities to negotiate and implement projects (Ferroni, 2002). The task of correctly accounting for the benefits and costs of cross-border infrastructure projects is also made correspondingly more difficult by these project characteristics.[14] Asymmetries in the benefit–cost incidence across countries must be delineated and addressed in the design and implementation of investments in cross-border transport infrastructure, such as those currently under way in the GMS.

The Northern Economic Corridor (NEC) Project is being implemented in Lao PDR under financing from the Thai and Chinese governments, and the ADB. The project, which is in an advanced stage of construction as this chapter was being written, runs 228 kilometres from the Thai border town of Houayxai to the Chinese border town of Boten in Lao PDR. (This route can be found as part of the North–South Economic Corridor in Figure 7.1.) Most of its expected benefits are anticipated to accrue to Thailand and Yunnan Province via enhanced trade between these two large economies, while relatively smaller trade impacts are expected for Lao PDR. On the other hand, many of the costs associated with the road's construction and operation will likely be borne by stakeholders in Laos. In this section we take up this particular project to illustrate disaggregate impacts of a cross-border road investment in GMS and implicit compensation mechanisms involved.

Conventional project appraisal used by the ADB was carried out for the NEC Project in 2002. Its economic benefits were calculated based on the direct savings in estimated vehicle operating costs (VOC) associated with normal (or existing) traffic, generated traffic and diverted traffic (from river). The appraisal did not attempt to quantify indirect benefits such as new investments and increased employment opportunities. The project costs considered consisted of: civil works, project management and supervision, resettlement costs, environmental management plans, administrative costs associated with the collection of road tolls, and recurring maintenance costs. Valuation of benefits and costs were based on an anticipated project life of 30 years and an ADB-standard rate of 12 per cent was used to discount them to the present values in 2002 prices. Following previous ADB-supported projects in Lao PDR, a standard conversion factor of 0.84 was used to convert the value of non-traded/market components to an equivalent value of traded/market components. The appraisal assumed workers for the road construction would be drawn from the project area and that the opportunity cost of labour for the project workers was equal to the prevailing local market wage rate (that is, that there was no surplus labour in the project area), therefore, there are no net direct benefits to labourers working on the project. The toll charge in Lao PDR used for the analysis is US$0.17 per kilometre, which is of the same order in both China and Thailand and considered not to deter traffic considerably. Table 7.4 illustrates the benefit–cost distribution analysis based on these assumptions.

While the analysis indicates an overall positive outcome of the project, a disproportionate share of the benefits from saved vehicle operating costs, particularly with diverted traffic, are projected to accrue to Thai and Chinese stakeholders. This follows from the fact that the road will improve the transport link between these two larger economies and the majority of the diverted traffic on the road is expected to involve stakeholders based in China and Thailand. There are two implicit compensation mechanisms assumed in the project arrangement that make up for the otherwise

Table 7.4 Economic analysis of the Northern Economic Corridor Project: an illustration (US million, in 2002 value)

Benefit/cost item	Net benefit	Lao PDR				Thailand				China			
		Private Businesses	Consumers	Labour[2]	Government/Rest of Economy[3]	Private Businesses	Consumers	Labour[2]	Government/Rest of Economy[3]	Private Businesses	Consumers	Labour[2]	Government/Rest of Economy[3]
Saved VOC[1]													
Normal traffic	40.10	6.66	9.05		6.23	13.26	0.95		0.78	1.42	0.97		0.78
Generated traffic	12.21	6.64	0.87		2.21	0.59	0.18		0.40	0.63	0.21		0.48
Diverted traffic	33.92					4.04	7.10		5.82	4.04	7.10		5.82
Transit fee	30.20				30.20								
Construction costs													
Labour	−7.30			−7.30									
Equipment	−20.80			−20.80									
Material	−13.50			−13.50									
Other	−10.40			−10.40									
O & M	−7.60			−7.60									
Finance[4]	0				34.60			−17.30				−17.30	

Net benefits	56.83	13.30	9.92	13.64	17.89	8.23	−10.30	6.09	8.28	−10.22
By country	56.83		36.86			15.82			4.15	
(Share %)	(100)		(64.90)			(27.80)			(7.30)	

Notes:

1. Savings on vehicle operation cost (VOC) are estimated based on projected traffic growth and the operating costs by vehicle type – various sizes of buses and trucks.
2. To the extent that the project labour is drawn from 'surplus' labour whose opportunity cost is lower than the paid wage rate, the project labour would have positive benefits. In this particular case, it was assumed that there exists no surplus labour.
3. This can be considered the residual stakeholders who cannot be particularly identified. It is considered here that the benefits and costs accruing to the government are eventually borne by taxpayers or the rest of the economy.
4. Without the knowledge of the loan terms, it is assumed that Thailand and China share an equal amount of financial transfer. The ADB also provides a concessional loan to the Lao government but the ADB's net benefit is not included in the table as it would not count towards economic criteria for project decision.

Source: Modified from ADB (2003: 4–66).

unfavourable distributional outcome for Lao PDR. The first is the transit fee to be collected by the Lao government from the road users, including those originating from Thailand and China. The second is the concessional loans (net financial transfer due to more favourable terms than the market-based loans) provided by Thai and Chinese governments to the Lao government – captured in the 'Finance' row in Table 7.4. These arrangements would counter potential unfavourable social and environmental effects (discussed below) that would mainly accrue to stakeholders in Lao PDR and help ensure a win-win outcome of the investment in the project road.

The conventional analysis illustrated so far is based only on direct impacts on vehicle operating costs and project investments costs and does not capture wider impacts through changes in trade (as we have seen in the previous section), investment, and tourist flows, nor the value of social and environmental effects. While these effects are difficult to predict or quantify, they could be more substantial than what the conventional analysis could capture, and therefore worth discussing qualitatively here in the context of the project road.[15]

In terms of expected increases in trade volumes due to the improved overland linkage, proximate beneficiaries would include Chaing Rai Province of Thailand, Bokeo and Louang Lamtha Provinces in Lao PDR, and Xishuangbanna and Simao districts of Yunnan Province. The improved overland route is also expected to increase supply capacity for raw materials (that is, timber, rubber and coal) produced along the route. Temperate crop producers (especially fruits and vegetables) in China and tropical crop producers (for example, fruits) in Thailand are expected to benefit from improved access to large urban markets in Thailand and China, respectively. Lastly, more distant manufacturing centres in coastal China and surrounding metropolitan Bangkok in Thailand would benefit to some extent from increased trade along the route.

Improved access to markets will likely enhance income prospects for households in the project area in a number of ways. Lower market transaction costs can be expected to facilitate the transformation of agricultural activity in the project area away from subsistence-oriented production and towards commercial agriculture. Households that derive a substantial portion of their income from agricultural or small-scale forest extraction activities – which describes the vast majority of households in the area – will be able to command higher net prices for their output. Changes in farm cropping patterns from ones based on rice destined for home consumption to production of higher value crops for market sale (for example, vegetables or fruits) will enable households to earn more – even through it may expose them to great income insecurity. From the perspective of consumers, the road will likely reduce the cost of most goods brought in from outside and could increase competition between traders. Prospects for non-agricultural income are also likely to improve. Off-farm employment opportunities in service sector activities, such as restaurants and transport services, are likely to be enhanced by the greater accessibility of the area. Investments in small-scale manufacturing facilities would also be induced. These would result in overall increases in non-agricultural economic activities in the area.

The project is likely to enhance tourism in northwestern Lao PDR, particularly in eco-tourism forest areas and traditional hill tribe communities as the road will make it easier for tourists to visit them and for enterprises to cheaply ship the materials and personnel needed to upgrade tourist facilities. The project area has been attracting an increasing number of foreign tourists who generally spend a few days trekking despite inadequate infrastructure and accommodations. The number of guesthouses and restaurants to meet the needs of visitors has grown significantly in the past few years.

Improved access to the towns and villages in the project area also holds promise of improving public service provision and improving governance in the area. It will be easier for the government and non-governmental organizations to establish public health and social service infrastructure and to staff public facilities (that is, recruitment of teachers and medical personnel may be made easier when non-residents know they can more easily visit urban areas due to the road), and could help to improve the quality and cost-effectiveness of various development assistance programmes targetted at Lao PDR's north-western provinces. Thus the overall vulnerability of the residents to external shocks along the project road will be reduced. Furthermore, greater entry of outsiders and news media may act to open up the area and facilitate reporting of corruption.

On the other hand, a number of environmental and social changes could result from the road that would adversely affect the welfare of households in the project area. First, the road could raise the value of land in the project area by making more profitable the cultivation of certain crops and raising value of land for non-agricultural uses. In the face of an immature land titling regime and unclear land tenure rights, rising land values threaten to cause displacement of tenure by poor households and to lead to a loss of household access to forest areas held as common (usually state) property as propertied private interests are attracted to opportunities in the area and seek to acquire available land. Loss of access to public forest land, in turn, could diminish the income prospects of poor households that depend upon the collection of materials from the forest for a sizeable portion of their subsistence or income.

Second, by raising income generating prospects in the area, the road may lead to higher income inequality as households with relative higher endowments of financial or human capital (usually households from the Lao

Loum majority ethnic group that live in the largest towns and villages in the project area).

Third, the road could induce further destruction of native forest areas by making large-scale extraction of timber and commercial cultivation of industrial tree crops (that is, rubber and oil palm) more profitable. Better road access due to the project may also lead to increased wildlife trade in the region. In anticipation of these effects, the Lao government introduced new policies of gradual phasing out of logging quotas in 2000 and the project mandates the establishment of three forestry checkpoints – one in each district – and strengthening local capacity to enhance detection of illegal logging. An increase in ecotourism activity that depends upon maintaining the quality of local flora and fauna might enhance incentives for local people to take the lead in environmental preservation efforts.

Fourth, the road could increase the risk of communicable diseases, particularly sexually transmitted diseases, as greater numbers of people transit through the area. The road could also lead to commercialization of traditional cultural practices of minority hill tribe communities under the aegis of cultural tourism. These negative social impacts can be counteracted by local residents' better access to public health and education services. Tourist interest in traditional culture can also act to raise respect for traditional culture and create economic incentives for preservation of traditional cultural practices and handicrafts.

V.   CONCLUSION

In this chapter we examined the role of road infrastructure for regional integration in the GMS. Among alternative analytical approaches, we first applied a gravity-type model to a panel data collected from the GMS to investigate the impact of cross-border and domestic road infrastructure on regional trade and FDI flows, and then applied a benefit–cost analysis to an ongoing specific cross-border road project to illuminate disaggregate impacts accruing to different stakeholders concerned.

The main findings from our econometric analysis were: (1) economy size appears to be a dominant driver of both trade and FDI; (2) the elasticity of trade in major exports likely to be transported over land between GMS economies with respect to developments in cross-border road infrastructure is estimated to be in the range of 0.6–1.4; (3) when the variable of domestic road infrastructure is included in the gravity model separately, we find a positive association between the two with an estimated elasticity of about 1.0; (4) when both variables of cross-border and domestic road infrastructure are included in the model, cross-border roads have a positive association and domestic roads have a negative association with trade flows (both major exports and total trade); and (5) barriers to trade captured by weighted average tariff rates failed to yield significant associations with trade flows, which may suggest a relatively greater impact of unmeasured non-tariff barriers.

Despite the severe data constraint we faced, our analysis shows that the development of cross-border road infrastructure in the GMS has had a discernible positive effect on the regional trade. The result that cross-border roads have distinct effects from domestic road infrastructure suggests promotion of regional trade may require deliberate policy shifts towards investments in roads in border areas. In this light, cross-border road infrastructure becomes an important part of a broader effort to encourage regional integration to benefit GMS economies that are less endowed with natural seaports such as Lao PDR.

While our research finds region-wide evidence on the positive impact of cross-border road infrastructure, it does not follow that all parties in the region will benefit equally from investments in cross-border roads. The incidence of benefits and costs of regional public goods must be considered in addition to aggregate benefits and costs. To investigate this issue, this research supplemented its country-level econometric analysis with a case illustration of benefit–cost distribution across stakeholders in China, Lao PDR and Thailand under the Northern Economic Corridor (NEC) Project. While direct benefits associated with reduced vehicle operating costs can be expected to accrue disproportionately to stakeholders in China and Thailand, there are compensation mechanisms that favour Lao PDR: transit fee revenues and inter-governmental transfer in the form of concessional loan finance. These mechanisms ensure that the outcome of the investment will be beneficial for all three economies concerned. However, there may be indirect effects not captured in traditional benefit–cost analysis. These include improved income generating opportunities due to increased trade and easier access to markets, enhanced tourism, and improved public service provision. On the negative side, there can be loss of access of the poor to forest resources and other common property resources as a result of heightened commercial land values, greater income inequality, more illegal logging and extraction of resources from the road area, and increased transmission of communicable diseases. More analysis is needed to consider these effects in projects involving infrastructure investments of a regional nature, such as the NEC Project, than for investments in domestic infrastructure.

NOTES

1. An earlier version of the chapter was presented at the LAEBA Third Annual Conference on 'Regional integration and regional cooperation in Asia and Latin America: the role of regional infrastructure' organized by the Asian Development Bank Institute (ADBI) and the Inter-American Development Bank (IDB), in Seoul on 16–17 November 2006. The authors thank financial support ADBI provided to the research behind this chapter. The views expressed here are the authors' alone and the usual caveats apply.
2. For example, see Kawai (2005) and Urata (2001).
3. Members of GMS are Cambodia, Lao PDR, Myanmar, Thailand, Vietnam and two southern provinces of China: Yunnan and Guanxi. Guanxi Province joined the GMS in 2005. Owing to scarcity of detailed data documented (for example, in Guanxi statistical yearbooks), particularly on transport infrastructure, empirical analyses in this research had to exclude data specific to Guanxi Province.
4. Distance variable represents distance between capital cities in each pair of the economies except that Ho Chi Minh City was used for Vietnam in relation to Bangkok and Phnom Penh.
5. The data-set used in this study features too few observations to permit simultaneous estimation of equations (trade and FDI) with a panel structure.
6. However, caution is warranted in interpreting results when asymmetric coefficients for exporting and importing economies are obtained, since these may to a considerable extent be driven by imbalance in the panel.
7. ADB (2004: 14).
8. A number of other points can be offered with respect to the issue of unmeasured trade within the GMS and its impact on our findings. Improvement in the availability and quality of roads at borders may reduce incentives for smuggling by increasing relative cost of transport via undocumented channels (by making transport via primary roads through international crossing relatively more cost-efficient vis-à-vis smuggler routes) and by capacitating customs enforcement. Also, to the extent that major international roads are used by smugglers, estimates of trade effects of cross-border road improvement will underestimate the true positive effect of the road on trade, so examining official trade figures would offer a conservative test of road improvement's influence on trade flows. Lastly, it is reasonable to assume that the economic incentives for smuggling of some goods between GMS economies have fallen over time as they have lowered tariff rates on many imports from their neighbours, which would be expected to reduce smuggling over time (other things being equal).
9. Data sources (and data years available) are: Committee for Development of Cambodia (CDC) for Cambodia (1995–2002), Department of Roads, Ministry of Communication, Transport, Post and Construction (MCTPC) for Lao PDR (1992–2003); Department of Highways, Ministry of Transport for Thailand (1994–2003); and transport section of statistical yearbooks for Myanmar (1984–1996), Vietnam (1993–2002) and Yunnan Province (1990–2002), respectively.
10. For Cambodia, road data by province were available only for 1995. This data was extrapolated to recent years based on the available data on total road length. For Thailand, road inventory data are not recorded by province but by the route of national highways that run through multiple provinces. Therefore, adjustment was made by the estimated provincial shares of road length of each highway based on the GIS-based *Road Inventory of ASEAN Highways* developed by UNESCAP (2004). For Vietnam, road inventory data was available for only 1994. This data was extrapolated based on the available administrative data on freight tonnage and distance carried. Justification for this treatment is that freight carriages reflect to some extent 'revealed' quality of roads that are used.
11. For example, our estimation results are broadly comparable to those reported in Frankel and Romer (1999), Soloaga and Winters (2001), Clarete et al. (2003), Rose (2004), and Yamarik and Ghosh (2005).

12. Given high covariance between available measures of domestic and cross-border road infrastructure, coefficient estimates that include both these variables must be interpreted with caution (that is, multicollinearity problem), which is why we present models that include the cross-border and domestic road variables separately. Unfortunately, no usable instruments for either of our road measures could be identified and other approaches to solving potential problems of multicollinearity between these two variables of interest proved impractical.
13. In addition to the explanatory variables discussed here, models estimates examined a number of variables (for example, dummy variables characterizing the export, import and foreign investment environment), but these were not found to have statistically significant effects on trade and FDI under various specification, and are not reported in this chapter.
14. A methodological framework for economic analysis of sub-regional projects such as Adhikari and Weiss (1999) has been available, but operational practice has been limited to date due to data constraints.
15. The following discussions reflect observations made by the authors during their brief field trip along the project route in 2005. A detailed field trip report was submitted to ADB Institute in December 2005.

REFERENCES

Adhikari, R. and J. Weiss (1999), 'Economic analysis of subregional projects', *EDRC Methodology Series*, No. 1, Asian Development Bank, March, Manila.

Asian Development Bank (ADB) (2003), 'Preparing the Northern Economic Corridor', consultant final report submitted to ADB, February, Manila.

Asian Development Bank (ADB) (2004), 'The Mekong Region: an economic overview', ADB, Manila, available at www.adb.org/Documents/Reports/MREO/default.asp.

Clarete, R., C. Edmonds and J.S. Wallack (2003), 'Asian regionalism and its effects on trade in the 1980s and 1990s', *Journal of Asian Economics*, **14**, 91–131.

Ferroni, M. (2002), 'Regional public goods in official development assistance', in M. Ferroni and A. Mody (eds), *International Public Goods: Incentives, Measurement, and Financing*, Dordrecht: Kluwer Academic, pp. 157–86.

Frankel, J. and D. Romer (1999), 'Does trade cause growth?', *American Economic Review*, **89** (3), 379–99.

International Monetary Fund (IMF) (2005), *Direction of Trade Statistics (DOTS)* (CD-ROM), IMF, Washington, DC.

Kawai, M. (2005), 'Trade and investment integration and cooperation in East Asia: empirical evidence and issues', in ADB (eds), *Asian Economic Cooperation and Integration*, Manila: ADB, pp. 161–93.

Limao, N. and A.J. Venables (2001), 'Infrastructure, geographical disadvantage, transport costs and trade', *World Bank Economic Review*, **15**, 451–79.

Oldfield, D.D. (2004), 'Border trade facilitation and logistics development in the GMS: component I – review of logistics development in GMS', report submitted to UNESCAP, Asia Policy Research Co. Ltd, UNESCAP, Bangkok.

Radelet, S. and J. Sachs (1998), 'Shipping costs, manufactured exports, and economic growth', paper presented at the 110th annual meeting of the American Economic Association, Chicago, Illinois, 3–5 January.

Redding, S. and A.J. Venables (2004), 'Economic geography and international inequality', *Journal of International Economics*, **62**, 53–82.

Roland-Holst, D. (2006), 'Infrastructure as a catalyst for regional integration, growth, and economic convergence: scenario analysis for Asia', *ERD Working Paper*, No. 91, ADB, Manila.

Rose, A.K. (2004), 'Do we really know that the WTO increases trade?' *American Economic Review*, **94**, 98–114.

Soloaga, I. and A. Winters (2001), 'Regionalism in the nineties: what effect on trade?', *North American Journal of Economics and Finance*, **12**, 1–29.

Statistics Canada (2005), *Trade Analyzer Database* (CD-ROM), Statistics Canada, Ottawa.

United Nations Economic and Social Committee for Asia-Pacific (UNESCAP) (2004), *Road Inventory of ASEAN Highways* (CD-ROM), UNESCAP, Bangkok.

Urata, S. (2001), 'Emergence of an FDI–trade nexus and economic growth in East Asia', in J.E. Stiglitz and S. Yusuf (eds), *Rethinking the East Asian Miracle*, Washington, DC: World Bank and Oxford University Press, pp. 409–59.

World Bank (2005), *World Development Indicators* (CD-ROM), World Bank, Washington, DC.

Yamarik, S. and S. Ghosh (2005), 'A sensitivity analysis of the gravity model', *The International Trade Journal*, **19**, 83–126.

8. Meeting the MDG water target in Asia: the role of regional co-operation[1]

P.B. Anand

I. INTRODUCTION

Access to water is a high-priority policy issue from both human development and human security perspectives. Lack of access to water and sanitation is an important characteristic of poverty. This has been recognized, for instance, in the construction of Human Poverty Index. Improving access to water and sanitation has a significant influence on decreasing the disease burden due to diarrhoeal and other water-related health risks and on improving overall quality of life. In recognition of these factors, the Millennium Development Goals include the aspiration to reduce by half the proportion of population without access to water and sanitation by 2015.

According to the World Health Organization and United Nations Children's Fund (2004) assessment, globally, 77 per cent of the population had access to water in 1990. This proportion has increased to 83 per cent in 2002, thus, is on track to achieve the target of halving the proportion of population without safe access by 2015. Much of this global increase comes from very significant improvement in access to water in India and China. However, that report also notes that in 2002, two-thirds of the 1.1 billion people lacking access to an improved source of water were also in Asia. For example, among the six countries worldwide with the lowest proportion of population having access to water and sanitation in 2002, three countries[2] were in Asia. The Millennium Task Force (UNDP, 2005) report highlights a number of factors why it is important to pursue the water and sanitation targets. Other studies, notably, Hutton and Haller (2004) and Rijsberman (2004) argue that water and sanitation investments should be considered a priority from the economic point of view too because benefit–cost ratios are in excess of 2.0. The Asian Development Bank (2006) study focuses on progress with target 10 of the Millennium Development Goals (MDGs) in Asian countries and estimated the costs of three alternative policy packages based on packages and unit costs developed by Hutton and Haller.

II.   AIMS AND OBJECTIVES

Against this background, I would like to examine the following research questions:

1.   Based on progress between 1990 and 2002, which countries of the Asian region are likely to meet the water and sanitation targets of MDG7 and which countries are likely to miss these targets?
2.   What role has aid played in improving access between 1990 and 2002? And if the effectiveness remains at a similar level, what is the magnitude of aid required for water and sanitation sector in Asian region to achieve the MDG target 10?
3.   Which policy variables have a significant impact on improving access to water and sanitation? In particular, from the data available, what can we say about the role of technical infrastructure and 'hardware' in promoting access? For example, is there synergy between development of irrigation infrastructure and improving access to water and sanitation?
4.   Is there a role for international co-operation and regional strategies in promoting access to water? To a large extent, water supply and sanitation are matters of domestic policy in countries. However, in relation to international water resources, as the Helsinki Rules and Seoul Rules emphasize, co-operation between nations is crucial.
5.   What are the implications of these findings for both policy and further research? In particular, how can these findings help in improving targeting of water and sanitation investments to help achieve MDG target 10?

Data and Methodology

This study uses secondary data sources and published resources, namely, WHO-UNICEF (2004) Food and Agriculture Organization (FAO)-Aquastat, World Bank privatization database, OECD Credit Reporting System (CRS), and the Asian utilities data (McIntosh and Yniguez, 1997). For issues under items 1, 2 and 3 above, I will be mainly using such secondary data and regression analysis. With regard to issues under items 4 and 5 above, I would like to examine these briefly using case studies and identify issues for policy and further research.

III. WATER AND SANITATION IN ASIA AND THE PACIFIC

In a number of developing countries in Asia, over 80 per cent of the population has access to improved sources of water in 2002. The ADB (2006) study estimates that approximately 758 million people have gained access to improved sources of water in the region since 1990. Despite this progress, some 670 million people in the region were without access to water by 2002. With regard to sanitation, the ADB study noted that there had been little change between 1990 and 2002 in the proportion of the population with access to sanitation. Nearly 2 billion out of 2.6 billion people without sanitation worldwide were in the Asian region. Figure 8.1 summarizes the picture in 2002. Most of the Asian countries are to the right of 60 per cent coverage as far as water supply is concerned. However, access to sanitation remains a major challenge.

Another message from Figure 8.1 is that although there is synergy in access to water and sanitation, countries seem to consider these in sequence with a higher priority accorded to improving access to water in the first instance and after this has been achieved, then improving access to sanitation in the second instance.

There is a positive and significant relationship between income per capita and proportion of population with access to water and sanitation. This is evident from Figures 8.2 and 8.3.

Variation in the proportion of population with access to water or sanitation is determined significantly by per capita GDP. This so-called 'environmental Kuznets curve' explanation can lead to alarming policy recommendations. Does this mean that it is futile for countries to worry about access to water and sanitation? Are they better off focusing their energies in the pursuit of economic growth and let structural change take care of improving access? Does policy matter? Preliminary analysis suggests that while per capita GDP is significant, other policy variables may also be important. Among other things, GDP growth rate, population policy, aid per capita and (control of) corruption are important too.

With regard to water and sanitation, the starting point does matter and this means that it is a very big challenge for countries with little or limited water and sanitation infrastructure to begin with. Figure 8.4 captures this aspect. The proportion of population with access to water/sanitation in 1990 is measured along the horizontal access; the corresponding figure for 2002 is shown on the vertical access. There is an enormous backlog with regard to sanitation, particularly in South and Southeast Asia. Even in countries such as India, Pakistan and China which have made significant progress with regard to water, access to sanitation remains a major

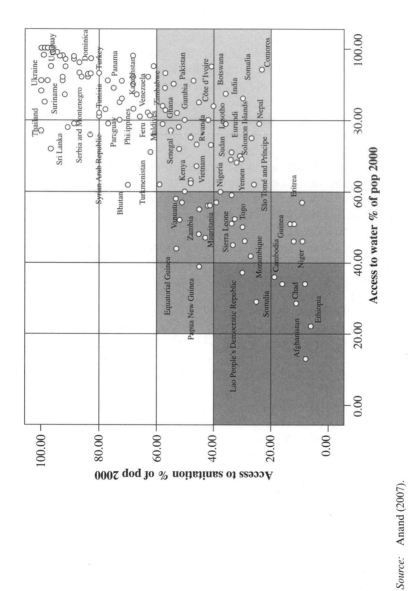

Source: Anand (2007).

Figure 8.1 Access to water and sanitation

176

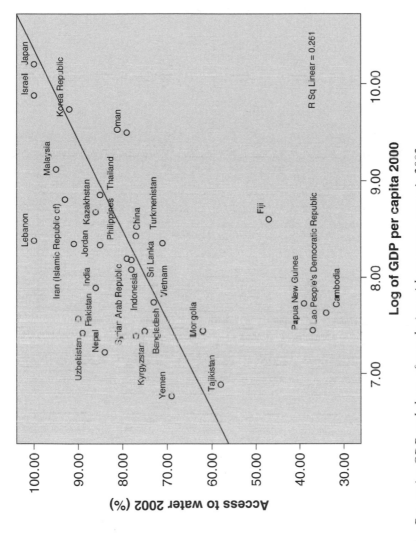

Figure 8.2   Per capita GDP and share of population with access to water in 2002

177

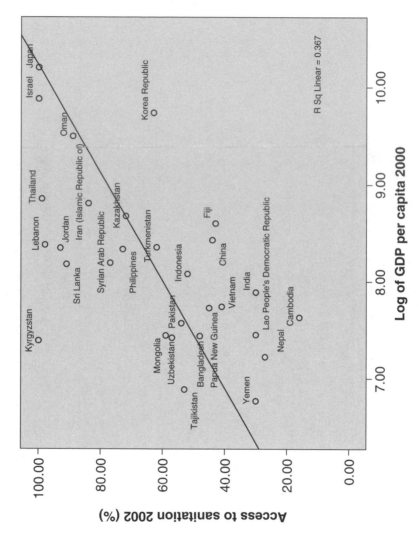

Figure 8.3   Per capita GDP and share of population with access to sanitation 2002

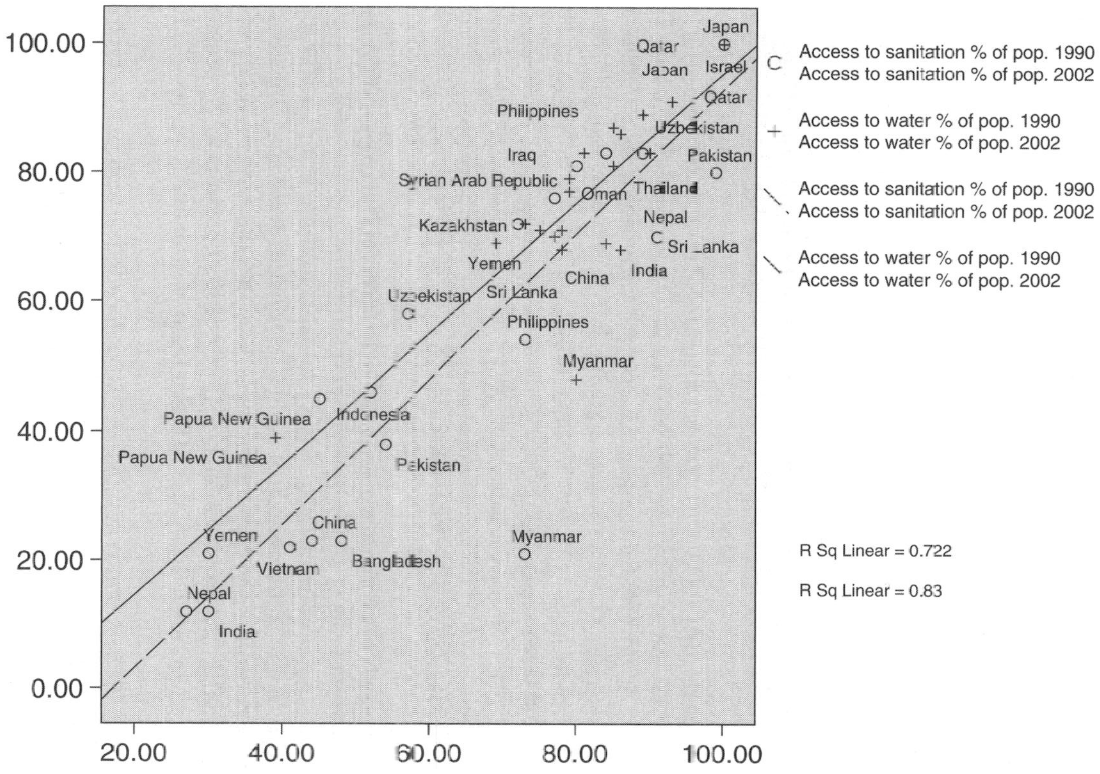
Access to sanitation % of pop. 1990
Access to sanitation % of pop. 2002
Access to water % of pop. 1990
Access to water % of pop. 2002
Access to sanitation % of pop. 1990
Access to sanitation % of pop. 2002
Access to water % of pop. 1990
Access to water % of pop. 2002
R Sq Linear = 0.722
R Sq Linear = 0.83
100.00
80.00
60.00
40.00
20.00
0.00
20.00
40.00
60.00
80.00
100.00
Japan
Qatar
Japan
Israel
Qatar
Philippines
Uzbekistan
Iraq
Pakistan
Syrian Arab Republic
Oman
Thailand
Kazakhstan
Nepal
Sri Lanka
Yemen
India
China
Uzbekistan
Sri Lanka
Philippines
Myanmar
Papua New Guinea
Indonesia
Papua New Guinea
Pakistan
China
Yemen
Myanmar
Vietnam
Bangladesh
Nepal
India

Figure 8.4 *Access to water and sanitation in 1990 v. access to water and sanitation in 2002*

challenge. The estimated fit lines also help explain why countries increase water access first before dealing with sanitation: the slopes of the two lines suggest that expanding access to water is easier than increasing access to sanitation.

Based on the discussion so far, Asian region countries seem to fall into one of three categories, namely:

- Group 1: countries with significantly high proportion of population (> 60 per cent) having access to both water and sanitation (for example, Sri Lanka, Thailand, Oman, Iran, Syria and Kazakhstan);
- Group 2: countries where access to water has improved significantly but access to sanitation remains low (for example, India, Pakistan, Vietnam and Nepal); and
- Group 3: countries where access to both water and sanitation remains low (for example, Lao, Cambodia and Afghanistan).

The policy priority for the first group of countries is to sustain the progress already made and continue to provide access with the goal of reaching 100 per cent. The priority for the second group of countries is to maintain the pace of increasing access to water but simultaneously give high priority to sanitation. The policy priority for the countries in third group is to pursue both of the targets as a high priority.

IV. FORECASTING PROGRESS

Based on regression models, it is possible to forecast the likely proportion of population to have access to water and sanitation in a number of countries and compare this with the MDG target. From the results so far, it is clear that a significant number of countries will miss the water target and a large proportion of developing countries will miss the sanitation target.

Non-availability of data is a major hurdle in forecasting progress with regard to target 10 of the MDGs. Data is available from the WHO-UNICEF joint monitoring programme for two points in time, namely, for 1990 and 2002. A small number of previous studies such as the interim assessment by Joint Monitoring Programme of the WHO-UNICEF (2004), UNDP (2005) and the ADB (2006) forecast progress based on the trend between 1990 and 2002. The basic methodology in these studies can be summarized as follows.

Let the proportion of population with access to water in country i at time $t1$ be w_{it1} and at time $t2$ be w_{it2}. Thus, the progress made between years $t1$ and $t2$ is:

$$dw = w_{it2} - w_{it1} \tag{8.1}$$

It is assumed that a similar level of progress will be made between $t2$ and $t3$ (as $t3 - t2 = t2 - t1$ and all other things remain the same). The proportion of population at the end of $t3$ is estimated as:

$$w_{it3} = w_{it2} + dw \tag{8.2}$$

The Millennium Development Goal target for this country is calculated on the basis of proportion of population lacking access to water in 2002.

$$MDG = 0.5*(100 - w_{it2}) \tag{8.3}$$

If the target is to be met, the country needs to achieve by 2015 ($t3$):

$$^{e}w_{it3} = w_{it2} + MDG \tag{8.4}$$

By comparing the estimated proportion of population with access, namely, w_{it3} with the target of $^{e}w_{it3}$, conclusions are drawn whether the target will be achieved or not.

My estimation procedure differs with regard to equation (8.2). Instead of simply adding dw to the figures related to 2002, I have used regression models. In the first instance, I try to estimate access to water in 2002 based on data for 1990 and other explanatory variables including per capita GDP, GDP growth rate, water resources per capita, health expenditure in GDP, population growth rate and so on for the years between 1990 and 2000. In these models,

$$w_{it2} = \alpha + \beta_1 w_{it1} + \beta_2 GDP_{it1} + \beta_3 GDPgrowth_{i,t1,t2} + \beta_4 HealthGDP_{it1} \ldots \tag{8.5}$$

Now, using the parameters from this model, the proportion of population with access to water in 2015 (w_{it3}) is estimated using relevant figures for other independent variables from the years 2000–04. This method captures the structural relationship between economic performance and improvement in access to water and sanitation better than the WHO-UNICEF method. Models W1, W2 and W3 relate to access to water; models S1 and S2 relate to access to sanitation. These regressions are reported in Tables 8A.1 and 8A.2 in the appendix to this chapter.

The forecast for Asia-Pacific countries based on models W2 and W3 with regard to water target is shown in Table 8.1. Similar results with regard to sanitation target are shown in Table 8.2.

Table 8.1 Forecast of progress with access to water, 2015, using regression models W2 and W3

Country	Access to water % of pop. 1990	Access to water % of pop. 2000	Addl % of population to be provided water to meet MDG (half of 100 minus wat2000)	MDG % of population with access to water in 2015 = Access in 2000 + ID Target	Projection 1 for 2015 based on model W1	Projection 2 for 2015 based on model W2	Gap (projection 1 minus MDG)
Saudi Arabia	90	—	—	—	—	97.62	—
Japan	100	100	0	100.0	98.46	—	−1.54
Israel	100	100	0	100.0	98.57	100.00	−1.43
Lebanon	100	100	0	100.0	—	89.18	—
Malaysia	—	95	2.5	97.5	99.25	93.57	1.75
Iran (Islamic Republic of)	91	93	3.5	96.5	95.60	90.25	−0.90
Korea Republic	—	92	4.0	96.0	93.38	100.00	−2.62
Jordan	98	91	4.5	95.5	91.83	85.86	−3.67
Pakistan	83	90	5.0	95.0	92.48	72.71	−2.52
Uzbekistan	89	89	5.5	94.5	90.52	69.15	−3.98
India	68	86	7.0	93.0	89.13	81.49	−3.87
Kazakhstan	86	86	7.0	93.0	89.49	—	−3.51
Thailand	81	85	7.5	92.5	90.16	92.01	−2.34
Philippines	87	85	7.5	92.5	90.58	82.25	−1.92
Nepal	69	84	8.0	92.0	88.90	69.08	−3.10
Syrian Arab Republic	79	79	10.5	89.5	—	82.29	—
Oman	77	79	10.5	89.5	—	97.83	—
Sri Lanka	68	78	11.0	89.0	83.37	100.00	−5.63
Indonesia	71	78	11.0	89.0	84.28	80.72	−4.72

Kyrgyzstan	—	77	11.5	88.5	82.03	65.65	−6.47
China	70	77	11.5	88.5	83.76	93.73	−4.74
Bangladesh	71	75	12.5	87.5	81.45	72.24	−6.05
Vietnam	72	73	13.5	86.5	80.48	79.66	−6.02
Turkmenistan	—	71	14.5	85.5	78.96	72.28	−6.54
Yemen	69	69	15.5	84.5	75.20	64.90	−9.30
Mongolia	62	62	19.0	81.0	72.75	69.79	−8.25
Tajikistan	—	58	21.0	79.0	68.25	78.90	−10.75
Lao People's Democratic Republic	—	37	31.5	68.5	53.95	70.37	−14.55
Cambodia	—	34	33.0	67.0	51.84	—	−15.16

Source: Author's calculations based on regression models.

Table 8.2   Forecast of progress with access to sanitation, 2015

Country	Access to sanitation % of pop. 1990	Access to sanitation % of pop. 2000	Addl. % of population to be provided sanitation to meet MDG (half of 100 minus san2000)	MDG target	Projection 1 for 2015 based on model S1	Projection 2 for 2015 based on model S2	Gap (projection 2 minus MDG)
Israel	100	100	0	100.0	100.00	98.82	−1.18
Japan	100	100	0	100.0	—	98.79	−1.21
Kyrgyzstan	—	100	0	100.0	100.00	97.70	−2.30
Thailand	80	99	0.5	99.5	100.00	100.00	0.50
Jordan	—	93	3.5	96.5	96.27	93.72	−2.78
Sri Lanka	70	91	4.5	95.5	99.12	97.27	1.77
Oman	83	89	5.5	94.5	—	94.68	0.18
Iran (Islamic Republic of)	83	84	8.0	92.0	89.51	88.60	−3.40
Iraq	81	80	10.0	90.0	—	80.86	−9.14
Syrian Arab Republic	76	77	11.5	88.5	—	86.13	−2.37
Philippines	54	73	13.5	86.5	83.49	82.40	−4.10
Myanmar	21	73	13.5	86.5	—	77.62	−8.88
Kazakhstan	72	72	14.0	86.0	77.48	77.57	−8.43
Bhutan	—	70	15.0	85.0	—	71.56	−13.44
Korea Republic	—	63	18.5	81.5	—	77.70	−3.80
Turkmenistan	—	62	19.0	81.0	66.75	66.63	−14.37
Mongolia	—	59	20.5	79.5	65.62	64.72	−14.78
Maldives	—	58	21.0	79.0	—	63.93	−15.07
Uzbekistan	58	57	21.5	78.5	67.37	65.63	−12.87
Pakistan	38	54	23.0	77.0	65.30	62.52	−14.48

Tajikistan	—	53	23.5	76.5	64.77	62.63	−13.87
Indonesia	46	52	24.0	76.0	69.07	67.58	−8.42
Bangladesh	23	43	26.0	74.0	63.32	61.09	−12.91
China	23	44	28.0	72.0	59.72	60.67	−11.33
Fiji	—	43	28.5	71.5	—	60.73	−10.77
Vietnam	22	41	29.5	70.5	61.40	60.02	−10.48
Timor-Leste	—	33	33.5	66.5	—	38.66	−27.84
India	12	30	35.0	65.0	46.63	46.03	−18.97
Lao People's Democratic Republic	—	30	35.0	65.0	47.40	44.86	−20.14
Yemen	21	30	35.0	65.0	47.08	43.45	−21.55
Nepal	12	27	36.5	63.5	45.81	44.11	−19.39
Cambodia	—	15	42.0	58.0	33.24	31.88	−26.12

Source: Author's calculations based on regression models.

From Table 8.1, it is clear that a number of countries will miss the water target; however, in most cases, the gap between what is likely to be achieved and the MDG target is less than 5 per cent of the population. The shortfall in terms of gap between the target and what is likely to be achieved is greater than 5 per cent for eight countries, namely, Bangladesh, Vietnam, Turkmenistan, Yemen, Mongolia, Tajikistan, Lao PDR and Cambodia.

The forecast with regard to the sanitation target presents a grim picture. The sanitation target is unlikely to be met in most of the countries in the Asia-Pacific region. In many countries, the gap between the estimated coverage and MDG target ranges from 10 to 25 per cent of the population.

Studies of benefits of water and sanitation improvements such as those by both Hutton and Haller (2004) and Rijsberman (2004) suggest that benefit–cost ratios for water and sanitation programmes lie in the region of 3 to 4.5. However, a significant share of such benefits is from the positive health impacts and reduced child mortality. The ADB study, however, indicates that convenience benefits are likely to form the major share of benefits of water and sanitation improvement programmes. The message from such studies is that to maximize benefits from water and sanitation programmes, it is essential that improvement takes place in all components of the package, namely, access to water, access to sanitation, and hygiene behaviour and awareness. The forecasts presented here suggest that while Asia region countries will continue to make a significant progress in improving access to water, full benefits in terms of health impacts may not be realized unless the sanitation target is also given a high priority.

V.   FINANCING WATER AND SANITATION IMPROVEMENT: THE ROLE OF AID

The benefits of water and sanitation improvements include private benefits which accrue mainly to the households gaining such access and public good benefits from health impacts, reduced morbidity and improvement in school attendance by children. While the two main domestic sources of water and sanitation sector investments are government funds and investment by consumers,[3] the two main international sources of finance throughout the 1990s were aid and loans. According to Rijsberman (2004: 511), 80–90 per cent of current funding in water and sanitation sector comes from domestic funding, much of this from the public sector. According to the Camdessus Panel report: 'In the mid-1990s the breakdown of financial sources was estimated to be: domestic public sector 65–70%, domestic private sector 5%, international donors 10–15% and international private companies 10–15%' (Winpenny, 2003: 6).

Water and sanitation sector portfolio during the period 1990–2001, based on data available from the Credit Reporting System of the OECD is presented in Appendix Table 8A.3. The CRS data pertains to commitments rather than actual disbursals. It is likely that the actual amount of investment based on disbursement is smaller than the figures indicated here. Throughout the period, approximately US$900 million to US$1 billion of aid was committed by donors to water and sanitation sector worldwide.[4] While the total amount of aid has remained more or less constant, the number of recipients increased from about 60 in the early 1990s to 100 towards the end of the decade. The average magnitude of aid given to a country has thus gradually decreased from about US$40 million to around US$30 million. Loan financing has increased significantly. It is important to note that aid has provided only a small segment of total investment in water and sanitation.

It can be seen from Figure 8.5 that the composition of financing changed in the mid-1990s when the volume of financing for water sector projects through loans increased substantially. At the beginning of the 1990s, water sector loans were approximately US$1000 million (and comparable to the total volume of aid). However, the volume of loans jumped to the highest value of nearly US$3000 million by 1996 but thereafter decreased. Asian region countries accounted for approximately US$313 million per annum of aid, approximately a third of all aid for water and sanitation sector worldwide.

Loans have been an important source of financing water and sanitation projects in Asia throughout the 1990s – of about US$1800 million per annum of water and sanitation sector loans worldwide, the Asian region accounted for approximately US$991 million. From Figure 8.5, it appears that there is no significant difference between global and Asian trends.

Recall the earlier categorization into groups 1, 2 and 3 in the previous section. Almost all group 1 countries (where a significantly high proportion of population has access to both water and sanitation) did not receive a high volume of aid during 1990–2001. Many group 2 countries did receive a significant volume of aid – it is plausible that aid was crucial in some of the countries in increasing coverage in terms of access to water. Some group 1 and group 3 countries are in the bottom-left quadrant in Figure 8.6 (low volume of aid/low volume of loans in 1990s). In Sri Lanka and Iran, the proportion of population with access to water and sanitation was already high in 1990. It seems that they were able to maintain this and increase coverage without external funds. The exception is Myanmar where the proportion of population with access to water and sanitation increased phenomenally during the 1990s with little aid or external loan financing.

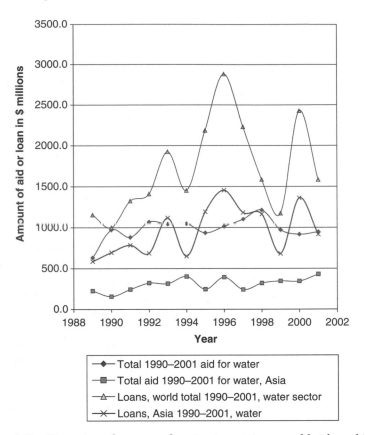

Figure 8.5   *Financing of water and sanitation projects worldwide and in Asia*

The main messages from Figure 8.6 seem to be that (a) aid may have played a role in the significant increase in access to water achieved by some countries; (b) if so, a similar strategy may be needed for countries in group 3 where the proportion of population with access to water and sanitation is presently very low; and (c) however, some of the countries that made very significant progress (group 1 and group 2) seemed to have depended on loans rather than aid. Loan financing suggests that in such countries, some extent of water charges or other payments from consumers may have been introduced to raise funds for repayment. Balancing between the goals of financial sustainability on the one hand and that of progressive charges for public services with some form of protection for the poor is a challenge. Aid can play a role in developing such protection mechanisms

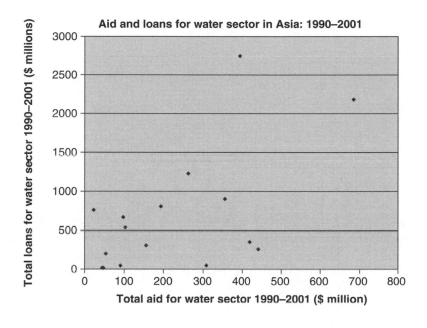

Volume of aid – low *Volume of loans – high*	*Volume of aid – high* *Volume of loans – high*
Malaysia, Thailand	India, China, Philippines, Indonesia, Vietnam, Jordan
(a) Sri Lanka, Pakistan, Nepal, Syria, Iran, Myanmar (b) Lao, Uzbekistan, Turkmenistan, Tajikistan, Bhutan *Volume of aid – low* *Volume of loans – low*	Bangladesh, Yemen *Volume of aid – high* *Volume of loans – low*

Figure 8.6   Aid–loan mix for water sector for countries in Asia, 1990–2001

while loan financing can focus on water sector reform and improving services on the basis of financial viability.

A caveat needs to be highlighted. While aid may be necessary, it appears that the relationship between aid and outcomes is complex. It appears from Figure 8.7 that for the period 1990–2002 the volume of aid does not determine the extent of change in the proportion of population with access to water or sanitation.

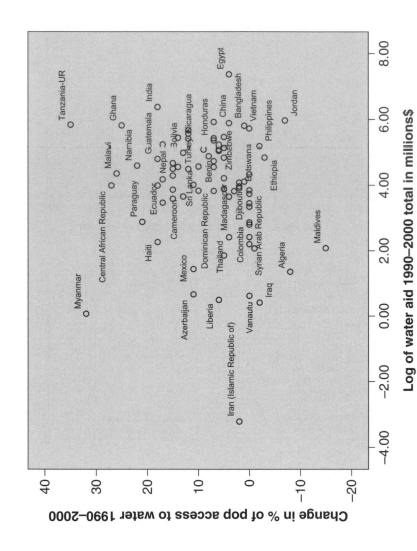

Figure 8.7   The extent of change in proportion of people with access to water and aid

VI. THE ROLE OF POLICY VARIABLES

From the analysis in section III, it was clear that (1) access to water and sanitation were highly correlated with per capita national income, and (2) that starting point matters – improving access is much harder for countries further away from the target where less than 50 per cent of population has access to the services. Here, the role of some of the policy variables is considered briefly.

Economic Growth

Does economic growth matter in increasing access to water and sanitation? There is considerable literature on the growth–poverty relationship. In regression model W3, it was seen that economic growth during 1990–2000 was significant and positively associated with proportion of population having access to water in 2000. Since both the dependent and independent variables are in percentages, the parameter is akin to elasticity. This seems to suggest that a 1 per cent increase in GDP per capita growth rate is likely to lead to an additional 1.3 per cent of population being provided with access to water. This suggests that sustained growth in combination with other factors can have an impact on achieving MDG target.

Inequality

Lack of access to water and sanitation is in itself an indicator of inequality in different countries. Therefore, an increase in the proportion of population with access to water and sanitation contributes to a reduction in an aspect of inequality. Though the parameter of Gini coefficient was not significant in many of the regressions, in most cases, it had a negative sign.

Social Sector Spending and Public Expenditure on Health

This variable was not significant in regressions related to access to water. However, it was highly significant and had a negative sign in some of the regressions related to access to sanitation. This is not surprising, given the link between lack of sanitation and child mortality rate (reported in Anand, 2006). Improving access to sanitation is likely to lead to a reduction in health impacts in terms of disease burden. Similarly, when only a few people have access to sanitation, high disease burden may lead to high health spending. This highlights the potential negative consequences of missing the sanitation target in most of the countries in Asian region and the urgent need to give a high priority to improving access to sanitation.

Privatization

In the previous section we saw that many of the high achievers in the Asia region used water sector loans rather than aid to increase access. In some countries in the region, privatization was a third route to increasing investment in infrastructure. Privatization of water utilities is likely to have played some role in increasing coverage in some countries, particularly in Southeast Asia. However, as compared to Latin America, the extent of privatization of water utilities in Asian region remains low. As per 1997 data (McIntosh and Yniguez, 1997), only two out of 50 water utilities in Asia were private concessions; in another 10 utilities the private sector was involved in water production. Some utilities use the private sector mainly for metering and billing. In countries where there is considerable inequality in access to water or where increasing access in cities requires transfer of water over long distances, privatization of water utilities tends to be opposed by some groups. If pursued at all, the privatization process needs to be managed with care so that the necessary covenants and institutional guarantees are in place to protect access for the poor. Private sector is more likely to be involved in terms of service contracts while overall management remains in the public domain.

Apart from privatization of the water sector, there is another route to mobilizing funds, namely, through privatization of infrastructure (other than water). Data reported in Table 8.3 suggests that it is likely that some of the increased government spending on water and sanitation sectors in countries in the region was made possible by the windfall incomes from privatization of other infrastructure (energy, telecommunications, ports). Although this variable is not included in the regressions reported in the appendix, in other models, it was noted that the parameter of the independent variable measuring the volume of proceeds from privatization of infrastructure was positive and significant (Anand, 2007).

Governance and Corruption

All other things remaining constant, corruption can inhibit performance of public services. This is likely to be the case in the water sector too. The data on the Corruption Perception Index (CPI) for various countries for the period 1995 onwards is available from Transparency International. The CPI is measured on a scale of 1 to 10, with 1 being most corrupt and 10 being least corrupt. From Figure 8.8 it can be seen that there is a positive

Table 8.3   Infrastructure privatization proceeds, 1990–2001

Region/country	Total infrastructure privatization proceeds 1990–2001 US$million	Proportion of population with access to water 1990	Proportion of population with access to water 2002	Proportion of population with access to sanitation 1990	Proportion of population with access to sanitation 2002
Latin America and Caribbean	107 844	83	89	69	75
East Asia and Pacific	32 076	72	78	24	45
Europe and Central Asia	24 863				
Middle East and North Africa	3 293	83	88	79	79
South Asia	3 104	71	84	20	37
Sub-Saharan Africa	2 978	49	58	32	37
China	19 143	70	77	23	44
Malaysia	6 751	—	95	96	—
Indonesia	4 688	71	78	46	52
Thailand	1 816	81	85	80	99
India	1 589	68	86	12	30
Pakistan	1 236	83	90	38	54
Philippines	973	87	85	54	73
Kazakhstan	779	86	86	72	72
Jordan	508	98	91	—	93
Oman	475	77	79	83	89
Sri Lanka	278	68	78	70	91
Fiji	2	—	—	98	98
Vietnam	1	72	73	22	41

Sources: Privatization proceeds from World Bank Privatization database; access to water and sanitation from WHO-UNICEF (2004).

correlation between the CPI score for 1990s and the proportion of population with access to water at the end of that decade.

Some water utilities in the region have taken steps towards increased
transparency. Performance indicators are displayed on websites of some
organizations, while a small number of utilities have issued 'citizen charters'.

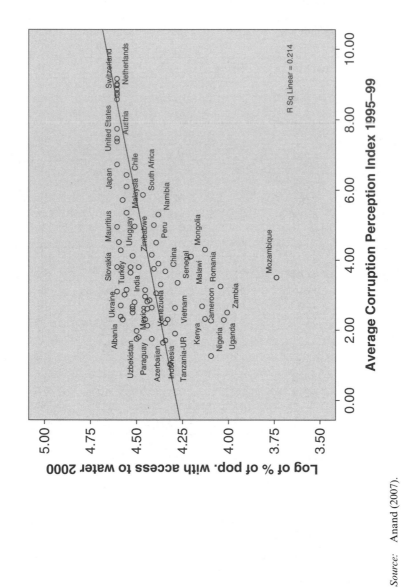

Source: Anand (2007).

Figure 8.8 Less corruption – more people have access to water

194

However, improving governance of water institutions remains an important issue at macro as well as micro levels. The data of 50 water utilities in Asia (McIntosh and Yniguez, 1997) shows an enormous variation for example in staff per 1000 connections (from 1.1 in Kuala Lumpur to over 500 in Ulaanbaatar).

An alternative route to improving accountability is the approach of 'right to water'. The General Comment 15 of the United Nations (issued in 2002) provides a broader interpretation of the concept of human right and dignity enshrined in the Universal Declaration on Human Rights and on this basis it is argued that a right to water emanates from a right to a life of dignity and health. South Africa has been at the forefront in implementing a right to water approach and some countries in sub-Saharan Africa and Latin America have also introduced provisions towards a right to water. It is early days but my preliminary assessment suggests that a right to water has not yet made a significant difference in increasing the proportion of the population with access in the countries where it has been introduced. A right to water is likely to be most effective in countries such as those in group 3 where a large proportion of the population does not have access to water, and in some countries in group 2 where a substantial majority already has access to water but extending coverage to the remaining population may pose challenges as almost all allocable water resources are committed.

Water Resources and 'Scarcity'

Some countries are better endowed than others in terms of water resources. In arid regions, all existing water resources may have already been committed to different uses/property right holders. Increasing the proportion of the population with access to water in such regions can trigger local level conflicts between rural and urban groups or between upstream and downstream users.[5] Where such water resources are internal, national level mechanisms may be needed. The issue can be even more challenging when the resource in question is international in scope. (This is examined in the following section.)

In general, in the regression analysis, it was observed that the proportion of population with access to water does not seem related to per capita annual renewable freshwater resources of the country. However, this may not fully reflect the reality. For example, in some Central Asian countries, the statistic of per capita freshwater resources would suggest that such countries have a lot of water resources. However, this is unequally distributed or accessing such water would require substantial investments (for example, due to mountainous terrain). In countries such as Pakistan and

India, the amount of freshwater available per capita in some arid regions is less than a third of the national level statistic.

Population

There are two dimensions to a relationship between population and the water and sanitation targets (which are defined in terms of reducing the proportion of population without access). The first dimension is of population size: increasing the proportion of population with access in a populous nation such as China, India, Bangladesh or Indonesia would require a significantly large level of resources as compared to a similar level of increase in the proportion of population with access to such services in a less populous nation. The second dimension is that of population growth rate: how fast we need to run to stand still. However, both these variables were not significant in the regressions.

VII. IMPLICATIONS AND PRIORITIES FOR REGIONAL CO-OPERATION

Water and sanitation improvements may seem to be the unlikely candidates for regional co-operation. However, from the discussion presented in this chapter, it appears that regional co-operation can make a significant contribution in helping countries achieve the MDG target.

1. *Priority groupings.* We have already seen that countries in the region seem to fall into one of three groups. There is some commonality but there is also difference in policy priorities for these three groups of countries. From the viewpoint of the region as a whole, there is an urgent need to focus on countries in group 3 (where the proportion of population without access is less than 50 per cent). Aid is likely to be more crucial than loan-financing for these countries.
2. *Creating a regional benchmarking system.* For countries in group 2 (where a significantly high proportion of the population has access to water but access to sanitation remains low and needs to be improved significantly), a regional benchmarking system is likely to be useful. While aid can have some role, loan-financing is likely to contribute to a major share of financing such a programme. At the same time, cost recovery and performance management remain major challenges to improving sanitation. A regional-level benchmarking system can help in comparing performance and identifying and sharing best practice. An example of such benchmarking is the ADB's work in the past

related to Asia's water utilities (McIntosh and Yniguez, 1997). What is being suggested here is much more than information dissemination, more akin to a network. For example, the analysis on corruption and access suggests that there is synergy between anti-corruption strategies and achievement of outcomes with regard to water and sanitation services. While much of the anti-corruption work focuses on judicial and regulatory reform, the implications for the water sector can be translated and discussed through policy briefs or conferences and publications by such a network. There is also a need for creating an information exchange with regard to approaches to promote accountability and participation, for example, through the use of instruments that can be used by water utilities (such as citizen charters or web portals) and through legal and universal instruments which can be used by the consumers (such as a right to information or a right to water).

3. *Facilitating co-operation for international water resources.* Many countries in the region share water resources. The most well-known cases are the Mekong River Commission (MRC) established by Cambodia, Lao PDR, Thailand and Vietnam (1995); the Indus Water Treaty between India and Pakistan (1959); the Ganga-Brahmaputra-Meghna accords (1996) between India and Bangladesh; the Jordan water-related treaties between Jordan, Israel and Occupied Palestine Territories (1995); and the Tigris-Euphrates-Shatt al Arab-related treaties between Syria and Turkey and between Iran and Iraq. There is some evidence to suggest that when two or more countries have a significant share of an international water resource, the proportion of population with access to water increases in countries with stable agreements for sharing of such waters than in countries without stable agreements. For this analysis, I used data available from the Oregon State University's basins at risk programme. These are preliminary findings. Pursuing the development of such treaties and water sharing institutions is likely to contribute to achieving MDG target in particular for Central Asian Countries (Aral Sea basin rivers), Afghanistan, Cambodia and Lao PDR (which are already party to the MRC). There is also another message from this analysis, to the effect that regional co-operation in the form of sharing of 'software', best practices and know-how is likely to maintain water and sanitation high on the policy agenda and promote convergence in outcomes.

4. *For some countries in group 2, and others in group 1, sustaining the significant progress that has already been made is the main issue.* Loan financing and privatization have been the main channels of financing water sector investments in such countries, and this is likely to be the case in the future too. A regional network for sharing best practice with regard to privatization, identifying thresholds only above which

privatization should be considered a policy mechanism, may be helpful for such countries.

The discussion here highlights the importance of creating a regional infrastructure of 'software' for promoting and sustaining water sector reforms in order to achieve MDG targets. Such networks are clubs that produce regional public goods (Anand, 2004b; Sandler, 1998). The design of incentive mechanisms is crucial for fostering and maintaining such clubs.

VIII.   LIMITATIONS AND ISSUES FOR FURTHER RESEARCH

The discussion in this chapter was based mainly on national-level aggregate data on access to water and sanitation. There are problems with the definition of access and there is considerable variation in access within each country – for example, between rural and urban settlements, within urban areas for those living in slums, and those living close to or far from perennial water resources such as rivers or lakes. Therefore it is important that the MDG target is taken both in letter and in spirit. Some of the relationships examined here may be indicating association due to endogeneity. Countries committed to good governance and reducing inequality tend to be less aid dependent and tend to give a high priority to social sector services such as water and sanitation. Therefore, the regressions should be seen as indicative of possible correlations rather than as definitive indicators of causality.

With regard to access, it is clear that definition of such access must be broad enough to include entitlements and opportunity to participate. Therefore, improving access to water and sanitation should not be seen only as a target for technical interventions in the form of pipelines or hard infrastructure but also in terms of the 'soft' infrastructure of collective action institutions to conserve and manage water and to promote well-being.

NOTES

1. The author is grateful to the ADBI for the opportunity, and to LAEBA workshop participants, and in particular to John Weiss and Jayant Menon for comments. The usual disclaimers apply.
2. Afghanistan, Cambodia, and Lao People's Democratic Republic.
3. In some Asian countries, where the public water supply is unreliable or unavailable, some individual consumers invest substantial sums in money-making alternative arrangements, such as in wells and tube-wells. Apart from investments to increase quantity, there is also

the issue of investments to improve the quality of water, such as UV filtration systems. While better-off consumers 'exit', the poor do not have the exit option. A detailed case study is reported in Anand (2007).

4. According to Camdessus Panel report (Winpenny, 2003: 23): 'The share of aid to water supply and sanitation in total ODA remained relatively stable in the 1990s at 6% of bilateral and 4–5% of multilateral ODA. In recent years, total aid allocations to the water sector have averaged about $3 billion a year. An additional $1–1.5 billion a year is allocated to the water sector in the form of non-concessional lending by the major MFIs.' The figures in CRS data are smaller as information for CRS classification is not available for all ODA projects.

5. See Anand (2004a) and (2007) on these.

REFERENCES

Anand, P.B. (2004a), 'Water and identity: an analysis of the Cauvery River dispute', BCID Research Paper number 3, Bradford Centre for International Development, University of Bradford, available at www.brad.ac.uk/acad/bcid/research/papers/Paper 3.pdf.

Anand, P.B. (2004b), 'Financing the provision of global public goods', *World Economy*, **27** (2), 215–37.

Anand, P.B. (2007), *Scarcity, Entitlements, and the Economics of Water in Developing Countries*, Cheltenham, UK and Northampton, MA, USA: Edward Elgar.

Anand, P.B. (2006), 'The Millennium Development Goal 7: an assessment of progress with respect to water and sanitation – legacy, synergy, complacency or policy?', WIDER Research Paper RP 1 of 2006, Helsinki: UNU/WIDER.

Asian Development Bank (ADB) (2006), *Asia Water Watch 2015: Are Countries in Asia on Track to Meet Target 10 of the Millennium Development Goals?*, Manila: Asian Development Bank.

Hutton, G. and L. Haller (2004), *Evaluation of the Costs and Benefits of Water and Sanitation Improvements at the Global Level*, Geneva: World Health Organization.

McIntosh, A. and C. Yniguez (1997), *Second Water Utilities Data Book: Asian and Pacific Region*, Manila: Asian Development Bank.

Rijsberman, F. (2004), 'Sanitation and access to clean water', in B. Lomburg (ed.), *Global Crises, Global Solutions*, Cambridge: Cambridge University Press, pp. 498–527.

Sandler, T. (1998), 'Global and regional public goods: a prognosis for collective action', *Fiscal Studies*, **19** (3), 221–47.

United Nations Development Programme (UNDP) (2005), 'Health, dignity, and development: what will it take?', UN Millennium Project Task Force on Water and Sanitation, London: Earthscan.

Winpenny, J. (2003), *Financing Water for All: Report of the World Panel on Financing Water Infrastructure*, chaired by Michael Camdessus, Washington, DC: World Water Council and Global Water Partnership.

World Health Organization and United Nations Children's Fund (WHO-UNICEF) (2004), *Meeting the MDG Drinking Water and Sanitation Target: A mid-term Assessment*, Geneva: WHO-UNICEF Joint Monitoring Programme.

APPENDIX

Regression Models Used for Forecasting

Table 8A.1   Regression models used for estimating access to water

Description of independent variable	Independent variable	Model W1		Model W2		Model W3	
		Parameter	Collinearity diagnostic	Parameter	Collinearity diagnostic	Parameter	Collinearity diagnostic
Constant		12.436 (0.687)		16.146*** (2.645)		−8.539 (−0.499)	
Access to water as % of population in 1990	WAT1990	0.579*** (6.341)	0.467	0.763*** (16.197)	0.646	—	
Annual population growth rate 1975–2000	POPGROW	1.670 (0.706)	0.443	—		−1.661 (−0.936)	0.669
Per capita GDP – average for 1997–1999 in US$ in 2000 prices	LogGDPCAP	2.131 (1.027)	0.473	—		12.310*** (6.877)	0.530
Per capita GDP growth rate 1990–2000	ECONGROW	0.676 (1.000)	0.579	—		1.365*** (2.567)	0.957
Health expenditure (public sector) as a share of GDP average for 1998–2000	HEALTH	1.010 (0.859)	0.453	−0.153 (−0.261)	0.698	0.119 (0.914)	0.643
Gini coefficient	GINI	−0.047 (−0.283)	0.374	0.123* (1.535)	0.817	—	

		Coefficient (t)	Tolerance	Coefficient (t)	Tolerance	Coefficient (t)	Tolerance
Aid as % of GDP in 1990	AID2GDP	−0.100 (−0.638)	0.696	—		—	
Malnourished people as % of population 1990	MALNURISH	−0.043 (−0.406)	0.725	—		—	
Fresh water resources available cubic metres per capita (Log)	LogWATRES	0.690 (0.783)	0.636	0.475 (0.403)	0.886	−1.126 (−1.338)	0.948
Adjusted R square		0.754		0.845		0.551	
F value		13.237 (0.000)		96.305		22.834	
Sample n		57		71		90	

Note: For models W1 and W2, the dependent variable is the proportion of population with access to water in 2002. Collinearity diagnostic, tolerance is the percentage of the variance in a given predictor that cannot be explained by the other predictors. When the tolerances are close to 0, there is high multicollinearity and the standard error of the regression coefficients will be inflated. Variance inflation factor was also estimated but not shown here. A rule of thumb is when the value of collinearity diagnostic is less than 0.5 (or VIF above 2) some degree of collinearity is present. In the above cases, all variables have VIF less than 2.

Table 8A.2 Results of multiple regression analysis: dependent variable is access to sanitation (% of population) in 2000

		Model S1		Model S2	
		Parameter	Collinearity diagnostic	Parameter	Collinearity diagnostic
Constant		38.573*** (4.180)		35.392*** (8.972)	
Access to sanitation as % of population in 1990	SAN1990	0.754*** (10.325)	0.282	0.731*** (16.373)	0.282
Population in 1990 in millions	POP1990	−0.00006 (−0.010)	0.615	—	—
Annual population growth rate 1975–2000	POPGROW	1.259 (0.495)	0.534	—	—
Per capita GDP – average for 1987–1989 in US$ in 2000 prices	LogGDPCAP	—		—	
Per capita GDP growth rate 1990–2000	ECONGROW	—		—	
Health expenditure (public sector) as a share of GDP average for 1998–2000	HEALTH	−1.974* (−1.947)	0.528	−1.543*** (2.645)	0.618
Gini coefficient	GINI	−0.103 (−0.792)	0.678	—	—
Aid as % of GDP in 1990	AID2GDP	0.091 (0.510)	0.651	—	—
Child mortality rate 1990	CMR	−0.103*** (−3.367)	0.361	−0.098*** (−5.698)	0.329
Adjusted R square		0.913		0.936	
F value		67.324 (0.000)		466.376 (0.000)	
Sample n		45		97	

Note: For For models S1 and S2, the dependent variable is the proportion of population with access to sanitation in 2002.

Table 8A.3 *Financing of water and sanitation sector in Asia, 1990–2001,*
            aid and loans

Country	Total water aid 1990–2001	Average aid per year	Water sector loans total 1990–2001	Average loan 1990–2001 per annum
Afghanistan	7.1	1.0	—	—
Bangladesh	419.6	35.0	348.7	58.1
Bhutan	15.9	2.3	—	—
Cambodia	—	—	50.9	25.4
China	394.2	32.8	2 745.1	228.8
India	684.4	57.0	2 181.2	181.8
Indonesia	262.3	21.9	1 227.2	102.3
Iraq	2.0	0.4	—	—
Israel	—	—	118.6	59.3
Jordan	441.5	44.1	256.3	28.5
Kazakstan	9.1	1.5	29.5	14.7
Kyrgyz Rep.	6.2	1.2	15.0	15.0
Laos	90.4	8.2	45.0	11.2
Lebanon	53.9	5.4	199.5	22.2
Malaysia	4.7	0.9	595.6	198.5
Maldives	8.1	2.0	—	—
Myanmar (Burma)	6.9	3.5	—	—
Nepal	156.0	13.0	304.8	50.8
Pakistan	97.5	8.9	667.6	83.4
Papua New Guinea	44.5	8.9	15.3	15.3
Philippines	193.6	16.1	805.6	100.7
Sri Lanka	102.7	8.6	536.7	48.8
Syria	47.6	7.9	13.6	13.6
Tajikistan	0.3	0.1	3.6	3.6
Thailand	22.9	2.3	759.6	126.6
Timor-Leste	17.0	4.2	—	—
Turkmenistan	1.4	0.3	—	—
Uzbekistan	11.6	2.3	19.2	9.6
Vietnam	355.6	29.6	901.2	100.1
Yemen	308.6	25.7	47.2	15.7
Total – Asia	3 765.4	313.8	11 892.1	991.0
Average – Asia	199.8	16.6	457.4	100.4
World total	12 112.1	1 009.3	21 175.3	1 764.6

Source: Author's calculations based on data from OECD-CRS.

9. Infrastructure financing: impacts on macroeconomic balances[1]

Douglas H. Brooks and Fan Zhai

The public sector is still the dominant source of infrastructure financing in developing countries, although public–private partnerships play an expanding role, as does foreign direct investment. Changes in technology have led to unbundling of services in the power sector and huge private investments in telecommunications, but most of the burden of ensuring an adequate level of infrastructure services to support growth and development still lies with the public sector. Even there, there are myriad combinations of revenue-raising, expenditure decentralization, financing mechanisms and risk management practices.

This can be seen most clearly in large, rapidly growing developing economies. Rapid growth has been accompanied by increasing urbanization, rising incomes in the growing urban middle class and a shift towards greater consumption of services. All this has led to strong demand growth for urban infrastructure, in particular.

This chapter compares and contrasts the recent experience of the People's Republic of China (PRC) with that of India in terms of infrastructure financing and resulting implications for macroeconomic growth. Similarities and differences are highlighted, and then each country is considered in more detail. A computable general equilibrium model is employed to examine the macroeconomic implications of alternative financing experiences. In particular, options of financing through a consumption tax, a labour income tax or through debt are considered. Differential macroeconomic impacts of these options are revealed as dependent on differences in economic structure in the base period.

There are key differences and special characteristics within individual infrastructure sectors or projects, but it is beyond the scope of this chapter to attempt to address those in detail. The quantitative analysis here looks at the macroeconomic impact of total public infrastructure investment, while much of the background discussion focuses on urban infrastructure as a leading, dynamic example to illustrate likely future developments.

I. COMPARISON OF INFRASTRUCTURE DELIVERY AND FINANCING BETWEEN THE PRC AND INDIA

The PRC and India are the two most populous countries in the world. They have many similarities in infrastructure financing, but also important differences, most notably the scale of investment. India's infrastructure spending is only about one-seventh of China's (Table 9.1). In 2005, total capital spending on electricity, railways, roads, airports, seaports and telecommunications was US$28 billion in India (3.6 per cent of GDP), compared with US$201 billion in China (9.0 per cent of GDP). While the PRC economy in 2002 was roughly two and a half times the size of India's, Beijing made 13.8 times the capital investment in infrastructure of Mumbai, an Indian city of roughly similar size (Mahadevia, 2006).

There is a high degree of fiscal decentralization in the PRC, associated with administrative decentralization. In India, the lowest levels of government do not have much taxation power. There is still greater centralization of the entire fiscal system, which then percolates down with local infrastructure provision becoming, to a great extent, state governments' responsibility. Both countries could benefit from greater legal, policy and contractual standardization in relation to infrastructure investments.

In both the PRC and India, the municipal government is an important entity in infrastructure provision and maintenance. While in the PRC infrastructure is constructed, operated and maintained by separate companies

Table 9.1   Infrastructure investment

(As of 2005/F2006)	India		China	
	US$ bn	% of GDP	US$ bn	% of GDP
Transport	10.9	1.4	95.7	4.3
Railways	3.5	0.4	15.2	0.7
Roads	5.8	0.7	67.1	3.0
Ports	1.2	0.2	9.7	0.4
Airports	0.4	0.1	3.7	0.2
Communication	8.1	1.0	19.0	0.9
Electricity	8.4	1.1	80.1	3.6
Urban Infrastructure	1.0	0.1	6.4	0.3
Total	28.4	3.6	201.2	9.0

Source: CEIC, Morgan Stanley Research, www.ibef.org/artdisplay.aspx?cat_id=349&art_id=11887.

Table 9.2   Infrastructure financing in India and China

	PRC	India
Decentralized revenue raising	Yes	No
Decentralized expenditure authority	Yes	In transition
Adequate retention of user fees	Yes	Questionable
Private sector involvement	Very little	Very little
Foreign investment allowed/encouraged	Yes, but difficult	Somewhat

set up by local governments, in India, it is the local government itself that carries out these functions through its own departments. As a consequence, cost recovery has been more efficient in the PRC than in India.

Private sector funds are not yet very important in infrastructure systems in the two countries in aggregate terms (Table 9.2), although they may occasionally contribute critical technology, project design or management skills. However, the potential remains enormous. For example, out of 483 private sector projects in the PRC's energy, telecommunications, transport, water and sewerage sectors that reached financial closure from 1990 to 2005, only four were in the telecomunications sector (PPI database).

Infrastructure Financing in the People's Republic of China

In recent decades, the PRC has to a significant extent devolved governmental authority from central to lower levels (including provinces, prefectures, counties, towns and townships). Local government units (LGUs) now have the authority to determine the structure of local expenditure and are responsible for the provision of local public goods. Partly as a consequence, 99 per cent of the population now has access to electricity and 77 per cent to an improved water source (PPI database).

In terms of fiscal decentralization, LGUs have relatively long-term (usually five-year) revenue-sharing contracts with higher-level governments and can keep a share of the revenue collected. In addition, LGUs are authorized to collect extra-budgetary funds not incorporated in the budgetary process. Since these extra-budgetary funds are entirely at the LGUs' expenditure discretion, they have become an important financing source for municipal infrastructure development.

In 1985 the Urban Maintenance and Construction Tax (UMCT), a systematic source for financing urban infrastructure investment, was launched nationwide. This tax for government services is collected as a surcharge on the consolidated industrial and commercial tax levied on the income of private enterprises, and therefore fluctuates with output levels. While full proceeds of the tax are retained by LGUs for local infrastructure development, the tax's share in total LGU revenue collection has declined from 26 per cent in 1991 to 10 per cent in 2002 (see Table 9.3). Consequently, non-tax methods of raising revenue started increasing in 2001 to supplement the UMCT (Mahadevia, 2006).

Another source of infrastructure financing has been domestic loans, primarily from the banking sector, which increased from 9 per cent of revenue for the Urban Maintenance and Construction Fund in 1991 to 28 per cent in 2002. Self-raised funds (for example, through a utility company's own efforts) increased from negligible amounts in 1991 to 19 per cent in 2002. Foreign investment in PRC infrastructure remains low (2 per cent in 2002) and is concentrated in the coastal areas.

Except for national-level cities and those qualifying for central assistance, all cities must rely on their own, and their provincial government's, finances for capital and maintenance expenditures on infrastructure and public utilities. In large cities, urban districts and sub-districts are responsible for local level infrastructure such as special development zones. Generally, for city-level infrastructure, a separate company is set up, which receives grants from the city government or borrows with city government guarantees.

Promotion of private investment in the PRC's infrastructure

The PRC has experimented with many models for private participation in infrastructure. Most infrastructure projects involving the private sector have been negotiated and implemented through joint ventures between private enterprises and governmental or quasi-governmental entities. Such arrangements raise concerns over conflicts of interest between the government's roles as regulator and as a project participant.

In accordance with the 1995 build, operate, transfer (BOT) circular, three pilot BOT projects were procured through competitive public bidding. Most of the resulting project companies were wholly foreign-owned enterprises, which helped to reduce potential conflicts of interest (Bellier and Zhou, 2003). However, the pilot BOT projects were not all judged to have satisfactory outcomes, and other arrangements are still being explored. Weaknesses in the PRC's legal and regulatory framework, with underdeveloped property rights and limited means of legal recourse, remain obstacles to broader private participation in infrastructure. The complicated approvals process is slow and redundant. Of even greater concern is the lack of transparency, which has led to inefficient investment at local levels, increased and misallocated financing risks and an inefficient pattern of infrastructure investments at the national level.

Table 9.3 Sources of urban infrastructure financing: China (*revenue for urban maintenance and construction fund in percentage*)

	Central financial allocation	Foreign investment	Self-raised funds by enterprises and institutions	Urban Maintenance and Construction Tax	Local financial allocation	Fees of utilities	Water fee	Domestic loan	Other revenues	Total
1991	3.8	4.0	0	26.1	10.4	10.1	1.3	8.6	35.6	100.0
2000	5.8	4.3	16.8	11.9	10.5	2.7	0.5	20.9	26.7	100.0
2001	3.5	2.2	16.2	10.7	12.8	1.9	0.4	29.4	22.7	100.0
2002	2.4	1.9	19.0	10.0	12.4	1.6	0.4	27.7	24.5	100.0

Source: Mahadevia (2006), based on Department of Finance and Ministry of Construction data.

Risk allocation remains inefficient in PRC infrastructure projects. Too often, private investors face legal and regulatory risks, government units face excessive commercial risks, and counterpart credit risk constrains private project financing. At the same time, constraints on the banking system mean that domestic banks play a limited role in financing infrastructure projects (Bellier and Zhou, 2003).

Infrastructure Financing in India

Public financing is more streamlined in India than in the PRC. India is a federation with constitutional demarcation of functions and taxation powers between central and state governments. Urban development in India, including urban housing and land and infrastructure development, is primarily the sole responsibility of state governments. They may pass on this responsibility to LGUs, in whole or in part, through state legislation. State governments set up parastatals to perform certain functions, such as water supply and sewerage boards, or public transport corporations. State governments may make capital investments and authorize the parastatals with partial cost recovery authority (Mahadevia, 2006). Some kinds of infrastructure that benefit broad or diffuse areas, such as airports and some railways, remain the responsibility of the central government.

Tax bases are assigned exclusively either to the centre or the states. Most broad-based and progressive taxes are assigned to the central government. States have the right to levy value added tax (VAT), and to authorize LGUs to collect certain taxes such as property tax or the Octroi.[2] The states are primarily responsible for ensuring the necessary legal and regulatory framework for private provision of urban infrastructure in India.

Although the major share of taxes collected goes to the central government in the first instance, state governments have the major share of expenditure responsibilities. The constitution provides for the sharing of revenue from personal income tax and VAT, while the states are given grants as additional assistance, together with some tax devolution as decided by the Finance Commission. Large cities may be able to access loans from various public sector, private sector and multilateral financial institutions. Municipal bonds debuted in 1997 and have spread in larger cities. Other localities may have to depend entirely on grants and soft loans from their state governments, although some innovative efforts at pooled financing show promise.

State Finance Commissions first decide on the proportions of state revenues to be distributed between rural local governments, and urban local governments, and then devolve state finances either on an ad hoc basis or according to a formula. There are also mechanisms for transfers between different government departments and access to financing windows such as the Rural Infrastructure Development Fund. The end result is that it is very difficult to get a coherent picture of the amounts going into public infrastructure development in the country as a whole.

Municipalities can charge for the services they deliver and can also charge for the use of municipalities' assets by private persons. Municipal authorities are empowered to borrow from banks and other financial institutions, and can raise funds in the capital markets, as per the provisions of the state municipalities' legislations. However, no uniform model of empowering or entrusting infrastructure functions to municipal bodies has emerged in India (Garg, 2005).

Underdeveloped pension and long-term debt markets have also restricted project finance. Lack of available debt with sufficient maturity has led to front-loading of tariffs to ensure debt repayment capacity, negatively influencing both users and project competitiveness (Secretariat for the Committee on Infrastructure, n.d.). To partially alleviate such problems, the India Infrastructure Finance Company was created to raise funds on the basis of government guarantees and provide financial assistance through long-term debt, primarily to private companies participating in public–private partnership projects.

There is thus an asymmetry between revenue sources and expenditure responsibilities. For example, over half of expenditures in 2002 were made by state governments, when they collected just 37 per cent of total revenue (Mahadevia, 2006). The states have commonly borrowed to supplement their expenditures and have consequently become faced with mounting debts and deficits, limiting their ability to increase their allocations for infrastructure projects.

While gross domestic savings remain roughly 25 per cent of GDP, the public sector continues to be a net dissaver. Consequently, infrastructure services such as telecommunications, where the private sector is very active, or banking, where there is a high degree of competition, are growing rapidly to meet the growth in demand. But services that are essentially provided by or through the public sector, such as water and sewerage, electricity and roads, are lagging in both quantity and quality (Garg, 2005).

Promotion of private investment in India's infrastructure
Since 1991, India has had a policy of attracting private investment into infrastructure. In 1997, the Infrastructure Development Finance Corporation Limited (IDFC) was incorporated as a specialized financial intermediary for infrastructure. The IDFC covers a wide range of infrastructure services, including energy, telecommunications and information

technology, integrated transportation, urban infrastructure, and health, education and tourism infrastructure. Through lead arranger mandates and key advisory assignments, the IDFC undertakes initiatives to rationalize policy and regulatory frameworks, and remove impediments to the movement of capital to infrastructure sectors.

Claims that the public sector must be responsible for infrastructure services to ensure access for the poor have been largely discredited by repeated failures to fulfil that ensured access. At the same time, projects involving private sector participation (including privatizations) have demonstrated significant efficiency gains (including in project design efficiency), enhanced quantity and quality of infrastructure services, and benefits for the poor (Mukhopadhyay, 2004). Fortunately, the rapid economic growth in recent years facilitates reform, as it both draws on and encourages private sector investment.

II. THE MODEL

This section describes the model used for simulating the macroeconomic effects of different infrastructure financing mechanisms. The model economy is populated by 72 overlapping generations with uncertain lifespans. The agents are rational, forward-looking and face no liquidity constraints. A representative, perfectively competitive private firm produces output using labour, private capital and public infrastructure capital. Installing new capital is assumed to be costly. Government owns public infrastructure and supplies it to firms for free. The economy is open to international trade of goods and services, but financially closed to international capital flows, implying the interest rate is determined by the domestic capital market. The supply of labour is elastic, reflecting the labour leisure choice of agents. The long-term steady state rate of output growth is exogenous at rate g, which is driven by labour-augmenting technological change and population growth. For notational simplicity, the time subscript t is omitted in what follows where doing so does not lead to confusion.

Households

The modelling of household behaviour follows the life-cycle approach. Agents are born at age 1 and live a maximum of 72 years, corresponding to adult ages 18 to 89. The probability of surviving between age j and age $j + 1$ is s_j. All agents have identical preferences over consumption and leisure that are given by the following utility function:

$$\sum_{j=1}^{72} \beta^j \left(\prod_{i=1}^{j} s_i \right) u(c_j, l_j) \tag{9.1}$$

where β is the subject discount rate. The period utility function $u(c_j, l_j)$ is of the constant relative risk aversion class with constant elasticity of substitution utility over consumption and leisure, where γ is the coefficient of relative risk aversion, $1/\gamma$ is the intertemporal elasticity of substitution, and ρ is intratemporal elasticity of substitution between consumption c_j and leisure l_j.

$$u(c_j, l_j, 1) = \frac{(c_j^{1-1/\rho} + \alpha l_j^{1-1/\rho})^{\frac{1-\gamma}{1-1/\rho}}}{(1-\gamma)} \tag{9.2}$$

The agent maximizes (9.1) subject to the following sequence of period budget constraints for each age $j = 1, \ldots, 72$:

$$PC \cdot c_j + (1+g)a_{j+1} = (1 - \tau_n)(e_j - l_j)\varepsilon_j w + t + (1+r)(a_j + b) \tag{9.3}$$

together with $0 \le l_j \le e_j$, $l_j = e_j$ if $j \ge 53$, $c_j \ge 0$ and $a_{j+1} \ge 0$ if $j = 72$. In the above budget constraint resources are derived from asset holdings a_j, labour endowment e_j, a lump-sum transfer t and an unintended bequest b. Assets pay an interest rate r. Labour receives a real wage $w \cdot \varepsilon_j$ and is taxed at rate τ_n, where the efficiency parameter ε_j reflects the skill difference across age. In the absence of annuity markets, assets of individuals who die in a given period are assumed to be distributed to all living individuals as lump sum transfer b. Expenditures in the left-hand side of (9.3) include the purchase of consumption goods and acquisition of assets for next period. PC is the tax-inclusive consumer price. There are no liquidity constraints, so the assets in (9.3) can be negative, although the terminal wealth must be non-negative if the agents survive up to terminal period ($j = 72$). Leisure may not exceed time endowment and may not be negative. In addition, agents are forced to retire at the age 53 (that is, the real age 70). The model calculates a shadow wage, which represents the excess over the efficient wage per unit of leisure forgone, to solve the problems of kinked budget constraints.[3]

Firms and Technology

Production technology is characterized by a Cobb-Douglas function with two private factors of production (aggregate labour L and private capital K_p) and public capital, K_g:

$$Y = AK_p^{\kappa}L^{\theta}K_g^{1-\kappa-\theta}\overline{K}_g^{\gamma}, \ 0 \leq \gamma < \theta < 1, \tag{9.4}$$

where Y is gross output and A is total factor productivity. κ and θ represent output share parameters of private capital and labour, respectively. Public capital generates a positive externality for private production, which is regulated by parameter γ. The condition $\gamma < \theta$ precludes the possibility of endogenous growth.

In each period, the firm decides on the intensities of labour input, taking as given the price of labour and the current stock of public and private capital, to minimize their cost. Thus, the firm employs factors according to marginal productivity rules.

$$R = \kappa AK_p^{\kappa-1}L^{\theta}K_g^{1-\kappa-\theta}\overline{K}_g^{\gamma} \tag{9.5}$$

$$w = \theta AK_p^{\kappa}L^{\theta-1}K_g^{1-\kappa-\theta}\overline{K}_g^{\gamma} \tag{9.6}$$

where R is the marginal product of private capital and w is the wage rate. As the production function exhibits decreasing returns to scale for private inputs, the firm earns an economic profit, Π, equal to the return to public capital.

$$\Pi = (1 - \kappa - \theta) \cdot Y \cdot P \tag{9.7}$$

where P is the price of the good.

The firm alters its private capital stock through investment I_p to maximize the value of the firm, V, defined as the present value of net cash flow. By assuming a quadratic and homogenous adjustment cost function, the investment expenditure J_p, can be defined as:

$$J_p = \left[1 + \frac{\psi}{2}\frac{I_p}{K_p}\right] \cdot I_p \cdot PA \tag{9.8}$$

where PA is the price of the composite good and reflects the replacement cost of capital. The dynamic optimization problem of firms leads to the following two arbitrage conditions: (i) marginal cost of new investment is equal to the shadow price of installed capital, that is, Tobin's q:

$$\partial(J_p)/\partial(I_p) = q, \text{ that is, } \frac{I_p}{K_p} = \frac{1}{\psi}\left(\frac{q}{PA} - 1\right) \tag{9.9}$$

and (ii) returns to financial and real investment are identical:

$$r_t q_{t-1} = (1 - \tau_k)\left(R_t + \frac{\Pi_t}{K_{p,t}}\right) + \tau_k \cdot \delta \cdot PA_t \qquad (9.10)$$

$$+ \frac{\psi}{2}\left(\frac{I_{p,t}}{K_{p,t}}\right)^2 \cdot PA_t + (1 - \delta)q_t - q_{t-1}$$

where δ is the depreciation rate of capital and τ_k is the corporate income tax rate. The right-hand side of (9.10) defines the total return to capital, including the after-tax marginal product and capital gains.

Government

The model specifies a general national government. At each period, the government purchases of goods and services, G, and public investment in infrastructure, J_g, are financed by tax revenue and debt issue, D. The government budget constraint in period t is:

$$G_t + J_g + t_t \cdot N + (1 + r_t)D_t = \tau_k(R_t - \delta \cdot PA_t)K_{p,t} + \tau_k\Pi_t + \tau_m M_t \qquad (9.11)$$
$$+ \tau_n w_t L_t + \tau_c PA_t (C_t + G_t) + (1 + g)D_{t+1}$$

The left-hand side of (9.11) represents uses of government revenue, where

$$N = \sum_{j=1}^{72} n_j$$

is the total number of the population. Government purchases, G, are assumed to be unproductive and generate no utility to households. Government revenue in the right-hand side of (9.11) includes corporate income tax, labour income tax, consumption tax, tariff revenue for imports M, and newly issued debt. Corporate income tax is levied on the profits of firms net of depreciation. By assuming a fixed world price of imports and choosing the exchange rate as numeraire, the import price is omitted in (9.11).

Public investment is also assumed to entail adjustment costs similar to (9.8).

$$J_g = \left[1 + \frac{\psi}{2}\frac{I_g}{K_g}\right] \cdot I_g \cdot PA \qquad (9.12)$$

The government also faces a no-Ponzi-game constraint, that is,

$$\lim_{T \to \infty}\left(D_T \bigg/ \prod_t^T (1 + r_t)\right) \leq 0,$$

implying that the present value of government expenditure must be less than or equal to the present value of revenue plus the initial stock of government debt. To ensure the intertemporal budget constraint holds, we fix the ratios of G and D to GDP throughout the transition period, and let the personal income tax rate or lump-sum transfer to households be endogenous to balance the period budget.

Foreign Trade

Demand is for composites of foreign and domestic goods. A CES function is utilized to specify the aggregation of composite goods, implying that products are differentiated by region of origin, that is, the Armington assumption (Armington, 1969).

$$C + G + (J_p + J_g)/PA = [(1 - \alpha^m)(Y - E)^{(\sigma-1)/\sigma} \qquad (9.13)$$
$$+ \alpha^m(M)^{(\sigma-1)/\sigma}]^{\sigma/(\sigma-1)}$$

where C denotes aggregate consumption and E denotes exports.

The corresponding price index PA is a combination of the price of imports (normalized to 1) and the producer price of the composite domestic good, P. It is specified as a unit cost function.

$$PA = [\alpha_m^\sigma + (1 - \alpha_m)^\sigma(P)^{1-\sigma}]^{1/(1-\sigma)} \qquad (9.14)$$

Export demand is in accordance with constant-elasticity demand curves, that is,

$$E = \eta \cdot P^{\sigma_e} \qquad (9.15)$$

Aggregation

Total consumption equals the sum of consumption by each cohort:

$$\sum_{j=1}^{72} c_j n_j = C \qquad (9.16)$$

Aggregate labour input is given by:

$$\sum_{j=1}^{72} \varepsilon_j (e_j - l_j)n_j = \sum_s L_s \qquad (9.17)$$

The clearing condition in the capital market requires that total national wealth, including total private wealth and government net wealth, equals the value of domestic firms plus net foreign assets F. F is determined by the exogenous current account balance, B.

$$\sum_r \sum_{j=1}^{72} a_{j,r} n_{j,r} - D = F + V \qquad (9.18)$$

Equilibrium

For a given government policy $\{G_t, D_t, J_{g,t}, \tau_n, \tau_k, \tau_m, \tau_c\}_{t=0}^\infty$, net foreign capital flows $\{B_t\}_{t=0}^\infty$ that ensure that net foreign assets F satisfy the no-Ponzi-game restriction, and $\{K_{p,0}, K_{g,0}, F_0\}$, the model's dynamic competitive equilibrium is the sequences of prices $\{w_t, r_t, R_t, q_t, P_t, PA_t, PC_t\}_{t=0}^\infty$ and allocations $\{b_t, c_t, l_t, L_t, K_{t+1}, Y_t, \Pi_t, C_t, J_{p,t}, I_{p,t}, I_{g,t}, E_t, M_t, V_t, F_{t+1}, t_t\}_{t=0}^\infty$ such that:

1. The allocation solves the dynamic programme (9.1)–(9.3) for all agents, given the prices and government policy.
2. The allocation satisfies (9.5)–(9.10) to maximize the profits of firms.
3. The allocation and government policy satisfy the government's budget constraint (9.11) given the prices.
4. M_t satisfies the first order conditions of the optimization problems of minimizing the costs of composite goods.
5. Capital and labour markets clear, that is (9.16) and (9.17) are satisfied.
6. Unintended bequests equal lump-sum transfers b.

III.   CALIBRATION

We implement the model separately for the PRC and India. The model parameters are determined through a dynamic calibration process, which finds a set of data to replicate the base year data and satisfies the intra-period and inter-temporal equations of the model. The dynamic calibration assumes the base year is on a temporal equilibrium along a dynamic adjustment path, rather than a stationary steady state, and therefore is more appropriate for fast-growing developing economies like the PRC and India.

The year of 2002 is chosen as the base year for the PRC. For India, the base year is 2003–04. The static benchmark equilibrium data are compiled from national account data and demographic statistics. Some

Table 9.4   Benchmark parameters of the model

		PRC	India
Extraneously specified parameters			
$1/\gamma$	Inter-temporal elasticity of substitution	0.330	0.330
ρ	Elasticity of substitution between consumption and leisure	0.800	0.800
γ	Externality parameter of public capital in production	0.000	0.000
$1-\kappa-\theta$	Share parameter of public capital in production	0.070	0.070
σ	Elasticity of substitution between imports and domestic goods	2.000	2.000
σ^e	Price elasticity of export demand	−6.000	−6.000
ψ	Capital adjustment cost parameter	2.000	2.000
δ	Depreciation rate	0.100	0.100
g	Long-term growth rate of effective labour	0.025	0.025
Endogenously calibrated parameters			
$(1-\beta)/\beta$	Long-term time preference rate	−0.048	−0.045
	Base year time preference rate	−0.107	−0.045
α	Utility weight on leisure	1.830	2.570
κ	Private capital share parameter in production	0.355	0.380
θ	Labour share parameter in production	0.575	0.550
τ_n	Labour income tax rate (%)	1.800	2.700
τ_k	Corporate income tax rate (%)	18.800	20.200
τ_c	Consumption tax rate (%)	41.500	11.000

parameters, mainly elasticities, need to be determined extraneously for model calibration. Most of these parameters are selected by drawing on a large number of empirical studies. Other parameters, like share parameters in production functions, tax rates and so on, are calibrated to replicate the base year data. Table 9.4 summarizes the major parameters in the model.

In calibration of the household sector, the inter-temporal substitution elasticity and intratemporal substitution elasticity between consumption and leisure need to be set. There has no been no empirical study trying to estimate these parameters for the PRC and India, while the international evidence on these parameters is controversial. We choose the value of 1/3 ($\gamma = 3$) in our model, which is close to the upper end of the range of empirical studies. The intra-temporal substitution elasticity between consumption and leisure is set at 0.8 in line with Auerbach and Kotlikoff (1987). The age-earning profile, ε_j, which is assumed to be hump-shaped, is also taken from Auerbach and Kotlikoff (1987). As the age-specific wealth distribution is not available, US data is used to approximate this distribution in the base year. All these parameters are assumed to be identical across the two countries.

For India, the household discount rate is endogenously determined in the model calibration to match the base year consumption. Given the high saving rate in the current PRC economy, we adopt a different method of calibrating the discount rate of PRC households. We assume that the long-run discount rate in the PRC is different from its base year level. The long-run discount rate is computed residually to generate a steady-state real interest rate of 3 per cent, a value that is close to the average value of real long-term interest rates in the OECD countries (Botman et al., 2006). The discount rates of all cohorts in the base year are endogenously determined in the model calibration to match the base year consumption in each region. We gradually lower the discount rates of successive cohorts so that the cohorts that reach adulthood in 2032 and thereafter have the long-run time preference rate. The different calibration approaches for household discount rates result in a higher long-term interest rate of 4.9 per cent in India, consistent with its lower saving rate. We set the relative parameter weights of leisure against consumption so that on average 40 per cent of available time endowment during work years are spent at work in base year.

The externality parameter of public capital γ is set to be zero, implying constant returns to scale for all inputs. This specification is the same as that used in Aschauer (1989), Cassou and Lassing (1998) and Canning and Pedroni (2004). It can be viewed as incorporating an implicit congestion effect associated with the scale of private capital. The empirical evidence for the value of output elasticity with respect to public capital, $1 - \kappa - \theta$, has been mixed. We choose a value of 0.07 which lies in the lower range of these estimates. This value is consistent with the recent cross-country estimates by Canning and Bennathan (2000).

The value of adjustment cost parameters is taken to be 2, which corresponds to the low end of some estimates, and implies that adjustment costs are 12.5 per cent of the value of gross investment in the steady state, under our assumptions on the depreciation rate and technical progress. The depreciation rate is assumed to be 10 per cent. The values of private and public capital stock in the two countries are estimated by means of the perpetual inventory method. The estimated private capital-output ratios are 1.83 for the PRC and 1.60 for India. The rest of the world elasticities of export demand are set at −6. The elasticities of substitution between imports and domestic goods, that is, the Armington elasticities, are set equal to 2.0.

In constructing the baseline scenario for model calibration, it is necessary to make some hypothetical assumptions on all exogenous variables for the period after the base year. The number of people newly entering into adulthood before 2050 is taken from the projection results of a separate demographic model. We assume that this number will be constant after 2050 and this results in the population being stationary after 2122 for the PRC and 2123 for India.

The GDP growth rate, which is exogenous in dynamic calibration, is assumed to decline from 8 to 2.5 per cent from the base year to 2050, and be stable at 2.5 per cent afterwards. We introduce two types of labour-augmented technical progress in this model. The first type of technical progress follows the definition in Altig et al. (2001), that is, the technical progress is assumed to cause the time endowment of each successive generation to grow at a constant rate, namely, 2.5 per cent in our model. The second type of technical progress is the standard assumption of labour-augmented technical progress, which entails multiplying the labour input by a factor that grows through time. The rate of the second type of technical progress is endogenously adjusted to match the pre-specified GDP growth rate.

All tax rates, which are calibrated from base year data, are held constant over the baseline. The government debt as a fraction of GDP is kept constant at the baseline level and the lump-sum transfers from government to households in each period after the base year are endogenous to maintain the government budget constraint. Since we assume non-steady state equilibrium in the base year, time-variant discount rates, and non-steady state growth of population and productivity, the endogenous variables from the baseline change over time along a transition path.

IV. SIMULATIONS

Empirical work has repeatedly confirmed that public infrastructure plays an important role in promoting productivity and output growth. However, infrastructure investment does not come without costs. As the main financier, government has to either raise distortionary taxes or cut other expenditures to finance its investment in infrastructure, which would offset some of the positive effects of public infrastructure investment. Therefore the net effects of public infrastructure investment vary across countries, depending on their fiscal positions, tax structures, indebtedness levels, infrastructure endowments and other country-specific factors. To explore the interaction of these factors and evaluate the implications of alternative financing modes, we conduct three policy experiments of expanding public investment for both the PRC and India using the dynamic general equilibrium model described in section II. In all three experiments, we assume that public infrastructure investment as a fraction of GDP is doubled from the baseline levels to 5.1 per cent in the PRC and 4.7 per cent in India, roughly in line with the OECD average.

The three experiments differ in their ways of financing the additional investment expenditure. The first two experiments assume a tax-financed, balanced-budget policy under which the increase in public spending is financed by adjusting the rates of either consumption tax or labour income tax on a period-by-period basis. The third experiment assumes the government runs deficits to fund the investment expenditure during a ten-year period from the base year, and then raises the consumption tax rates on a period-by-period basis to stabilize the debt-to-GDP ratio thereafter.

People's Republic of China

Table 9.5 presents the evolution of major macroeconomic variables through transitional dynamics to final steady state under the scenarios of increasing public infrastructure investment in the PRC. All these variables are presented as deviations from the baseline. Generally, the increased public infrastructure leads to a higher return to private capital, stimulating more private investment. As a result, private capital increases by 4.5 per cent to 7.4 per cent and output increases by 6.2 per cent to 7.5 per cent under the three scenarios. High investment also raises the long-term interest rate, which rises by 2.9 per cent to 5.5 per cent in the scenarios of labour income tax financing and debt financing. However, the long-run interest rate barely changes in the consumption tax financing scenario.

Despite the higher wage, labour input in the steady state is slightly lower than the baseline, as work efforts in the long run are reduced by the positive wealth effect, which dominates the intra-temporal substitution effect arising from the higher wage and the inter-temporal substitution effect arising from the higher interest rate. In the long run, private consumption rises only 3.2 per cent to 3.5 per cent above the baseline, less than the corresponding gains in investment, reflecting the diminishing returns to public and private capital, as well as the larger tax burdens associated with higher public investment in infrastructure. To finance the increased investment spending or interest payments, the government has to raise tax revenue by 12.0 per cent to 12.9 per cent ultimately. Under the debt-financing scenario, the steady-state government debt is two times higher than that in the baseline.

The results reported in Table 9.5 clearly demonstrate the importance of public infrastructure to output and private investment. By comparing the

Table 9.5   Effects of doubling public infrastructure investment: PRC (% change relative to baseline)

	Year 1	Year 2	Year 3	Year 10	Year 20	Steady state
Public infrastructure stock	0.0	11.2	21.6	69.7	92.7	100.0
Consumption tax financing						
Output	−0.6	0.0	0.6	3.5	5.6	7.5
Private consumption	−5.1	−4.7	−4.2	−1.4	1.0	3.5
Private investment	−4.6	−3.4	−2.4	2.1	5.0	7.4
Private capital stock	0.0	−0.6	−1.0	−0.2	3.0	7.4
Labour supply	−1.1	−0.9	−0.8	−0.4	−0.3	−0.4
Interest rate	4.4	5.9	6.9	7.7	5.4	0.0
Wage	0.5	0.9	1.2	3.3	5.1	6.8
Tax revenue	13.8	13.6	13.5	13.0	12.8	12.0
Consumption tax rate*	11.6	11.0	10.7	8.2	6.6	4.8
Labour income tax financing						
Output	−0.8	−0.4	0.1	2.8	4.9	6.9
Private consumption	−3.5	−3.3	−3.0	−1.0	1.1	3.4
Private investment	−6.8	−5.6	−4.5	0.2	3.2	5.9
Private capital stock	0.0	−0.9	−1.5	−1.7	1.2	5.9
Labour supply	−1.4	−1.4	−1.2	−0.6	−0.5	−0.6
Interest rate	4.8	7.0	8.3	10.1	8.1	2.9
Wage	0.7	1.1	1.3	2.9	4.6	6.4
Tax revenue	13.5	13.7	13.6	13.1	12.9	12.0
Labour tax rate*	6.2	6.3	6.1	4.9	4.1	3.4
Debt financing						
Output	0.4	0.9	1.3	3.4	4.7	6.2
Private consumption	−0.7	−0.4	−0.1	1.8	1.1	3.2
Private investment	−6.3	−5.2	−4.2	−0.8	2.9	4.5
Private capital stock	0.0	−0.8	−1.4	−1.9	1.0	4.5
Labour supply	0.7	0.7	0.7	0.5	−0.6	−0.8
Interest rate	6.1	8.1	9.4	16.6	8.3	5.5
Wage	−0.3	0.0	0.3	2.3	4.6	6.0
Tax revenue	−0.3	0.2	0.6	2.7	12.5	12.9
Government debt	0.0	22.2	44.5	182.5	199.8	199.8
Consumption tax rate*	0.0	0.0	0.0	0.0	6.4	5.4

Note: * Absolute changes in tax rate (%).

macroeconomic effects under different financing modes, it is also clear that the financing mode does matter. Under the consumption tax financing scenario, private investment in the steady state rises strongly by 7.4 per cent in comparison with the baseline, two-thirds greater than under the debt-financing mode. The difference arises from their different impacts on saving. As older people tend to consume a larger fraction of their lifetime resources than do younger people, higher consumption tax rates impose larger tax burdens on older people. These inter-generational distributional effects increase total saving. The increased saving restrains the rise in the interest rate, in spite of a large increase in private investment. Under the labour income tax financing scenario, the response in saving rate is relatively small, resulting in a higher interest rate and less increase in investment. In the case of debt financing, the initial private investment is significantly crowded out by the enlarged government debt, inducing a lower level of capital stock and a much higher long-term interest rate.

The evolution of major macroeconomic variables over the short term is illustrated in Figure 9.1. In the short term, the increased public investment raises the interest rate and crowds out private investment. However, private investment turns to increase during 2007–09 in the two tax financing scenarios, as the positive externality generated by the expansion of public infrastructure gradually dominates the negative impacts of higher interest rates. The higher interest rate in the short term makes future consumption and leisure less expensive than current ones. The resulting inter-temporal substitution effect thus encourages a shift of consumption into the future, leading to less private consumption and more saving. Moreover, the values of the existing capital stock, as measured by Tobin's q, drop by around 1.0 per cent to 1.4 per cent in the initial phase of the transition. This generates a negative wealth effect, inducing a further increase in saving in the short term. In the case of debt financing, as the consumption of initial older generations is not impacted by the debt-financing policy, private consumption falls only slightly in the first three years, but increases thereafter until 2011. The anticipated tax hike on consumption after 2011 also contributes to the increases in consumption before 2011, as it leads consumers to substitute current, cheap for future, expensive consumption.

The same reason induces the larger labour supply in the short term under the debt financing scenario, as leisure is relatively cheaper after 2011. The short-term decline of labour supply under the two tax-financing scenarios is determined by the intra-temporal substitution effect arising from changes in the relative prices of consumption and leisure. In the case of consumption tax financing, the relatively higher price of consumption results in more leisure and less work effort. In the case of labour income tax financing, higher labour income tax lowers the opportunity cost of leisure, again resulting in less work effort.

One interesting finding from Figure 9.1 is that the short-term effects of debt financing on output and consumption are superior to those of tax financing. This result is exactly opposite to that in the long term. Therefore, policy-makers face a trade-off between short-term costs and long-term gains. This trade-off can be better illustrated through the effects on inter-generational distribution.

Figure 9.2 shows the effects of raising the public infrastructure stock on remaining lifetime utility for different generations. Following Auerbach and Kotlikoff (1987) and Altig et al. (2001), the change in remaining life-time utility is measured as the equivalent variation of remaining full life-time income. It represents the equivalent percentage change in each cohort's remaining full lifetime wealth (assets plus human wealth based on working full-time) needed in the baseline to produce its realized level of utility under the alternative cases of public infrastructure investment.

Overall, the figure suggests a redistribution of lifetime wealth from older to younger generations induced by doubling public infrastructure invest-ment. This inter-generational redistribution is modest under the labour income tax financing scenario and debt-financing scenario, but very significant under the consumption tax financing mode. In the latter case, cohorts that reached adulthood 36 years before the base year are worse off. This corresponds to the generations older than 53 in 2002. Older cohorts receive little or no labour income, thereby gaining little from the increased wage. They also suffer from the fall in the value of existing capital, which depreciates their accumulated savings. Under the consumption tax financing mode, greater tax burdens are borne by the old because they account for a disproportionately large share of consumption.

Young and future cohorts achieve welfare gains from the expanded public infrastructure stock. In the long run, future cohorts' welfare gain is equiva-lent to 1.5 per cent of their full lifetime wealth. Recall that full lifetime wealth includes the value of leisure and around two-thirds of lifetime resources are spent on leisure. This welfare gain is consistent with the long term increases in consumption reported in Table 9.5. The inter-generational welfare effects suggest that the larger long-term gain in output and welfare from consump-tion tax financing may come at the expense of current older generations.

India

Table 9.6 and Figure 9.3 present the major macroeconomic effects of dou-bling public infrastructure investment for India. It is not surprising that they follow a pattern similar to that obtained from the simulations for the

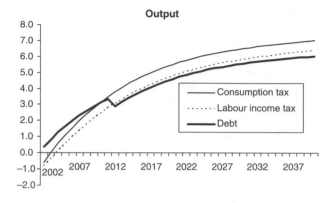

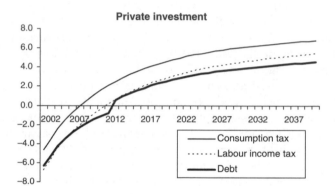

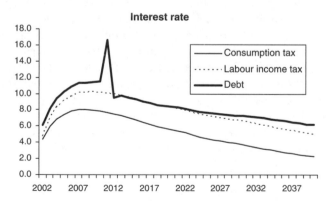

Figure 9.1   Short-term effects of doubling public infrastructure investment: PRC (percentage change relative to baseline)

Private consumption

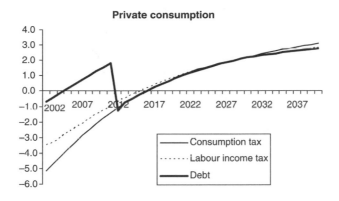

Labour Inputs

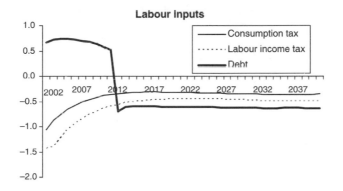

Tobin's *q*

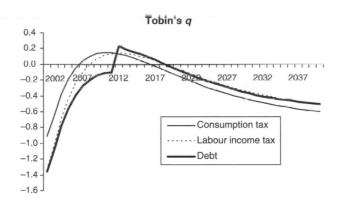

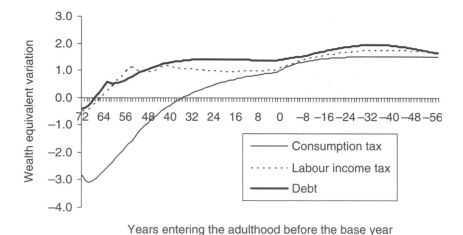

Figure 9.2   Changes in remaining full lifetime utility: PRC (equivalent variation as percentage of wealth)

PRC. However, some quantitative differences between the simulation results for the two countries are instructive in revealing differences in their underlying economic structure.

The first observation arising from the comparison of the two countries' results is that doubling the stock of public infrastructure would generally bring larger output gains in India than in the PRC. Among the three financing modes investigated, India's steady-state output expansion is larger than the PRC's under both tax financing scenarios. Only the mode of debt-financing scenario results in less output expansion in India than in the PRC. Two reasons account for this. First, India has a relatively smaller public infrastructure stock and public infrastructure investment in the base year. Doubling its public infrastructure investment would require less resources, and thereby impose smaller tax burdens on the economy in comparison with PRC. Thus, even assuming similar output elasticities of public infrastructure, countries with less developed infrastructure can gain more from increased infrastructure investment. Second, PRC has a higher initial ratio of investment to capital stock, which incurs higher adjustment costs when making further investments. This partly offsets the gains from expanded private and public investment, resulting in relatively smaller output and investment expansion in the PRC.

In further comparing the results across the three modes of public infrastructure financing, it is clear that India would gain most in the long run under the consumption tax financing scenario, mainly because of its higher steady-state level of private capital stock. In comparison with the simulation

Table 9.6 *Long-run effects of doubling public infrastructure investment:*
India (% change relative to baseline)

	Year 1	Year 2	Year 3	Year 10	Year 20	Steady state
Public infrastructure stock	0.0	9.8	19.0	66.2	91.6	100.0
Consumption tax financing						
Output	−0.4	0.1	0.5	3.4	5.9	8.0
Private consumption	−2.7	−2.6	−2.3	−0.1	2.2	4.5
Private investment	−4.9	−3.5	−2.3	2.5	5.7	8.3
Private capital stock	0.0	−0.6	−0.9	0.0	3.6	8.3
Labour supply	−0.7	−0.6	−0.6	−0.4	−0.3	−0.5
Interest rate	3.5	4.2	4.7	5.0	3.1	−0.8
Wage	0.4	0.7	1.0	3.2	5.2	7.0
Tax revenue	16.7	18.0	18.4	18.6	17.7	16.7
Consumption tax rate*	4.8	5.1	5.2	4.7	3.8	2.9
Labour income tax financing						
Output	−0.6	−0.5	−0.2	2.2	4.6	7.0
Private consumption	−2.5	−2.6	−2.5	−0.6	1.6	4.0
Private investment	−6.4	−5.6	−4.7	−0.1	3.3	6.4
Private capital stock	0.0	−0.7	−1.3	−1.8	1.2	6.4
Labour supply	−1.1	−1.6	−1.7	−1.2	−0.9	−0.9
Interest rate	2.5	4.0	4.9	6.7	5.5	1.4
Wage	0.6	1.2	1.5	3.1	4.7	6.6
Tax revenue	16.4	18.3	19.3	20.3	19.4	18.0
Labour tax rate*	4.6	5.7	5.9	5.2	4.1	3.3
Debt financing						
Output	0.3	0.7	1.0	2.4	3.9	5.8
Private consumption	−0.6	−0.4	−0.1	1.9	1.0	3.3
Private investment	−7.2	−6.1	−5.3	−3.5	2.1	3.9
Private capital stock	0.0	−0.8	−1.5	−3.1	0.1	3.9
Labour supply	0.6	0.6	0.6	0.0	−1.4	−1.3
Interest rate	4.6	5.7	6.5	19.7	6.1	4.4
Wage	−0.3	−0.1	0.2	2.0	4.6	6.1
Tax revenue	−0.1	0.4	0.8	2.9	25.7	24.5
Government debt	0.0	2.7	5.9	33.9	38.4	38.4
Consumption tax rate*	0.0	0.0	0.0	0.0	6.3	5.0

Note: * Absolute changes in tax rate (%).

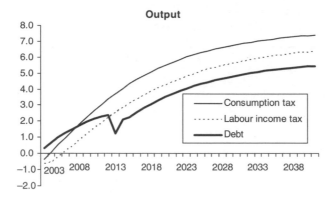

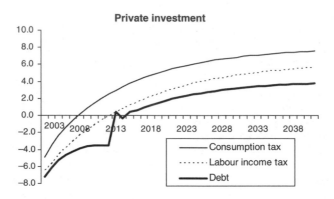

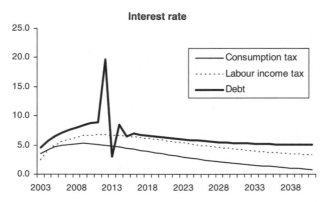

*Figure 9.3   Short-term effects of doubling public infrastructure investment:
India (percentage change relative to baseline)*

Private consumption

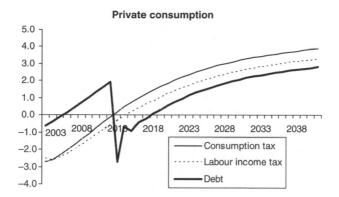

Labour inputs

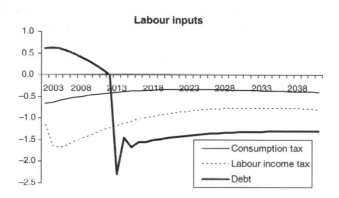

Tobin's *q*

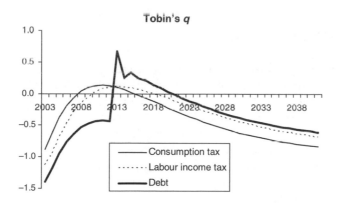

results for the PRC, India has only a modest additional gain from labour income tax. Labour income in India accounts for a relatively small share in GDP, thus financing public investment through a labour tax would require a higher tax rate. This leads to a stronger substitution effect against work effort, causing more shrinkage in labour supply. Consequently, the larger distortion from higher labour income tax rates in India partly offsets its potentially larger gains from increasing public investment in infrastructure.

The results in Table 9.6 of debt financing in India are most striking. Given its initial very high level of government debt, debt financing is very costly for India both because of the initial crowding-out effects on private investment and the long-term substitution effects away from work arising from higher consumption tax rates. Despite the initial smaller rises in interest rates in India than in the PRC, the high level of public debt in India causes a heavier interest payment burden and, consequently, a larger expansion in government deficits in the initial stages. This results in a stronger crowding-out effect on private investment. Moreover, the higher debt-to-GDP ratio eventually translates into a larger tax burden for households. The simulation results in Table 9.6 show that if debt is used to finance public investment in India, the required long-term consumption tax rate to stabilize the government debt-to-GDP ratio would be 70 per cent higher than that under consumption tax financing. This contrasts with the corresponding result obtained from the simulations for the PRC, in which the long-term tax rate under debt financing is only 12 per cent higher than that in the consumption tax financing scenario. The higher consumption tax rates induce stronger substitution effects towards leisure, reducing the long-term supply of labour in India.

V.   CONCLUSIONS

Infrastructure expansion is critical for sustaining rapid growth and employment generation in Asia's giant developing countries. The PRC and India have been pursuing infrastructure investment policies and patterns that are in many ways similar, but also different in critical aspects. The devolution of revenue generation and expenditure authority is one of the most obvious areas. Given the fungibility of revenue once raised, financing options to support the already large and expanding public infrastructure investment becomes important not just for raising revenue, but also in terms of macroeconomic impacts.

Using a dynamic general equilibrium model with overlapping generations, we examine the macroeconomic and intergenerational distributional impacts of increasing public infrastructure investment in the PRC and

India. Three alternative financing modes are considered: consumption tax financing, financing through a labour income tax and debt financing. The simulation results confirm that public infrastructure plays an important role in sustaining long-term output growth and private investment. However, its effects on the macroeconomy and inter-generational distribution heavily depend on the particular financing mode chosen by the policy maker. In general, the consumption tax financing option is the best in terms of promoting long-term output growth and investment, but it involves large short-term transitional costs for existing older generations. Debt financing is more favourable to ensure inter-generational equality, but may have undesirable long-term effects.

The comparison of simulation results between the PRC and India also reveals that some country-specific factors are important in determining the magnitude of these effects. In particular, due to its relative scarcity of public infrastructure, India can generally benefit more from increasing the public infrastructure stock. However, the high existing stock of government debt in India renders debt financing the least attractive mode of public infrastructure financing.

Two important limitations of this chapter need to be mentioned. First, some model parameters, such as the output elasticity of public infrastructure, which are central to the simulation results reported here, have been taken from cross-country studies. Obtaining country-specific estimates of these parameters would significantly improve the empirical and policy relevance of the model simulations. Second, our model and simulations consider public infrastructure financing only. However, in some infrastructure sectors private firms have actively participated in investment and the public–private partnership has emerged as a vital option for infrastructure financing. Incorporating private infrastructure investment in the model analysis would be an important topic for future study.

Similarly, more detailed examination of the two countries' debt and taxation policies, and the relationship of those policies with plans for infrastructure financing, would improve the realism of any such analysis. However, such a task is, like the two economies, huge and complicated. The present analysis is intended to be just an indicative step towards fuller understanding.

NOTES

1. The views expressed are those of the authors and do not necessarily reflect those of their organizations. They gratefully acknowledge research assistance by Mary Ann Magadia but claim full responsibility for any remaining errors. An earlier version of this chapter appeared as Brooks and Zhai (2008).

2. The Octroi is a tax on goods entering the area. It has been ended in many states but still persists in some locations.
3. See Auberbach and Kotlikoff (1987: 29–30), for details.

REFERENCES

Altig, D., A.J. Auerbach, L.J. Kotlikoff, K.A. Smetters and J. Wallser (2001), 'Simulating fundamental tax reform in the United States', *American Economic Review*, **91**, 574–95.

Armington, P. (1969), 'A theory of demand for products distinguished by place of production', IMF Staff Paper, **16**, 159–78.

Aschauer, D. (1989), 'Is public expenditure productive?', *Journal of Monetary Economics*, **23** (2), 177–200.

Auerbach, A.J. and L.J. Kotlikoff (1987), *Dynamic Fiscal Policy*, Cambridge: Cambridge University Press.

Bellier, M. and Y.M. Zhou (2003), 'Private participation in infrastructure in China: issues and recommendations for the road, water, and power sectors', World Bank Working Paper No. 2.

Botman, D.P.J., D. Laxton, D. Muir and A. Romanov (2006), 'A new-open-economy-macro model for fiscal policy evaluation', IMF Working Paper No. 06/45.

Brooks, D.H. and F. Zhai (2008), 'The macroeconomic effects of infrastructure financing: a tale of two countries', *Integration and Trade Journal*, **28**, 297–323.

Canning, D. and E. Bennathan (2000), 'The social rate of return on infrastructure investments', *World Bank Policy Research Working Paper*, No. 2390.

Canning, D. and P. Pedroni (2004), 'The effect of infrastructure on long-run economic growth', Economics Department Working Papers, Williams College, MA, USA.

Cassou, S.P. and K.J. Lansing (1998), 'Optimal fiscal policy, public capital, and the productivity slowdown', *Journal of Economic Dynamics and Control*, **22** (6), 911–35.

Garg, S.C. (2005), 'Mobilising urban infrastructure finance in India in a responsible fiscal framework', in *Practitioners' Conference on Mobilizing Urban Infrastructure Finance in a Responsible Fiscal Framework: Brazil, China, India, Poland and South Africa*, Jaipur, Rajasthan, India: The World Bank, http:www.worldbank.org/urban/mun_fin/uifpapers/garg.pdf.

Mahadevia, D. (2006), 'Urban infrastructure financing and delivery in India and China', *China & World Economy*, **14** (2), 105–20.

Mukhopadhyay, P. (2004), 'In the name of the poor: what role for PFI?', in *India Infrastructure Report 2004*, 3iNetwork, New Delhi: Oxford University Press.

Private Participation in Infrastructure (PPI) database, The World Bank and the Public–Private Infrastructure Advisory Facility, http://ppi.worldbank.org.

Secretariat for the Committee on Infrastructure (n.d.), 'Scheme: financing infrastructure projects the India infrastructure finance company', www.infrastructure.gov.in.

Index